Effective
DEFENSE

2nd Edition

by Gila Hayes

Published by
The Firearms Academy of Seattle, Inc.
Post Office Box 400, Onalaska, WA 98570
360-978-6100

Printed in the United States of America

First Edition 1994
Second Edition 2000

Neither the publisher nor the author assumes any responsibility for the use or misuse of any information contained in this book. Products and services referenced in this book are included to increase the knowledge of the reader. Mention should not be construed to constitute an endorsement, as the marketplace is constantly changing, with improved products continually introduced, taking the place of older products and services which become obsolete.

Dedicated to the memory of
Laura J. May

Foreword

In 1993, it was my privilege to write the foreword to Gila May-Hayes' first book, *Effective Defense: the Woman, the Plan, the Gun.* A lot has gone on since.

Gila has emerged as one of the nation's very best firearms trainers. She is particularly sought after by other instructors as an advisor on how to teach women and smaller-statured males to control powerful weapons. Her interactive hands-on courses have been extremely well-received by the seasoned police instructors who attended her courses at national seminars of ASLET, the American Society of Law Enforcement Trainers, and IALEFI, the International Association of Law Enforcement Firearms Instructors.

In addition to watching her teach in those venues, and attending some firearms industry seminars with her in her capacity as contributing editor of *Women and Guns* magazine and as a regular contributor to *American Guardian*, we teach together a few times a year. Gila and her husband Marty run the Firearms Academy of Seattle, which in addition to the excellent programs offered by their cadre staff annually hosts Jim Cirillo, Chuck Taylor, myself and others.

I've seen Gila interact with hundreds and hundreds of students, young and old, female and male, civilian and armed by the government. I have watched her give caring insight to a woman who was a rape victim, and reassurance to more than one woman who had shot and killed her attacker. Gila Hayes understands every element of the use of countervailing force to stop violent attackers.

She doesn't just talk the talk. She walks the walk and she fights the fight. Many "gun experts" are reluctant to shoot in front of the public. Gila has competed in major shooting events from Second Chance to the National Tactical Invitational (NTI) to state and regional championships. She didn't just shoot in those high-stress venues; she shot well.

How well? In the mid-1990s, I watched her win the Washington State Bowling Pin Championship in stock gun class. Not the woman's championship, but the overall title, beating a lot of highly skilled men. The pistol she used was a Mark Morris Custom Springfield Armory .45 automatic, not only without any sort of recoil compensator, but with powerful and hard-kicking Cor-Bon +P ammunition.

Gila has won the prestigious High Woman title at the NTI, an extremely difficult and complicated event that demands fast reactions, high tactical awareness, and skill at arms. Like every other woman who has won that title (including Lyn Bates, Cat Ayoob and Vicki Farnam) she also beat the vast majority of the male contestants, many of whom were combat-hardened, highly trained SWAT cops and SPECOPS troops.

Two days before my writing this, Gila and Marty and I managed to win the Tactical Team Event championship at the famous 3-gun shoot hosted annually by Washington State Law Enforcement Firearms Instructors Association. Each trio of practitioners could use but a single gun—one a rifle, one a handgun, one a shotgun—to combine tactical movement and use of cover with the neutralization of more than two dozen "hostile targets." Gila chose the shotgun, a 12 gauge Remington 870. A lot of the 3-man teams we beat were made up of men who looked burly enough to clean out a whole Gold's Gym with their bare hands, but this slender woman's manipulation of the powerful 12 gauge pump was so expert that we were able to amass the top score at the fastest speed. As she notes in her book repeatedly, skill can negate opposing strength.

Gila has combined her experience with that of other top female instructors in her orbit. She makes it clear that full-powered, responsible defensive capability can be integrated with the factors of female body shape, female wardrobe, and other problems unique to the armed woman. Above all, she is living proof that there is nothing unfeminine about strength and empowerment.

I've been recommending *Effective Defense* since the first edition came out. The second edition is even better. It is an act of love to share this book with women you love and wish to remain safe. This is why I shall give copies to my wife and my daughters.

Massad Ayoob
Concord, NH
July 22, 2000

Massad Ayoob is founder and director of the Lethal Force Institute, one of the best-recognized armed defense schools in the United States, and possibly the world. Training over 1,000 police officers and private citizens per year, Ayoob's instruction ranges from armed to unarmed combat, police officer survival, use of deadly force for both police and private citizens, as well as his StressFire shooting methods for handgun, shotgun and rifle.

In addition to nearly 30 years experience in law enforcement, he serves as an expert witness in court cases requiring testimony about the dynamics of a violent encounter, weapons and self-defense training, threat management tactics and more. A prolific author, Ayoob's byline is common in firearms publications ranging from Combat Handguns to GUNS Magazine. He is author of seven books, including In the Gravest Extreme, and The Truth About Self Protection, to name only a couple.

Recent awards and recognitions included winning the Outstanding American Handgunner award in 1998, filling the "parent" role in the National Champion Parent-Child team at Second Chance National Police Combat Shoot with his daughter Justine. Just days before writing this foreword, Ayoob won the handgun event at the Washington State Law Enforcement Firearms Instructors Association competition. He is the current New Hampshire state combat pistol champion.

Introduction

The work of rewriting and expanding *Effective Defense* into the second edition you now hold has afforded an interesting exploration into the changes in self-defense tactics, equipment and threats seen since 1994, when the first edition of this book was released. The exploration has been quite personal, as well, as I've vigorously critiqued and aggressively improved the chapters I wrote for that first edition so long ago.

The woman who for the first time considers her self-defense choices faces a complex endeavor entailing new responsibilities, concerns and decisions. Although I faced this challenge over a decade ago, I have not yet forgotten the evolution from an early decision to study martial arts for physical self-defense that grew into learning additional defensive methods up to and including the defensive firearm.

I had thoroughly enjoyed martial arts training for several years before a shift change at work gave me a choice: return home late at night or find a new job. Unable to immediately implement the latter option, I began a serious study of my self-defense choices. Unfettered by fear of or distaste for firearms, I decided that licensed carry of a concealed pistol would best buffer me against the violence that occurred daily in Seattle, WA where I then lived and worked.

Only blocks from the printing plant in which I was employed, the infamous Green River killer had abducted and killed an estimated 49 women between the years of 1982 and 1990. Remaining unsolved, the case was cause for fear that the killer remained active in the area. Less sensational crime occurred daily, with car jackings, rapes, robberies, home invasions and other attacks reported in each new edition of the news. Apartment building gossip spread reports of residents accosted at the front door of my security building, and attacked in the parking area and street.

Although I had grown up on a ranch where a rifle was readily available for varmint and predator control, I had no knowledge of self-defense firearms. The pursuit of an appropriate self-defense handgun, learning the skills with which to use it effectively, and discovering the legal and ethical constraints governing self-defense were simultaneously a huge challenge yet utterly fascinating. It was immediately apparent that possession of a firearm and its potential for deadly force was a much greater responsibility than I'd anticipated.

Dissatisfied with only basic marksmanship skills, I sought continuing training in the physical skill of shooting, as well as defense tactics and mental preparation. The job of learning to defend myself effectively was more involved than it appeared on the surface. My challenges, discoveries and solutions comprise the foundation of *Effective Defense,* both in its first edition and now in this second version.

What has changed in the six years that have passed so quickly since the first edition of *Effective Defense* came off the printing press? I believe the threats remain quite similar, but our understanding of the pervasiveness of violent crime has grown. The methods of defense remain basically unchanged, although certain models of firearms have been improved and new versions introduced, as the commercial machine grinds out its wares. I pray that women's attitudes have continued to change toward a more aggressive refusal to fall prey to those who view us as little more than objects for exploitation. Women's attitudes have not changed sufficiently, however, for we continue going about our daily lives, regularly subjected to concerns about violence, if not actually confronted by actual danger.

Unchanged is my personal conviction that self-defense is *more* than a right: that self-defense is a responsibility to ourselves, those we love, and to our society. We have a responsibility to aggressively *eliminate* the dangers that steal the peace and enjoyment from women's lives.

Predictably, my own continuing training is reflected in the content of the second edition of this book. As the rewrite comes to an end, I believe the changes mirror my exposure to additional techniques, threat assessment and other ideas from a variety of instructors and sources I've encountered since the first edition. I hope these further influences have made me more open-minded, recognizing that solutions that I, myself, might not employ may help another woman prepare to defend herself. Although the contents are expanded and in some cases changed, I hope to have maintained a tone of encouragement, urging the you and women about whom you care that you *can* and *should* defend against violence.

Pursuing this goal, I have added a new chapter on workplace violence, hoping to provide hardworking career women, working moms and women returning to the workplace skills beyond those merely required to do their work! Other topics expanded into separate and much longer chapters about shotguns and rifles for home-defense. I expect some of the handgun-savvy readers may find new shooting enjoyment by exploring these different types of guns. The vital subject of non-lethal defenses is expanded, and the discussion of threats and crimes against people is updated. Home security is covered in greater depth, and the chapter on concealed carry methods is brought up to date with this ever-changing marketplace.

While the second edition is expanded and reorganized, my philosophy that criminal victimization need not be inevitable remains as strong as ever. The woman who develops her own defensive capabilities should realize that we all too often acquiesce to victimhood, whether by quietly accepting verbal harassment or in failing to strike back before suffering physical injury. When the *tools* of self-defense are readily available, the *mindset* of self-reliance must be developed concurrently.

The words, sentences and paragraphs in this book are personal. I've tried to communicate the means, methods and mentality of self-defense as personally as if you and I sat in the same room, sharing a conversation. This is not to imply that the topics are simple or simplified, nor are all of the subjects easy to discuss. There exists between women, however, a shared style of communication. One hallmark of female communication is greater depth of detail. I hope this attribute serves to help readers grasp "why" as well as "how and when." Without determination to fight and mental clarity about the righteousness of your defense, the challenges of self-defense are more difficult to surmount.

None of the shooting techniques, operating methods or tactics are my original creation. They are, instead, drawn, distilled and learned from a wide variety of instructors. An enormous resource, every year these men and women train thousands of qualified private citizens, law enforcement professionals, military personnel and recreational shooters. Time- and street-proven survival methods are drawn from Massad Ayoob, John and Vicki Farnam, Evan Marshall, Jim Cirillo, Ken Hackathorn, Clint Smith, Chuck Taylor, Marty Hayes, the instructional cadres of Heckler & Koch International Training Division and Glock, Inc., Bill Burris, Vince O'Neill, Tony Scotti, Larry Smith, Louis Awerbuck, Jim Lindell and the instructors at National Law Enforcement Training Center, and many more. So many others have lent their influence and knowledge through training seminars, professional journals, books, magazines and other sources. Although they are too many to cite individually, my sincere gratitude to all who work to keep others alive, alert to danger and ready to fight when appropriate.

Finally, to the reader of this book: thank you for your interest in this topic. It is through your attitude and contribution to our society that changes will occur in women's perceptions of themselves, men's perceptions of women, and change will come most decisively when criminals learn that women are well-able to defend themselves from assault and exploitation!

Where ever you are on this path to self-sufficiency, I hope the discussions in the pages to follow will strengthen your resolve, lift your spirits and increase your preparedness to live a satisfying, happy and safe life.

Gila Hayes
Onalaska, WA
November 19, 2000

Acknowledgements

In additional to the professionals previously acknowledged, the individual contributions to this book are as numerous as they are varied. A great debt of loyal gratitude is due my husband Marty Hayes for guidance, encouragement and pushing me farther than I would have ever attempted alone.

A resounding thank you to Massad Ayoob, Heath Gunns, Jim Cirillo, Vicki Farnam for her friendship, Clay Whitehead, Clyde Caceres, Tom Haeflinger, Jay Vosburgh, Robert Zielke, Tom Thomas for personal encouragement, Elizabeth Kennedy, Roy Huntington, Art Mize for his insight into the psychological aspects of survival, Judith Weiss, and back through time to De Gasaway, who made karate fun. To Sonny Jones, my first editor at *Women & Guns*, and to my current editor of that publication, Peggy Tartaro, ever patient with my tardiness. John Barnett, also of the Second Amendment Foundation has given encouragement, publishing advice and saw to the purchase and sale of many of the first edition copies of *Effective Defense*. Additional publishing contacts, including Karen Mehall, Harry Kane, Kirby Smith and others have occasionally found room for my work in the magazines they edit, for which I am grateful. Thank you to Larry Rives, the long-suffering chief of police of the department at which I serve.

This book is greatly enhanced by the photographic and modeling support of Grant and Chris Cunningham, Brady, Heath and McKenzie Gunns, Richard Morgan, Norm and Kendra Aubin, Marty Hayes, DeAnne Orive, Marlys May, Clinton Hansen, Karl Wingren, Jim Pike, Jay Vosburgh, Loren Neill and others. Thank you all.

Finally, my appreciation to all the students who have shared their concerns, experiences and emotions with me. To each person who comes to a class, thank you for being part of my growth and experience.

Table of Contents

1

Women's Rights & Responsibilities

I grew up with my mother's repertoire of fears: attack by strangers, rape, and other violent acts by men against women. She warned me to avoid strangers, to keep window shades down and never go out alone at night, yet never was there any mention of fighting back. Behave quietly, dress modestly and bad men won't bother you, I was taught.

Common sense measures like protecting one's privacy are sensible, yet what could we do if someone attacked even the most careful, unprovocative woman? Our training was in avoidance; we had no game plan if evasion failed. Girls weren't taught how to fight, even in last-ditch self-defense. We feared violence but weren't allowed to respond with countervailing force.

A lot of things have changed in 40 years. Women now realize that rape and assault can happen to anyone, anywhere. Most women have wondered what they could do if attacked, and finding no satisfactory answer, have tried to ignore the worry. It is unwise to hope that some good fortune will separate us from the 75% of American women predicted by crime statistics to face violent assault, rape, or murder in their life time.[1] A more optimistic study, this one conducted by the Denver-based Center for Policy Research, reported that more than one-half of the nation's women at one time in their lives has been physically assaulted, by an armed or unarmed assailant.

As early as 1992, then-Surgeon General Antonio Novello identified physical violence as the leading cause of injuries to women between the ages of 15 to 44. Not automobile accidents or workplace mishaps, but physical violence.[2] A study of more current Uniform Crime Reports and other data show little change.

Politicians in the latter half of the 1990s began to brag that violent crime was sharply declining. Those sound bites failed to acknowledge that although between 1973 and 1997 the victimization rate for American men indeed did fall from about 65 to 50 incidents per 1000, during the same 24 year span, violent crimes against women actually increased slightly.[3] The figures peaked when nearly 44 of every 1000 female Americans became victims of violent crime in 1993. In 1997 at the end of the Bureau of Justice Statistics analysis, the numbers decreased to about 34 women per 1000, up slightly from about 32 per 1000 when the study began in 1973.

> *If violence against women is to decrease, each individual must be capable of effecting her own self-defense at any time and in any place.*

The study of statistics and crime reports is fraught with potential for erroneous conclusions from exaggeration or understatement. Not only is it far too easy to mis-interpret the data compiled, methods used to state the data vary from study to study, and all too often crimes are never reported and are not even considered in the analysis. For example, in 1995, according to data compiled by the Bureau of Justice, one in every 1390 American women reported that she was forcibly raped.[4] However, the definition of forcible rape excludes quite a wide spectrum of other sexual assaults, and compounding wrong conclusions is the estimate that only one third of sexual assault victims report the violence enacted against them.

Who's responsible?

In a world where women are responsible for earning their own living and often are sole support of their children, it is ironic that we have not embraced complete responsibility for our own self-defense. Women who are accustomed to a strong father figure find it easy to transfer responsibility for their well-being and the protection of their families to law enforcement officers, husbands, lovers, or friends. The decision may be conscious, in recognition of the safety they feel is provided them. Other times, it is an unconscious choice, coming from inaction and oblivion to the risks around us. We spend much of our time away from these protectors, in situations where none are near enough to respond in time to stop an assault. If violence against women is to decrease, each individual must be capable of effecting her own self-defense at any time and in any place.

Gun control proponents want Americans to relinquish their weapons and rely on the government for protection. Realistically, however, police forces are employed to patrol, maintain peace, investigate crimes after the fact, and rarely do circumstances allow officers to stop a crime in progress. This truth was emphasized in 1975, when three Washington, D.C women were raped, sodomized, and terrorized for fourteen hours in their home. The police were called in the initial moments of the attack. When four cruisers arrived at the home, none of the women were able to answer the door and after five minutes the officers left. A second call received a promise of help on the way. Later investigation determined that officers were never dispatched to answer the second plea for help. Fortunately, the women survived. Lawsuits ensued, and in 1981 the Court of Appeals for Washington, D.C., ruling on *Warren v. District of Columbia*, wrote that under American law the "government and its agents are under no general duty to provide public services, such as police protection, to any individual citizen."[5]

Citing *Warren vs. District of Columbia* is in no way an indictment of police officers. The men and women who work in law enforcement put their lives on the line every time they go to work. The private citizen must recognize that the police cannot provide moment-to-moment protection. The role of protector ultimately rests with the individual, for government is not capable of addressing individual emergencies. This we learned as early as the 1950's, after New Yorker Linda Riss sought police protection from a former boyfriend who made violent threats against her. The City of New York denied her request for a gun permit, as well as refusing repeated appeals for protection. After the harasser blinded and disfigured her with lye, Riss sued New York City for failing to protect her. All but one justice on New York's high court ruled against her case. The dissenting justice concluded that "by a rather bitter irony she was required to rely for protection on the City of New York which now denies all responsibility for her."[6]

The difference between a court-issued restraining order and actual protection generates unrealistic expectations when women appeal to the courts for protection. Too many women have been killed or injured while learning that their restraining order is merely legal protection, not bodily defense. In 1989, a Los Angeles, CA woman called police dispatch (911) when threatened by her estranged husband against whom she had a restraining order. When the dispatcher asked sarcastically if she expected a patrol car to park outside her home, Maria Navarro hung up. Within 30 minutes, a second call to 911 reported the murder of Navarro and a guest who was

> We must expand the feminine role to include defending life, as well as giving it birth.

in her home to celebrate Navarro's birthday. Before police officers could arrive, her estranged husband killed another guest.

Another California woman sued the Pacifica Police Department after she was beaten by her estranged husband. The courts found that the restraining order against the husband did not confer additional responsibility on the police agency for the victim's well-being. Additional court decisions affirm that unless an individual is **in police custody**, the government assumes no liability should they be killed or injured.

With a government that controls so many aspects of our lives, it is easy to understand how some come to believe themselves entitled to constant protection. Such expectations ignore the reality that at any given time approximately one police officer is employed for every 3,300 people.[7] The disparity is further compounded by the assignment of some of these officers to administration, investigations or juvenile services, as well as days off duty and vacations. Realistically, no police department will be able to respond instantly to the citizen's need, no matter how great an effort is made.

Learning to be a mother wolf

When women rely on police and others for their defense, we perpetuate a society that perceives, trains, and treats women as unequals and as victims. When women are perceived as meek, defenseless prey, all women–from the bravest to the most timid–are targets of victimization by strangers, acquaintances or mates.

To be female is to literally give life to the next generation. Instead of accepting the traditional role of the weaker female, we must expand the feminine role to include defending life, as well as giving it birth. That means, after deliberation and training, that each woman should learn defenses against anyone who would take her life or harm those in her care, even if that defense entails taking or threatening the attacker's life.

A perfect weapon for a woman, a magic bullet or any other optimum mode of feminine self-defense, would all be worthless without the individual woman's determination to preserve her own life and well-being if necessary, at the expense of her assailant's life.

The well-meaning woman who buys a gun, saying that she plans to use it to mere-

Vicki Farnam (right) teaches women and men alike the value of mental composure that comes from knowing what to do and possessing the skills to prevail in a self-defense situation.

ly threaten an assailant, harbors a dangerous misunderstanding of the mind of the victimizer. Like any predator, the rapist knows instinctively if his victim is mentally unprepared to defend herself. Going far beyond the general societal idea that women are weaker and less aggressive, the rapist views women as objects for him to exploit for his benefit. Men who victimize women do so in pursuit of power and domination, as well as the humiliation of their victims, acting out of hatred for women.

When women accept responsibility to the extent that we are willing to spill the blood of an assailant before sacrificing our own lives, I believe we will find fewer men who are willing to risk injury or death for the gratification they achieve by raping and killing. In a survey published in 1986, over a third of felons questioned said they worried about being shot by their intended prey, and over half agreed that "most criminals are more worried about meeting an armed victim than they are about running into the police."[8]

In my ideal world, anyone who assaults, terrorizes, or exploits a woman would challenge an individual of equal or superior defensive ability. How can this dream come true, when the female gender is physically smaller than the male? Disparity of force is ultimately balanced by mindset—the determination to defend one's life—and by training and acquisition of the appropriate tools to support that determination.

We are individually responsible for our own survival and well-being. Just as a woman exercises and eats wholesome food, she needs to prepare herself for the eventuality that she may need to defend against assault. Until we pursue and embrace that power and responsibility, we continue to *fuel* the violence and abuse that takes the peace and safety from our lives.

---

1 *Violence Against Women: A Week in the Life of America*, a majority staff report prepared for the Committee on the Judiciary, United States Senate, 102nd Congress, 2nd Session, Oct. 1992.

2 *Journal of the American Medical Association*, Vol. 267, No. 23, p. 3132, June 17, 1992.

3 U.S. Dept. of Justice, Bureau of Justice Statistics: *National Crime Victimization Report*, 1998.

4 U.S. Dept. of Justice, Bureau of Justice Statistics: *Sex Offenses and Offenders*, Feb. 1997, NCJ-163392.

5 *Warren v. Dist. of Columbia*, D.C. App., 444 A.2d 1 (1981).

6 *Riss v. New York*, 22 N.Y. 2nd 579, 293 N.Y.S. 2nd 897, 240 N.E. 2nd 806 (1958).

7 Wright, J. & Rossi, P., *Armed and Considered Dangerous: A Survey of Felons and their Firearms* (1986), published by Aldine de Guyter Press; based on data from a survey formerly released by the National Institute of Justice.

8 Don B. Kates, Jr., *Gun Control: A Realistic Assessment*, excerpted from *Guns, Murder and the Constitution*, 177 Post St., San Francisco, CA 94108.

2
Finding the Will to Survive

Women's responses to using deadly force in self-defense range from absurd to frightening to savvy.

"I want a gun so I can point it at a rapist to scare him away."

"There's no reason to practice with my gun: I only keep it by the bed in case someone breaks into the house."

Another response, one well-thought out, is: "I don't own a gun because I'm not sure I could shoot someone."

Or a different view: "I feel my life-style puts me at risk, so I need a gun and I need to know how and when to use it."

The doubt that asked, "Can I kill to preserve my own life?" finally left my mind after an immersion study of justifiable use of deadly force. I suggest similar studies for women plagued with questions about of their ability to use deadly force in self-defense. At a minimum obtain Tanya Metaksa's book *Safe, not Sorry*,[1] and read it well. Read and reread Massad Ayoob's *In the Gravest Extreme*;[2] attend his seminars if possible.

My mental determination began to take shape during firearms training that included videotaped lectures by Massad Ayoob, an authority on the lawful use of deadly force. His frank discussions of the danger, illustrated by case histories and their adjudication in American courts, confirmed my belief that I was at risk and at the same time strengthened my resolve to protect myself. The study forced me to confront a fear of attack that has been with me

The will to survive stems from honor for yourself, love for your family, and regard for the well-being of other women and the society we will leave behind for our children.

since earliest childhood. In the end, I became certain of my right to stop any threat to my life and my own right to survival.

I still find it hard to listen to story after story of victimization and assault, but my immersion in this study of self-defense has burned away much of the emotional baggage of feeling powerless. Gone is the part that believed that being female meant being weak.

Deciding to live

The will to fight has been trained out of socialized humans. If surprised by an assailant, do not expect either the intent or technique of a vigorous defense to surface automatically. If you have not confronted fears about your right to defend yourself, questions of legality and morality may be foremost in your mind, interfering with the concentration that should be directing your defense. I don't think an ethical person can blithely say "Sure, its OK to kill to save my own life," without understanding what it means to kill in self-defense. Read the work of Ayoob, John Farnam[2] and obtain Robert A. Waters' *The Best Defense: True Stories of Intended Victims Who Defended Themselves With a Firearm.*[3] Study the experiences of those who have been forced to use guns in self-defense and consider what they have experienced in the aftermath. Ponder reports of citizens' self-defense acts as reported in publications including the NRA publications' monthly Armed Citizen column or *Combat Handguns* and other magazines. You need to understand all the implications of using defensive force, accept the responsibility, and decide how you will fight back, based on actual information, not on your society's prejudices.

I don't think we can consider the self-defense mindset without first discussing the moral aspect of using deadly force. Each ethical woman who learns self-defense techniques must ask herself, "Is it right for me to take a life to save my own?" Interestingly, the question is answered affirmatively more easily when phrased, "Is it right for me to kill to protect the lives of my children or my geriatric parents?" Few would stand by passively and allow those in their care to be harmed. Now consider the following query: "Is it right to take the life of an assailant who would kill me, orphan my children, and widow my spouse?"

Fundamental to the self-defense mindset is: The assailant forfeited his right to live upon initiating an assault with intent to kill or cripple an innocent person.

Even Christianity, with its doctrine of unselfishly putting others first, requires only that you lay down your life for a friend. Biblical doctrine does not promote self-sacrifice to satisfy the desires of a deranged predator who would take not only your life, but may go on to harm others. How different recent history could have been if Kenneth Bianchi, Ted Bundy, or other serial killers had encountered an armed woman who put her survival first!

Your decision to fight back grows stronger as you come to understand the conditions under which the law and society condones use of deadly force. Killing to protect property will reap a grave punishment both in the legal arena and in the reaction of family, friends, neighbors, employers and others. And though killing in self-defense is also likely to earn societal disapproval, clear-cut cases of self-defense are court-defensible and the survivor can deal with the concurrent social fallout, because she is alive to do so.

A serious study of use of deadly force results in a mature conviction to use this ultimate power only to preserve innocent life, not to threaten or intimidate. THE DECISION, as this process is termed by Ayoob, is one that assigns the ultimate value to innocent human life, not self-image, pride or material possessions. Educate yourself and make the decision to survive. Make the decision out of honor for yourself, love for your family, for other women and for society. This is not a decision to become a cold-blooded killer; this is a resolution to preserve that unique spark of life that is you.

The mental process

As you internalize your survival determination, you may experience thoughts, dreams and day-time reveries about assault and self-defense—envisioning scenarios with varying outcomes. Defined by Ayoob as a process of inoculation, most experience it when beginning to grasp concepts of righteous self-defense. This seems to be the mind's way of dealing with concepts that run counter to our earliest training to "do no harm"

or "turn the other cheek." The thoughts and mental images are your social conscience weighing the propriety of your newly-embraced determination to survive. The best advice I can offer is to accept the process. Don't judge yourself harshly for your thoughts. Understand that your mind is judging your new belief that you have the right to survive unmolested against the unfair constraints society has imposed on women.

A student told me that although she had no nightmares during her first months of carrying a gun, she was weighed down with guilt because she thoroughly enjoyed shooting her new gun. It seemed terrible to like something capable of deadly results, she confessed.

Reservations about using force in self-defense are put to rest in Ayoob's Judicious Use of Deadly Force seminar, where these and other concerns are addressed in depth.

Like all of us, she needed the company of like-minded individuals who could share similar experiences and confirm that she had not become evil. Other students have reported uneasiness and feelings of unspecified anxiety, as they grapple with the concept of using deadly force in self-defense, or even just possessing a deadly weapon. Women often report that their friends are horrified by their interest in guns, contributing to their feelings of generalized disapproval.

You may find it difficult to discuss your growing belief that you have the right to employ deadly force to stop a lethal assault. Only a limited pool of people share this conviction. Parents, co-workers and friends may not be able to respond supportively to the concepts you need to discuss. Responsible armed citizens, particularly women, belong to a limited peer group who will do what is necessary to prevent rape, murder or violent assault. Our feminine support group is extremely limited. Beyond the practical aspect of training, shooting classes can provide fellowship with like-minded people. A class that meets *your* needs will likely contain other women who are dealing with many of the same issues. Women's self-defense groups listed below can put you in contact with groups and instructors who share your concerns.[4]

At last, it is time for the good news: women are far less likely than men to be damned by society and their peers if forced to use a gun to stop a rape or assault. Men are often burdened with the macho ideal that they have to fight fairly, man-to-man. Society's unattractive portrayal of the helpless female establishes her need to use deadly force against a rapist or murderer. As a result, the woman who has determined to pull the trigger in self-defense may act more decisively if faced with an assailant who intends her harm. After the assault, she will suffer less condemnation from society and will answer fewer accusations that she used excessive force to save her life.

I am not going to regale you with tale after tale of rapes and assaults. I don't have the emotional fortitude to tell the stories, and there are already several good sources of this information.[2,3] What I am going to tell you is when and why it is all right for you to use a gun and other defensive tools and methods to stop a threat against you or other innocent life.

1 Metaksa, Tanya, *Safe, Not Sorry,* 1997 HarperCollins Publishers, Inc., 10 East 53rd St., New York, NY 10022.
2 Ayoob's *In the Gravest Extreme* and *The Ayoob Files,* and Farnam's *The Street Smart Gun Book* often available in retail gun stores or by order from Police Bookshelf, 800-624-9049.
3 Waters, Robert A., *The Best Defense,* Cumberland House Publishing, 431 Harding Industrial Park Drive, Nashville, TN 37211, 888-439-2665.
4 *Arming Women Against Rape and Endangerment* (AWARE), P.O. Box 242, Bedford, MA 01730-0242, *American Women's self-defense Association,* 713 N. Wellwood Ave., Lindenhurst, NY 11757, *National Rifle Association of America, Women's Issues and Information,* 11250 Waples Mill Road, Fairfax, VA 22030 703-267-1413.

3

When Am I Allowed to Shoot?

I don't think very many first-time gun owners immediately realize the power and resultant responsibility they have assumed. I know long-time gun owners who talk as though they haven't a clue about their responsibilities if a situation prompts them to draw a gun. I'm as uneasy with people who loudly proclaim "If anyone tries to break into *my* house, I'll shoot the *#@^ right through the door," as I am with someone who has a gun but is convinced they could never shoot another human, even to stop a lethal assault.

When does the law allow me to use my gun in self-defense? The question deals with issues of legality, morality and just plain common sense. The first issue, legality, varies from state to state, and is subject to the mood of the prosecutors and judges currently serving in your area. In our current age of Internet computer access, there is little excuse for ignorance of the laws governing possession and defensive use of firearms. Absent the convenience of browsing laws and statutes posted on many states' websites, an afternoon spent at the county courthouse reading through the applicable codes is a necessary responsibility for the armed citizen.

There are some broad parameters that define justifiable use of lethal force, however, and I credit Massad Ayoob's excellent instruction and writings for the information that follows. Meeting Ayoob, listening to his lectures, and later assisting in teaching his classes has strengthened both my determination and my caution in matters of self-defense. As we discuss the concepts of justifiable use of lethal force, I think you'll discern the constant interplay of caution and courage.

American women are products of our society's conditioning and the conscience of most raised in our culture is inevitably molded by certain moral values and ethics. Members of most Western societies behave in accordance the basic tenet of respect for life. Exceptions are diagnosed as psychopathic. Out of this societal code we—and the society that judges our actions—react to the defensive use of lethal force.

Both the legal and the moral codes have some foundation in plain old common sense. We will answer to the standard of reasonability in deciding when to employ lethal force. "What would be the actions of a reasonable and prudent person, under the same circumstances and knowing what you knew at the time?" This yardstick is the concept of reasonableness as introduced by Ayoob in his lectures on judicious use of deadly force.

Most instructors who address lethal force teach that the presence of three elements are required to justify using lethal force: ABILITY, OPPORTUNITY and JEOPARDY. If using lethal force in self-defense, the survivor must be able to show that the attacker had the ability to kill or cripple. Presence of a deadly weapon, superiority in numbers, or greater physical size and strength all exemplify ABILITY.

Women and elderly people are at increased risk from unarmed assailants, since a larger person can overpower and kill or seriously injure them with physical force alone. The concept that an unarmed but larger person can exert deadly force against a smaller person is called DISPARITY OF FORCE. Further applied to women's societal conditioning, this legal doctrine argues that women are conditioned to submissive behavior, to make peace and to avoid physical conflict. This feminine socialization, psychology and mindset put women at great risk from even an unarmed male assailant.

Did the assailant have the OPPORTUNITY to harm you? You cannot shoot a person who verbally threatens to choke you from across a crowded street because they cannot enact the threat without laying their hands on you. Opportunity exists only when the threat can be acted out with such immediacy that the intended victim cannot escape.

Finally, has the assailant put your life in JEOPARDY? Verbal threats and gestures alone do not justify killing unless the assailant's actions make it clear he intends to kill or cripple you now.

We will illustrate these concepts with a hypothetical situation, discussing each element as the fictitious "event" unfolds. Suppose your car failed as you returned home from your 10-year old daughter's piano recital. The neighborhood through which you must pass to reach your home is one that harbors the city's most unfortunate and unsavory residents. You have gotten your car off the street and are wisely sitting inside, doors locked, waiting for the help you have summoned on your cellular telephone. Instead, you watch as two men approach your car. One carries a length of heavy pipe. Your heart beat accelerates.

ABILITY?

Do the men have the ability to cause grave bodily harm or death to you of or another innocent person?

Yes, two against one, or a man against a woman is disparity force; the pipe is an improvised street weapon.

Ability exists.

As the men approach the car, you order your daughter to lie between the front and back seats. You pull your revolver from your holster purse and hold it on your lap. "Get out! We're going to have some fun," orders one of the men. You respond with a forceful, "Go away, now!" but the passenger side window shatters under the impact of the pipe.

OPPORTUNITY?

Is the threat close enough to inflict harm? A person cannot kill you from across the street, unless they wield a gun or explosive device.

Yes. When the car window was broken they created the opportunity to hurt you and your child.

Opportunity is present.

You fling open your door, and fix the gun sights on the nearest assailant, ordering, "Don't move!" Instead, he sneers, "You'd never shoot me, woman," and begins to come around the front of the car, brandishing the pipe.

JEOPARDY?

Did the assailant take specific action against you, causing you to believe he intended to inflict crippling injury or death?

Yes. When the pipe-wielder smashed your window and disregarded your command to stop, his acts put you in reasonable fear of death or crippling injury.

Your life and well-being is in jeopardy.

Suppose, to continue this awful little tale, that the assailant rushes toward you and you pull the trigger. As the leader falls, the other man turns and runs away. Can you shoot him in the back as he flees? No, no, no! No matter how terrifying the experience, you may only shoot to *stop the assault.* You must not shoot a fleeing felon who has clearly broken off the assault.

Do different rules apply inside the confines of your own home?

Suppose you hear noises in the basement during the daytime. Home alone, you take your loaded gun to check out the intrusion. This is no time to burst in, gun drawn with your finger on the trigger. You must know the intruder's identity before firing a panicked shot into a landlord, repair worker or other person authorized to be there.

I had owned my first gun less than a year when early one evening my landlady entered my apartment unannounced. While she believed I was not at home, her good intent did not decrease the alarm I felt looking down the hall to the front door until it became apparent who was entering the apartment. Fortunately, I had received training that prompted me to issue a verbal challenge before pointing the gun at the opening door. Did I have a gun

in my hand? You bet. Did the landlady know that? No, nor did she need to know. As has proven true in so many situations, training provided the confidence to act with discretion and to take the time to fully assess the situation for the presence or absence of dangers.

Imagine a new scenario. You awake at 2 a.m. to hear noises coming from the ground-level dining room. You really should call 911, then gather all your dependents to one room where the family can wait for help or mount a defense if the intruder comes through the locked door.

Armed home-defense is undertaken only to defend the innocent lives of those living in the home and never to protect only property.

Unlike your duty to retreat if assailed on the street, there are few if any jurisdictions that require you to leave your own home to escape an intruder. Evan Marshall, a well-recognized author in firearms and law-enforcement publications now retired after 20 years with Detroit's police force, told me that during all his years as a homicide detective, he never saw a citizen prosecuted for shooting a criminal who had forced entry into an occupied home. We deal here with legal issues. The survival and safety tactics to weather a home intrusion are numerous and will be covered in depth in Chapter 7.

For now, imagine that you pause at the head of the stairs and see in the half-light a stranger with a gun in hand. This so greatly escalates the danger that you are not required by law to issue any warning before shooting a criminal who has invaded your home (unless in one of the few jurisdictions where possession of firearms even in the home is forbidden). A stranger with a gun is an identifiable and immediate threat. He has the advantage of being physically alert and pumped up on adrenaline; his eyes are adjusted to the dark. His reflexes will likely exceed yours because he is the actor, just as you are the re-actor. Your only advantage is surprise if he has not yet detected your presence. Get behind bullet-stopping cover or retreat to a safer location if doing so does not risk your life or the well-being of others in the home. If no other reasonable alternative exists, you are allowed by law to shoot without issuing a challenge.

The individual's right to defend the sanctity of their home is upheld by most state laws and municipal codes. In civil court, however, the intruder or his heirs can allege you acted recklessly and by your actions deprived them of the benefit of their son, husband or father's support.

Other concerns must ascertain if other people dwelling in the home might have gone into this area with a gun to check out a strange noise. The decision to shoot must be based only on an unescapable threat to yourself or other innocent occupants of the home, not panic.

If you or occupants of your home participate in illegalities that could cause police to raid your home, you must consider how to deal with law enforcement officers entering to serve an arrest warrant or a search warrant. Armed citizens *should* accept a responsibility to live by higher standards than the average, unaware individual. Part of this responsibility includes adopting a lifestyle that avoids entanglements like illegal drug use, theft and other crimes. If sharing a dwelling with roommates, you will to some degree share the peril of illegal activities in which they may engage. Choose your companions carefully. In any case, the frequency of "no knock" and surprise police raids is exaggerated by gunstore commandos and internet chat groups. While officers use surprise to successfully serve search and arrest warrants, *unannounced* entry is scarcely a common or accepted tactic.

Finally, you must not shoot a criminal as he flees from your home. You may not shoot him as he is escaping. Some argue that you may kill a burglar as he escapes with your television or VCR, but that seems pretty uncivilized to me and is expressly unlawful in numerous jurisdictions, according to attorney Andrew Branca, author of *The Law of Self-Defense*.[1] Let him and your property go; the cost of that television is tiny compared to the legal fees you could incur defending yourself from a civil lawsuit for crippling or killing this person.

Legal issues aside, there are a number of excellent reasons to earnestly avoid using deadly force. They don't use the word "aftermath" for nothing.

Post-shooting survival

If forced to shoot an assailant in self-defense, you should be prepared for a number of consequences, including interacting with the authorities, dealing with your psychological and physiological responses, and answering to a society that may not acknowledge the deadly danger that caused you to use deadly force.

To discuss dealing with the authorities, let's again draw up a hypothetical incident. Home alone, you must shoot to stop a knife-wielding criminal who breaks through your bedroom window screaming out his specific, evil intent. The criminal falls and is no longer an immediate threat, so you order him into a controllable posture, face down, hands palms up and fully extended from sides, ankles crossed, his face turned away from you. With the danger of continued attack reduced, you reload your gun and call the police.

Dial 911 (or your area's emergency number) and tell the dispatcher:
- that a home intruder is wounded and down at your address;
- that you are holding him at gun point;
- your physical description, to assure correct identification by the responding officers;
- your location in the home, giving permission for the officers to break a door or window if necessary to gain entry.

You must be aware of numerous safety concerns, including renewed attack from the intruder, how to approach responding police officers and how to explain what has happened.

Presume your assailant is still dangerous, even if he has fallen. Find a position behind furniture that would impede a lunge toward you, and keep your gun pointed at the assailant. Maintaining control remains paramount; a conscious intruder can be expected to resist verbally and physically.

You need to be able to safely put the gun away when police officers arrive. The police have no choice but to consider *any* gun a threat, for their information is extremely limited. If your assailant is actively threatening, you need to keep the gun pointed at him, while preparing to holster or drop the gun upon police orders when they enter the room. Be sure you maintain enough distance to drop the weapon beyond your assailant's reach.

Be mentally prepared for the entry of the police officers. This is just one reason to continue talking to the 911 emergency operator until help arrives. If responding officers surprise you and you turn, gun in hand, to see who is coming in, there is a very good chance you will unintentionally point your gun toward the officers. This is convincingly threatening to merit gunfire from the police, who cannot automatically determine that you are the innocent party. Don't let a startled response cost your life.

Next you have to be concerned with giving the responding officers a truthful account of what occurred. You must not appear secretive or uncooperative, yet must take care to avoid giving confusing information.

Why not tell the cops everything? If you have just survived a look into death's abyss you will be eager to talk, make human contact and eager to justify the horrible act you were forced to commit. The responding officer, who will file an official, court-admissible report is not the person with whom to share this emotional unburdening. Maintain emotional control—you can bare your soul to a religious advisor or professional counselor later to excise the emotions. Priests and psychiatrists are generally exempt from court subpoena, so are safe resources for post-traumatic event therapy.

Reports of self-defense shootings reveal that the perceptions of trauma survivors are extremely unreliable. A survivor who makes a lengthy statement to the first officer through the door will probably relate incorrect information, especially about exact lengths of time, specific distances and other details. During the stress of a violent encounter, the body and mind narrow their focus to just the threat. This phenomenon, called the "tachy psyche" effect, is demonstrated in tunnel vision, distortions in time and distance perceptions, degradation of fine motor skills, general muscle tightening, and tremors. In addition, hearing shuts down to only that which seems necessary for survival. Called auditory exclusion, this phenomena causes survivors to report that they did not hear the shots they fired or words yelled by a partner.

The tachy psyche effect is a documented part of the human survival system and can cause unnecessary inaccuracies in court-admissible statements made to investigators. The survivor who must now defend her self-defense actions in court needs the testimony of experts who can educate the judge and jury about mental and physical reactions like sensory exclusion in an emergency. With documented studies in hand, the triers of fact should better understand and recognize the justification for your act of self-defense.

When law enforcement officers arrive at the scene of a self-defense shooting, it is best to supply only general information to avoid reporting inaccurate details as a result of the tachy psyche effect. If pressed for details at the scene, it is appropriate to tell the questioning officer: "He attacked me. I was forced to shoot before he killed or crippled me. You know how serious this is. I wish to call my attorney before you ask me anything further." By invoking the right to counsel, answers you (as the suspect) give to continued or insistent interrogation is of questionable admissibility in a court of law. Remember, any information freely volunteered, even after requesting legal counsel, can be used against the suspect.

Evan Marshall once told me, "Cops hate to be told 'no,' but it is better for you to spend the night in lock-up than 20 years in the penitentiary because of (inaccurate) information you gave right after a shooting."

If a police officer must shoot someone, the officer is usually sequestered away from the press and other information seekers, to let them settle their minds and emotions before making a statement or answering questions. You deserve the same consideration, although you may have to insist that you receive it.

Have a thoroughly-researched survival plan—both against physical attack and to fend off any who would turn your survival into a crime. If you ever face this situation, when asked what happened tell the responding officers, "He broke in and assaulted me. I was forced to shoot to save my life." Ayoob defines this approach as telling "the active dynamic." It truthfully describes what occurred and how the assailant's death or injury transpired.

Weigh the strength of emphasizing your assailant's aggressive, active role against blurting "He was in the bedroom and I shot him twice" to the first cop on the scene. Both statements are true: the first gives a more accurate picture of who caused the shooting. You had to shoot to stop his assault. A statement underscoring that awful reality places responsibility for the outcome squarely on he who initiated the confrontation.

Marshall suggests admitting to fear and a wish to run away. He advises this kind of response to on-the-scene questions: "My first thought was to escape, but that wasn't possible, so I yelled at him to leave. When he came up the stairs toward me and my family, I had to fire in his direction."

Unless you are hospitalized as a result of the assault, you may be taken into police custody after shooting in self-defense. Women are sometimes treated more gently than men, who may find themselves behind bars. You may be allowed only one phone call. Be sure you have laid the groundwork to make that one call productive. You should know, *in advance,* your attorney's after-hours telephone number. This is no time for interference by an answering service paid not to disturb your lawyer during the hours that most self-defense emergencies transpire–dark of night or weekends. The best preparation is advance arrangements for a stable family member, trusted associate or friend to contact attorneys and investigators. Explain that you want to prepare for the possibility that you might someday need to defend yourself. Ask if they would be willing to help in an emergency, describing for them the events that may follow a self-defense shooting. If they

After leaving law enforcement, Evan Marshall (right) has been active in teaching and writing about armed self-defense.

agree to help, it is their number you memorize and to them you direct your emergency call. From their greater freedom and superior privacy, they can call your attorney, a private investigator and anyone else who can ease your way through a shooting investigation.

Your gun, and probably any other firearms in your home, will likely be seized by investigators. The police have no way of immediately determining your innocence, and may well choose to take custody of any firearms until you are completely cleared of suspicion. The gun fired will be held as evidence until the prosecutor determines if you will be charged with a crime.

And finally, remember that even if authorities decide that there is no reason to charge you with a crime, you may well be sued in civil court by the survivors of the person who assaulted you or by the assailant, if he survives. As incomprehensible as it may seem, rapists' families may surface to argue in court that their "boy" was a good student, active in his church and quite incapable of violence. By civil court rules of evidence, the plaintiff need only convince the judge or jury that there is a better than 50% chance that their arguments are the truth. In criminal court, evidence must convince the triers of fact "beyond a reasonable doubt," a far more demanding burden of truth.

The judge or jury will be faced with an additional puzzle: you appear before them alive, a survivor. It is difficult to view the survivor as a victim, too. They weigh your vitality against the grief of a bereaved family. An element of sympathy for the dead person or for their survivors is inevitable, in spite of atrocities committed by the deceased.

Attorney selection

The person who has chosen to possess the power of defensive deadly force is advised to have an attorney available, as we just underscored.

Evan Marshall recommends that individuals should understand their legal environment *before* they must interact with the courts as a defendant. In small towns, a private law practice may augment the prosecutor's salary. If this is the case in your area, Marshall suggests making an appointment with the prosecutor, and spending an hour asking questions and getting advice about armed self-defense and the mood of the court in such cases. "Get a receipt for the fee," Marshall advised. Not only does that prove that you seriously studied the legal ramifications of your self-defense provisions, Marshall further suggests that the prosecutor may not be able to bring charges against someone that he or she has advised.

Another alternative Marshall advises is to contact the lawyer who defends the police force after a shooting. This lawyer's connections with the law enforcement community are valuable, he said.

Finally, Marshall concludes, "know the lay of the land." Local politics, the personal beliefs and the political aspirations of your local prosecutor can influence charges brought against someone who uses force in self-defense. Ask the attorney you contact how courts in your area have treated recent self-defense shootings.

Massad Ayoob emphasizes that citizens should not *retain* a defense attorney, nor should they seek out a famous criminal attorney to lead their defense. He lectures that keeping an attorney on retainer suggests that you expected to shoot someone. Famous criminal attorneys are remembered for "keeping bad guys out of jail," planting the suggestion in jurors' minds that you are not innocent. Instead, he suggests a building a relationship with a retired judge who is likely to be well-connected and understand current judicial attitudes.

Few criminal defense attorneys have extensive experience representing innocent people, and may advise you to confess to a crime you did not commit, in exchange for a lenient sentence. A common tactic is pleading that the gun went off accidentally, instead of in an intentional act of self-defense.

Not only is a lie given under oath a crime, it compromises the entire self-defense premise, that of the affirmative defense. The self-defense argument asserts that the defendant performed the act of which they are accused: using deadly force against another citizen. But it also argues that the accused was justified in so doing, as they acted in defense of their own or other innocent life. This is a demanding legal strategy and requires absolute adherence to ethical behavior by both defendant and attorney.

Defense against an abusive partner

You can see that even after a lethal force attack, the survivor faces many on-going challenges. Preparing for and facing judgement in the courts can be an arduous process, especially in circumstances where the survivor's right to use deadly force is not entirely endorsed by the investigating police or courts. One of the most challenging deadly force scenarios is found in cases where women were forced to kill or injure domestic partners in defense or themselves or their children.

In her book *When Battered Women Kill*[2] author Angela Browne cites a study group of 42 female survivors of domestic abuse and battering, who were charged in the death or serious injury of a husband or boyfriend. Of this group, about half were sentenced to jail terms, twelve received probation or suspended sentences, and only nine were acquitted. Jail sentences ranged from six months to 25 years, and one woman was sentenced to 50 years in prison. Browne quotes FBI statistics showing that fewer men are charged with first- or second-degree murder when they kill women they know, than when women kill men known to them. Women convicted of murder of a spouse or live-in mate frequently receive longer prison terms than men who kill wives or girl friends, according to Browne.

The courts and juries have historically viewed the killing of a domestic partner as an avoidable danger, thus postulating that the homicide must have been "premeditated." Juries lacked the education and sensitivity to recognize that the female survivor's instinct indicated that this time the batterer intended to complete his murderous act. Further, the woman's reticence to act against the abusive mate is demonstrated in the length of time she refrained from taking action against him. If ever expert testimony about abused women's psychology is needed, it is in defense of battered women who kill to save their own or their children's lives.

Always tell the truth

If you are charged with a crime after an act of self-defense, your job and the job of your defense team is to show the jury the truth–the information and details that prove you acted in response an unavoidable threat of death or crippling injury. Entire responsibility for the incident must be shown to rest with the perpetrator. Elements of the defense should include specific information about your training–both marksmanship training and studies in rightful use of lethal force.

Verify that you faced a deadly threat. Demonstrate that you were forced to choose between your life or his. From your first report to the responding officer through testimony in the courtroom, you must always tell the truth. Lies and exaggerations will be uncovered, and if one falsehood is revealed every subsequent statement made becomes dubious. Your justified act of self-defense will be tarnished and forever suspect.

---

1 Branca, Andrew, *The Law of Self-Defense*, Operon Security, Ltd., P O Box 2805 Action, MA 01720
   pp. 198.
2 Browne, Angela, *When Battered Women Kill*, The Free Press, Division of Macmillan, Inc., 1987
   pp. 11, 12.

In additional to the above titles, home-study resources include *The Ayoob Files*, available from Police Bookshelf, 800-624-9049 and Ayoob's on-going column *The Ayoob Files* in *American Handgunner* magazine, 619-297-8032.

4

Post-Violent Event Trauma: After you live to tell about it

A survivor who employs deadly force in self-defense must prevail in several arenas—physical, legal and emotional. The news media dissects self-defense shootings and other tragedies with little regard for the survivor's feelings; in the courts, lawyers argue about the circumstances and question the survivor's actions; and the survivor herself must come to terms with the assault and her act of self-defense. You don't hear much about emotional recovery from a violent event, only physical recovery. I intentionally emphasized the word "survivor" in the first sentence. It is difficult to equate "victim" with "survivor," yet the person who is forced to shoot or otherwise fight in self-defense is simultaneously victim of a crime to which they did not contribute, and at the same time, a survivor.

The emotional aftermath largely results from our society's reaction to killing and is exacerbated by the physiological response to the monumental stress of a life-death emergency. The research leader on post-violent event trauma is Dr. Walter Gorski. Though he has published no books, his professional papers and studies have been distilled and taught extensively by leading instructors like Massad Ayoob and John Farnam, and are the basis for this chapter. A "must-see" reference is Calibre Press' video Ultimate Survivors[1] which reenacts the stories of several law enforcement professionals who survived deadly assaults and lived to relate their experiences and to discuss the aftermath.

The aftermath

After a self-defense emergency, the survivor's body must eliminate the adrenaline produced to power through the crisis. Adrenaline is a powerful substance, requiring hours to leave the body, and its side effects are the some of the first post-violent event trauma symptoms the survivor experiences. Directly after an emergency, adrenaline creates agitation and a heightened mental state that may be followed by nausea or lethargy as it is eliminated.

Survival puts a different perspective on day-to-day needs like food and sleep. Sleeplessness may continue for several nights after a crisis. Nightmares commonly afflict those surviving a violent event. The dreams are often terrifying replays of the shooting, with endless variations, bizarre twists and conclusions. The attacker may become a loved one at the moment the bullets are discharged; the gun may become a different object in the hand; or the bullets may have no effect. During waking hours, daydreams or flashbacks also replay the event.

Assault survivors generally suffer insomnia, first as the adrenaline leaves the body, and later as the mind sorts through the horror of the attack. Likewise, loss or exaggeration of appetite may occur after a life-threatening emergency. Alcohol or drug dependency is a pitfall, as "crutches" used during hard times. Those who are treated by several professionals simultaneously may receive conflicting medications. If simultaneously receiving help from a psychiatrist and a physician, tell each professional about other treatment, and advise them of prescriptions you have been given to avoid receiving conflicting drugs.

A period of sexual dysfunction or promiscuity is experienced by many shooting survivors and relationships or marriages may fall apart after a shooting. In addition to sexual difficulties, the relationship may be challenged by the survivor's need for introspection, excluding the partner who wants to assist in the loved one's recovery, for they, too, have nearly lost a precious part of their life. The survivor, however, often feels emotionally isolated, believing that no one understands their questions and emotions.

The isolation increases if friends stop visiting the survivor. Just as you may have searched for the words to comfort one who has lost someone to death, others may struggle to interact with a friend who has killed in self-defense. Despite concern, acquaintances clam up, fearful that they will say something to upset the survivor. Those who act as if nothing has happened risk the survivor's outrage at the suggestion of fun or recreation. Others become impatient with the excess precautions and fear of one who has survived a violent assault.

Affection and patience are required. While friends and acquaintances need not be counselors, they can give priceless assurance and support to a survivor who is struggling to overcome an uninformed public's judgements about her decision to save her life.

Casual acquaintances, business associates, and the general public are less discreet in their avoidance of one who has killed. Called the "Mark of Cain" syndrome by Dr. Gorski, this societal judgment of the survivor is evident in refusals to let the children play together, in cold shoulders at social functions, or in insensitive inquisitiveness as they try to understand "what kind of a person could kill someone else." Unfortunately, we form our self-image largely from the reactions of other

> *The emotional aftermath largely results from society's reaction to taking human life.*

people. Repeatedly tell a child she is stupid or homely, and she will grow up concerned that the slurs were true. In the same way, when news reports, prosecuting attorneys and insensitive neighbors call a survivor a murderer, she will also wonder if her actions were those of a cold-blooded killer.

Surviving a self-defense shooting is a long and arduous process. Healing can be facilitated by skilled counseling, so don't try to survive alone. A counselor, spiritual advisor or physician offers the survivor solace and assistance during the emotional and physical recovery. Seek help when the dreams, flashbacks and sleeplessness are ruining daily life. Do not continue counseling with a judgmental counselor or minister who is unable to affirm the necessity and righteousness of your defensive choices, at a time when you most need confirmation of your own decency. There are experienced counselors who specialize in helping defense shooting survivors. Ask for professionals' names from the firearms instructors who trained you, or ask the mental health association for referral to a counselor with experience in post traumatic stress disorder (PTSD).

One of the best sources of relief is peer counseling, time spent with others who have survived a traumatic event and dealt with the after-effects. This is a two-pronged resource, offering succor for those in crisis, and an outreach for those who have survived and want to help others do the same. Most cities have rape crisis hot lines and support groups for women in crisis, and constantly need volunteers. When you are ready, contact one of these groups and volunteer to help. The YWCA is a good starting place. If they don't have a women's crisis program in place, the staff may be able refer you to a women's organization that will welcome your help.

Strength from adversity

Survivors of self-defense shootings are forever changed. Massad Ayoob compares the changes to scar tissue: for those able to grow from their experience, the trauma leaves behind a stronger character. Policeman Steve Chaney, featured in a segment of Calibre Press' video tape *Ultimate Sur-*

vivors, relates his feelings after surviving a second line-of-duty shooting. At first he wondered, "Why me?" Then he realized he was still alive and uninjured. "Some of life's positive lessons are not learned in positive ways," he tells viewers.[1]

Just as the inoculation process discussed in Chapter 2 prepares you to face self-defense challenges, advance knowledge of experiences common to those who have shot in self-defense gives strength, should you ever face the aftermath. If experiencing symptoms reported by other survivors, you can observe that others have undergone the same challenges and come through them to live full, satisfactory lives.

In the final analysis, only the survivor can make the decision how an attack will effect the rest of her life. We see people who go on to define their outlook and their entire life based on the experience of being a victim. This is tragic. While the survivor's life is forever altered, the goal of emotional and psychological recovery is to grow beyond the incident, becoming stronger and more resilient through the experiences of recovery.

---

1 *Ultimate Survivors*, Calibre Press, Inc., www.calibrepress.com 800-323-0037.

5

Safety-Conscious Attitudes

Animals wisely put their physical survival before other considerations. Far more in touch with survival instincts than are we, the so-called "lesser creatures" often avoid danger with greater intelligence. Humans are tempted to deny the existence of danger or–if we admit that a threat exists–we follow that acknowledgment immediately by "I know, but..."

". . . but I can't afford a reliable car."

". . . but I can't afford an apartment in a safe, secure building."

". . . but I can't pay for self-defense training and a weapon."

Others who acknowledge the risk stop training short of the level of skill required to deal with a determined assailant. Early in my karaté training, I hoped I could fight off a one-on-one assault, although I knew two or more could overpower me. I had to be thrown to the mat a number of times before acknowledging that at that skill level, I could easily be overcome by just one.

After a woman acknowledges the danger, she needs to obtain the skills and weapons that will allow her to go where she needs, while behaving as safely as possible. What choices will she make that give her the maximum safety with the least restrictions? A hermit-like withdrawal from the vicissitudes of modern living is rarely practical or satisfactory. Instead, I am advising a critical, realistic assessment of your world and pragmatic decisions based on its dangers.

Even this small insect instinctively shelters itself from predators until its hard shell is developed. The lesson? As Clint Smith says, "If you look like food, you will be eaten."

Judith Weiss, a self-defense instructor I met through our mutual membership in the American Women's Self-Defense Association, offers the following explanation:

"All activities (driving a car, filling the bathtub, walking through the parking lot at night) entail some risk. We all have different attitudes toward risk. At one end of the scale is refusing to engage in an activity by exaggerating the risk involved. At the other end is engaging in very risky activities while refusing to take any precautions. Neither of these attitudes are useful for living an empowered life. What is useful is to accurately assess the risks involved, take whatever precautions make sense, and live as fully as possible."[1]

Ask yourself now: what compromises am I willing to make to assure my well-being? Living outside the United States for a time, I learned to blend in to avoid the hassles faced by a woman traveling alone. That habit, plus growing older and decreased sensitivity about others' opinions, has eased me into a comfortable style of dress that doesn't scream out for attention. Understand this well: if you want to be noticed, be assured you will receive attention from one and all, not just from sane, desirable people. My own beautiful sister told me of the day she realized this truth. "I was unloading the trunk of my car," she explained. In the heat of summer, she wore short cut-offs that attracted the attention of a vagrant. "Hey, sister, you sure do keep yourself in good shape," she heard in a slurred male voice. Acknowledging him with a surprised "Thank you," she rushed to her nearby destination.

I well understand that this advice sounds like the common accusation that a woman "asked to be assaulted" by how she dressed. That is, of course, untrue. Predators select victims for a variety of reasons. You must choose: will you deal with unwanted comments and even being followed by odd strangers as a side-effect of your choice of clothing? If you make this choice, do it consciously, understanding the results and possible dangers. If you will make different choices, I recommend reserving your Spandex® for the gym, your short shorts for home, and covering your jog bra with a t-shirt when in public. Showy or very expensive jewelry can also attract trouble.

Only the strong survive?

Predatory people can intuitively sniff out those they can overpower psychologically or physically. They observe body posture and levels of alertness, as underscored by interviews with prisoners made by Dr. Robert Anthony. When the prisoners described a victim profile for women they might assault, they cited slouching posture, head down, eyes averted, a shuffling pace instead of brisk walk, women who were looking through their purse or brief case and appeared distracted, lost or unable to find their keys.

Another female victim type is the flamboyant beauty, who emphasizes outward appearance, but is not alert to dangers around her. Her posture, gait and garments invite a sexual response. Both the unaware woman and the flamboyant beauty attract predatory interest. While the women identified by Dr. Anthony's study group projects fright, the flamboyant beauty is not sufficiently concerned.

Though few advance far enough in their training to mount an decisive unarmed defense against a committed assailant, the martial arts can transform bodies and attitudes. Karaté was the catalyst that changed my timid, submissive posture into an erect, confident stance. I have proven that a strong, confident posture discourages assailants and predators. Martial arts awoke my awareness to danger and heightened sensory perceptions of my surroundings.

A common characteristic shared by most vulnerable women is an oblivion to threat. A careless woman will wander right into the arms of trouble, engrossed in conversation or simply lost in her own thoughts and worries. Evolution may be to blame: in the bipedal mammal, males of the species are the aggressive hunters while women traditionally "gather" food looking down

Aware of her surroundings, this woman checks carefully around her as she unlocks the door to her home, prepared to respond appropriately.

and collecting the fruits of the earth. A successful hunter possesses a predatory instinct about surrounding resources. This skill can be developed in men and women alike, stemming from a desire on the part of the novice to gain mastery of her surroundings.

Unfortunately, nearly all the people I know suffer from a lack of awareness of their moment-to-moment surroundings. If you can't answer a pop-quiz about the area you passed through five minutes ago, you are caught in this oblivion. Inner contemplation is good, but not on the street where being deep in thought can cost your life. The woman who indulges in airheadedness experiences an immobilizing terror when surprised by danger. The stress of bare fear is debilitating, while the alertness of moment-to-moment awareness is invigorating and requires no additional energy to maintain.

And be truthful: most adults who look "lost in the clouds" and absent-minded usually aren't contemplating nirvana, they are more often worried about a relationship, concerned about a bank balance or calculating how many more miles they can drive before buying new tires! Now that is exhausting!

The most difficult question I am asked is "how can I convince the women in my life that they are at risk?" Denial is a hard condition to combat. Conversationally, point out crimes against women that have occurred nationally, in your own city and even in your own neighborhood. Take care to make your approach constructive, avoiding criticism. If the woman is your spouse, partner or roommate, use these examples to devise plans of how you and your loved one would combat and survive an assault, like a home invasion. Bring her in at the planning stage, giving her an active role, instead of announcing "here's how we'll do it!"

Without pressure, make available reading material including the titles listed in Chapter 2, especially Tanya Metaksa's book and the work of Robert Walters. An additional source of safety and defense advice is found in Walter Rauch's book *Real World Survival! What Has Worked for Me.*[2] Just as individuals respond positively to different personalities, different authors will resonate with varying effectiveness with different readers. Obtain as many personal safety books and brochures as possible and make them accessible to the women about whom you are concerned.

Continual pressure and criticism of your loved one's attitudes and actions will not change how she behaves. Gentle persuasion and making information easily available to her may do the trick. Genuine change will not be accomplished overnight.

Absolute awareness

I call it absolute awareness: the acknowledgment that danger exists; the moment-to-moment watchfulness for peril; the commitment to protect myself from danger; and the skill and training to back up that commitment.

Many schools of armed self-defense employ Colonel Jeff Cooper's color code to describe the states of awareness appropriate to different levels of threat. Col. Cooper, known to handgunners as the father of modern pistolcraft, adapted the color code used in military operations during World War II, when radio-transmitted reports on troop conditions were subject to interception by the enemy. The code has been altered by others, including Ayoob, to better suit the private citizen's choices of preclusion or retreat.

CONDITION WHITE describes circumstances in which you are completely oblivious to any threat. One enters Condition White in sleep or when indulging in the oblivion discussed earlier.

Awareness to the potential for danger even in the absence of any recognizable threat is CONDITION YELLOW. Psychologists tell us that humans can spend all their waking hours in Condition Yellow with absolutely no detrimental effects. Indeed, Condition Yellow should be your mental state while driving, chopping up vegetables, or hammering a nail into the wall. You are not threatened by any immediate danger, but are aware that your activity includes potential hazards.

Some activities are riskier than others. Circumstances may prompt you to switch into CONDITION ORANGE. This attitude is appropriate in situations that entail a higher degree of risk like driving on icy roads or entering your empty home late at night. In this mental state, all your senses are active, scanning for potential danger. You are prepared to take appropriate action should a specific threat appear. If an armed stranger approaches as you open your front door, you should switch to CONDITION RED, in which you have identified a specific life-threatening danger.

If Condition Red is embodied in the thought "Oh, no, they could hurt me!" CONDITION BLACK is "They are assaulting me!" Black indicates a lethal assault is in progress and justifies immediate use of any level of force necessary to stop the assault.

How does the defensive firearm fit into these conditions? In Condition White you should not have a gun available, since your lack of alertness makes the weapon vulnerable to a hostile or to a child's misuse. Secure it in a lock box or gun safe, since in Condition White you are not in command of its power. In Condition Yellow you may or may not have your gun readily available, however if you do have a gun, you must not drift into the unguarded Condition White. In Condition Orange it would be preferable to have immediate access to your gun or alternative defenses, like a trained guard dog at your side. Depending on the situation, the gun may or may not be in your hand. In Condition Red the gun should be in your hand if circumstances permit, even if it is only a small, five-shot revolver in your hand inside a coat pocket. You need to be ready and able to use it if a lethal assault pushes you into Condition Black.

Self-defense instructors tell me that the women most reluctant to learn defensive tactics (whether a martial art or the handgun) are those who feel secure in their marriage or relationship. Newly single women, they tell me, are among their most enthusiastic students. It makes perfect sense: the newly independent person learns to enjoy many fresh challenges. Providing for her own survival offers a lot in strength, positive self-image and pride.

I suspect that relying on a mate for personal safety indicates a dependency that characterizes other aspects of the relationship. Both marital partners contribute to the equilibrium of their relationship. As a woman accepts responsibility for her own survival, her move away from the comfortable dependency threatens the union's equilibrium. Accepting respon-

Condition Red: Lethal assault imminent. Escape if possible or prepare to fight back.

sibility challenges the woman's self-image as much as it challenges her perception of her strong mate (to say nothing of his self-image as the provider!) Married women who have accepted these challenges report that striking a new balance leads to a stronger, more balanced relationship in which each partner relies on the other in new, healthier ways.

Placing all the responsibility for family safety on a person who is gone 40-60% of every day is not only unfair, it is a con job. Not many men would accept this division of responsibility if the demand was voiced as: "You have to take care of me, even if I don't care enough to look out for myself!" Thankfully, some women have genuinely good partners who encourage them to exercise independence and develop survival skills. The woman fortunate enough to be involved with such an individual has a responsibility to take care of herself and their family.

Guns won't keep you safe

What? A book about guns saying that a gun won't keep you safe? Yep. Absolute awareness about your surroundings, tactical planning, and ability with an appropriate weapon are the factors that will keep you alive and well. *You* are the active party–your gun is an inert mechanical assembly, incapable of any action on its own.

An expensive gun or any other defensive device is useless if the owner is oblivious to threat. The prepared person, however, in addition to maintaining an appropriate level of awareness, will study, practice and perfect her defense tactics. In following chapters, we'll talk about basic tactical awareness and self-defense preparations.

---

1   Judith Weiss, http://www.yehudit.org/APINintro.html.
2   Rauch, Walter *Real World Survival! What Has Worked for Me*, self-published by Rauch & Co., PO Box 510, Layfayette Hill, PA 19444.

6

Victory is a Fight Avoided

Over-socialized humans are rarely prepared to respond instantly to assault. It is a huge shock to find a punch coming toward your face or find yourself immobilized by a bear-hug from behind. This element of surprise serves criminal assailants well, whether attacking men or women. Mental preparation coupled with physical training gives the advantage that avoids, escapes or wins the fight. As discussed in foregoing chapters, there are few places it is safe to lapse into Condition White.

Know who and what is around you. Practice this exercise: when driving or walking, train yourself to see all the details, all the people, doorways, windows and natural elements like thick foliage. Mentally re-create the scene through which you just passed as though designing a movie set. In your mind, describe the people inside a distance of 20 feet; describe cars and structures; detail objects you could use as bullet-stopping cover in a gunfight or obstacles to prevent contact with an unarmed assailant. As awareness of the scene ahead and around you becomes habitual, you'll rarely be frightened by the wino who lurches out of the doorway to ask for money. You will already have moved to the outside of the sidewalk, insulated among other pedestrians.

Walk purposefully, head up, eyes scanning your surroundings. Keep your hands free so you are ready to fight if surprised. Don't shove your hands into pockets or wrap your arms around your torso. Whenever possible, avoid carrying a big purse or filling your arms with packages. Briefcases, laptop computer bags and luggage need shoulder straps. Keep your limbs supple and relaxed, ready to move quickly. Stay loose and alert.

Make brief eye contact with other pedestrians. Let potential predators know you have recognized them. Abusers prefer anonymity. Walk away from catcalls and let casual comments from strangers pass unanswered.

One of the harsh facts of life in the '90s was the massive proliferation of people living on the city streets. The presence of these poor, desperate people drastically altered the mood of the streets in most American cities. I was out of the United States from January through July of 1990. When I returned to the States that summer, I took up residence near downtown Seattle. Imagine my surprise to encounter nearly as many beggars in my first morning stroll as I would have on a walk to the vegetable market in India! But there was a difference: the Seattle beggars were physically aggressive. They took offense if ignored. Some would physically block the sidewalk or verbally assail those ignoring their demands. Others worked in pairs, flanking the person they had targeted. It would be wrong to blame all the street crime on homeless people, since many of the predators "working" streets and city parks do not share the street dweller's fate.

Learn a few basic rules for dealing with aggressive approaches from strangers: Whether overseas or in America, one of the most common approaches a criminal takes is to ask an innocent question. A stranger will approach you as you unlock your car in a parking lot. "Excuse me, do you know the way to the bus station?" Without pausing, open the car door before the stranger gets too close and quickly enter the safety of a locked car. Only then, and only if you feel strongly compelled, should you respond. The problem is, it never ends with the first question. The predator prolongs the exchange, asking other questions about landmarks or events, anything to distract you until they have a chance to slip through your defenses and get what they want: your possessions or your person.

If unable to immediately get away, create distance between you and the stranger and respond firmly "Sorry, no," as you leave the area. Experience tells me that ignoring a harasser is usually perceived as fearfulness. Make eye contact, politely and forcefully answer that you cannot help them, and quickly move away to a safer place. Assaults happen lightening fast–usually in three to five seconds. Too often the female prey is knocked to the ground before she realizes what is happening.

Where is it written that you have to be nice to strangers?

While the Bible directs believers to turn the other cheek, love thy neighbor as thyself, lay down your life for a friend, and other selfless ideals, nowhere does it advocate sacrificing innocent life for the gratification of evil doers. I firmly believe that the Creator placed an excellent survival instinct in all creatures, and would prefer you and I exercise that ability to assure our daily survival. Today's reality requires a guarded response to strangers. Giving help to those in need is admirable, and can and must be accomplished in sensible, safe ways.

One of our century's mass killers, Alton Coleman and his accomplice Debra Denise Brown, approached a number of victims by asking for rides to church or prayer meetings. The victims were robbed, raped and usually murdered by the criminal pair. Serial rapist-murderer, Theodore Bundy, viciously exploited the human desire to help others by pretending to be injured. It is thought that he accomplished his first double-murder by asking women at a lake near Seattle to help him load a boat onto his car. They believed he needed help with the task, because he wore an arm sling. After capturing one young woman with this ruse, it we are told that Bundy returned and successfully abducted a second victim. Two young women visiting a popular park lost their lives that day because they did not question the safety of going with a stranger to give him a bit of help.

First, recognize the predatory stalking technique of stepping in close to engage the prey in unnecessary conversation. There are phone numbers to call for the correct time; directions can be obtained by reading maps or asking at gas stations. Two muggings at a security apartment building where I lived occurred when a man asked for directions while our residents were unlocking the front door. One woman lost her purse for her courtesy; the other found herself wrestling with a man who threw her to the ground before she could give directions to a public park.

"Gotta light?" Common courtesy does not require you to respond to wolfish approaches from strangers who can easily get a match, receive directions or the time of day elsewhere.

If circumstances don't allow an immediate escape from your stalker, face your harasser and order in a firm, loud voice: "Go away! Don't talk to me!" or "Leave me alone, now." Couple your command with forceful eye contact. Your unwavering gaze shows your assailant you are not afraid to take whatever action is necessary to rid yourself of him. Use a decisive, commanding voice, expelling the words with air from the diaphragm.

The first women's self-defense course I took many years ago, taught us to cuss and swear loudly at assailants. Role-playing a stalking event, the prey was to swing around and yell "What do you want, asshole? Leave me the fuck alone." The premise was that the bad language would shock the harasser into breaking off the pursuit. Experience has since shown that gutter language is more likely to anger the assailant, escalate the assault and make you appear to be the instigator or an active participant in the fight. Your abusive language will be perceived by witnesses as active involvement in a two-sided dispute.

A young advertising professional with whom I once worked learned this lesson the hard way. What began as a purse-snatching attempt rapidly escalated to an all-out assault when she screamed obscenities at a man who initially only wanted her wallet. She had been knocked to the ground and would have sustained a beating, but a police officer rounded the corner and stopped the assault before she was badly hurt. Your pre-emptive strength lies in an unabashed gaze, confident stance and body language, not in bravado expressed by foul language. In all instances, you must be able to back up your aggressive attitude with your physical skills or an appropriate weapon.

If your assailant disregards your command to leave, take evasive action if you have not already tried to escape. In crowded public spaces, uninvolved bystanders can serve as a distraction while you get away. Move around other pedestrians so they and others have to step between you and your harasser, giving you time to escape. Other urban features that provide escape routes are people-filled malls, stores and public buildings. Here, buffered by onlookers, you can find a telephone and call for police help.

Even if you carry the firepower to "win" a fight, you must avoid drawing your gun unless the threat to your life is immediate and unavoidable. One winter evening I waited with a companion at a Seattle bus stop. Several others gathered to wait for the bus, including a small-statured fellow who began "working" the crowd for change and other hand outs. In parts of Seattle, begging is a normal activity and people tend to forget the danger its less savory participants pose. We rebuffed the fellow, only to become re-involved when he began to touch a young woman who seemed unable to fend him off.

In retrospect, intervention may have been foolhardy, but we stepped in and moved the man into the street. As his verbal abuse escalated, he reached under his coat for the weapon he kept in the small of his back. At that moment, the bus arrived. Keeping one eye on him, we took seats toward the front of the bus. To my horror, he boarded, took a front-row seat and started threatening to "cut up some rich young yuppies." When the bus driver refused to discharge the man, I told my companion that we should disembark only at a busy, well-lit stop and when other passengers were exiting the coach. At a downtown bus stop, a trio of college-age boys rose to disembark, so we also arose and made a safe exit, keeping the uninvolved boys between us and the harasser.

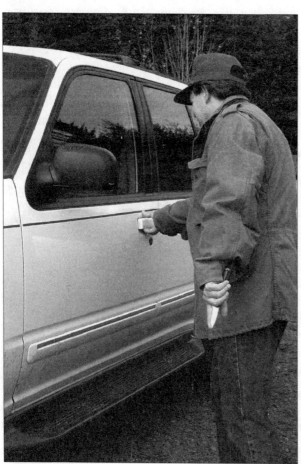

A knifer rarely reveals his weapon until in close, where the chances of stopping him before he cuts you are minimal.

Had I owned a gun then, I would have made the same decision. There are no winners in a street fight. At close quarters and against a committed fighter a gun against a knife may not save you. The knifer may die from your bullet, yet not before he has cut you repeatedly with his blade.

Street fights are further complicated by the presence of innocent bystanders. My bullet might have passed through the vagrant to harm the bus driver or another. And finally, having finessed our way out of the situation, we were free to go. Had we fought, we could have been held accountable for the harasser's injuries. Always try to escape a confrontation; join the fight only if the alternative is unavoidable death or crippling injury.

React decisively if your instincts tell you something is wrong. If you feel scared or uneasy, leave the area. Be prepared to fight back immediately and viciously if you are assaulted. A small revolver in your pocket, a can of pepper spray or a mini-baton and keys in your hand, may deflect an assailant long enough for you to reach safety. Whatever your defensive tools, their value is only as great as your pre-established defensive plan. Have simple, vicious responses planned and mentally rehearsed. "I will do 'A' if that oddly behaving teenager does 'B'."

Danger signs

Ability to react dynamically relies on recognizing danger. Too often denial or air-headedness blinds women to predictable predatory approaches. As outlined earlier, Condition Yellow codifies the appropriate level of awareness vital to knowing what threats may be present. Your guard should go up if an attempt is made to block your path—whether as a pedestrian or driver. By maintaining a good danger scan, this ploy is avoidable. Observed far enough ahead, you have room to cross the street rather than step around an impediment into an alley or bushes.

It is essential that you know what people around you are doing. Take care that you are not "blinded" by your stereotype of criminal appearance. Youth crime is rampant. Be aware of teens and young adults of either gender, as well as people in all manner of dress and grooming.

Be alert to followers who match your pace, pausing when you do, or walking faster to keep up. A car that follows slowly, or pulls ahead and stops near the sidewalk you must

A small, lightweight revolver holstered in a jacket pocket can be carried with the hands on the grips when moving through areas of potential danger.

tread should raise an alert. A car that has passed you several times is cause for concern. Unless an escape route is accessible, do not look away if targeted: the predators have already chosen you. Instead, pointedly look inside the car, do your best to memorize features or characteristics of those inside. Remember, anonymity not recognition serves the criminal.

Be aware of predatory team-work in which one member distracts you as the other attacks. Look for exchanged glances, nods or signals between two pedestrians who do not appear to be together; watch out for circling or flanking moves. A stranger who pushes or bumps you deserves an extra wide berth. The contact may be a distractionary move to channel you into a partner's grasp, may indicate mental instability, intoxication, or simply a rude, aggressive person with whom you do not need to exchange words. Whatever the problem, you need not become part of it. Likewise, move away from drunken or excessively boisterous groups to avoid being the prey of dog-pack mentality. In many situations a solid tactic is to interpose obstacles between the group activating your early warning alarm. This may be as simple as stepping around others in a crowd, crossing a busy street, getting behind a car in an immediate danger. A large planter, trash container or any other object may prevent the person you fear from rushing you. Finally, neither is the absence of crowds reason to let down your guard. All an empty street provides is the absence of witnesses about which an assailant need worry.

Faced by any of these predictable predatory warning cues, wishing that it "ain't so," won't change anything. Do something, and do it NOW to avoid, escape, or if necessary strike back before you are injured.

Choose your pleasures

A woman needs to weigh the events she attends to determine if they entail a greater-than-ordinary threat because of location or the type of crowd. Is the level of threat manageable under the circumstances of the event? For example, I might skip a popular band's concert, since concert security personnel usually frisk spectators, making it impossible to carry a defense weapon. I might decline to attend a theatre production held in a neighborhood with a high crime rate. These decisions are extensions of the acknowledgment that dangers exist. They represent the mindset embodied in Condition Yellow, in which you consciously avoid things that might cause you harm.

Choose your dangers. For example, I despise those huge multi-floor concrete parking garages. I'm not the only one who feels at risk going there. A clerk at a gun range told me that after feeling threatened in a hospital's underground parking facility he started parking on the street or in an open-air lot, even though it was considerably less convenient. Parking garages don't generate enough foot traffic for the relative safety of crowds, and aren't patrolled nearly often enough to deter the opportunist looking for a victim.

If you must park in public garages, walk in the driving lane, avoiding the close confines between parked cars, and have your gun immediately accessible. Park in a garage with live attendants and drive right back out if anything looks or feels threatening once you are inside. Park near the attendant and in a brightly lit area. If you are delayed at work, ask a trusted co-worker or a security officer who you know to escort you to your car. Follow your instincts: they will keep you alive.

Public elevators are another location in which I exercise guarded caution. A few years ago, I'm told, numerous Seattle women began using the stairs after a series of muggings and molestations in the downtown highrise elevators. These ladies exercised (no pun intended) admirable awareness of danger, and probably got a little extra muscle tone as a bonus. Seriously, give me a crowded elevator, with all its discomforts, instead of an elevator car containing only one or two people. While it is a situation-specific decision, I have been in several incidents like the one at a Seattle community college when I boarded an elevator alone, only to be followed in by a fellow who I had seen waiting nearby although several elevator cars had come and gone. I couldn't say exactly what alarmed me about him, so I exercised the "be smart and act like an idiot" option, pressing the "open" button and saying, "Silly me! I don't need to go up!" as I left the car. Don't board an elevator with a single occupant; wait for the next car. When you get in an elevator, stand near the control panel, keeping a weapon in hand: a revolver in the pocket, your Persuader mini-baton on your keys held ready in your hand.

I see women taking more risks while jogging and exercising than during nearly any other activity. Women exercise along deserted running paths, in parks replete with hiding spots, and wearing garments that a courtroom lawyer can construe as sexually inviting. Again, I don't advocate locking yourself away in a cloister: I do suggest responsible awareness. If possible, walk or jog with several companions and a protective dog. Even in groups, maintain awareness of your surroundings, don't drift off in a haze of burning muscles or music from your sports radio. I would not cut off my auditory warning system by wearing headphones in public, whether jogging, riding the bus or waiting in a queue.

Jogging paths are a more difficult subject. Many running paths follow scenic, yet remote and dangerous routes. Bushes, trees and ravines offer concealment for an assailant and a place to which he may drag his victims. In urban areas jog on a public track around an open playing field. And use the track only during daylight and at times when other people are about. In Spokane, Washington, Kevin Coe enjoyed a lengthy career as a rapist, preying on solitary joggers who ran at night or dawn.

Let me re-emphasize the importance of immediate access to your handgun whenever you are out in public. Shop for a good concealment holster, or carry your gun in a belly band, a holster-fanny pack or a gun purse tucked snugly against your body. The extremely light alloy and Titanium revolvers are perfect sports guns, as the lighter weight bounces and moves less as you run or work out. A bobbed-hammer revolver can be hidden in a pocket with your hand on it, ready for immediate use if your awareness rises to Condition Red.

Automobile safety AAA never told you about

The aware woman uses everyday equipment to maintain her safety, understanding that the gun is actually a very small part of the personal safety equation. A locked car surrounds you with an added ring of safety, if you are alert to tactical advantages. Maintaining a safe car that will not fail you is critical. This, as with home safety, is a matter of priorities. Forego buying a few CDs, in favor of getting a tune up. Keep the gas tank more than a quarter full, so you don't absent-mindedly run out of gas and

At traffic lights or when stopped by heavy traffic, check for proper distance from the car ahead, by asking "Can I see its rear tires over the hood of my car?"

become stranded. At gas stations, exercise alertness, observing the area carefully before starting to pump gas and remaining aware of the surroundings while pumping. Chose a pump at which you cannot be blocked in from front and rear, and use a credit card to pay at the pump as a way to minimize your exposure and time out of your car's safety.

Learn basic car maintenance skills, like changing tires. The ability to replace a flat tire and get your car to a service station greatly increases your safety. If you cannot repair the car's problem, do not leave the safety of your locked car. If you have a cellular phone, dial 911 to summon help. If not, put up the hood and wait for the state patrol. Do not open the door or window for anyone but an identified law enforcement officer. If, for any reason, you are unsure of the officer's legitimacy, remain in the car and ask him to call a tow truck.

Your safety begins before you get in the car. Your personal vehicle should always remain locked, even when you are in it. Look beneath the car from a distance while approaching, and check between the seats for an intruder before getting inside. Once in the car, lock all the doors to keep unwanted "passengers" out. Never pick up hitch hikers or allow a stranger into your car. If flagged down to help at an apparent emergency, remain in your locked car and call the highway patrol for assistance. Drive away after reporting the location and situation.

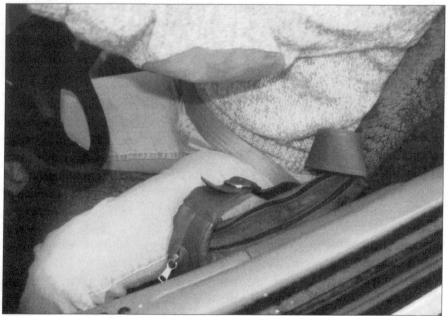

If you carry a handgun in a holster handbag, take extra care inside your car that the gun and purse are tightly lodged where they will remain available, even after a minor accident.

When you are stopped at a traffic light, glance around to see who and what is within striking distance. At traffic lights, maintain distance between your car and the one ahead. A good visual cue is to stay far enough back to see the rear tires of the car ahead. This space will allow you to pull around the car and escape if an attack is initiated while you are stopped. If first in line at the light on a multi-lane street, leave half a car length between you and the stop line. Most drivers will simply stop somewhat ahead of you, increasing your anonymity and making you a less attractive target to the occupants of cars in the adjacent lanes. And, by the way, before pulling out into that intersection when the light changes, check in both directions then count "thousand one, thousand two," to be sure the yellow-to-red light jumpers all get through before you drive through, as wisely advocated by Curt Rich in his outstanding book *Drive to Survive!*[1] which I highly recommend.

Tony Scotti's video tape on "defensive" driving is another excellent source of additional car safety information. While Scotti addresses the driver/bodyguard's responsibilities, protecting yourself and your family is equally important and many of the skills taught are very applicable.[2] One of the highlights of my own training remains several days spent in a driving course with Scotti, a charming man who drew on his experience in the executive protection business and time spent racing cars.

While driving remain alert to cars that may be following you. Taking down a license plate number and checking in the rear view mirror may worry an opportunistic assailant who prefers easier prey. If you are followed, do not go home. Make at least three right- or left-hand turns, then go to the nearest occupied public facility, stop close to the door and run inside, calling out loudly, "Call the police, I'm being followed!"

If you are attacked while stopped in traffic, take any escape route available—at times like this it's OK to break traffic laws. While you must remain aware of others' safety, you need not sit immobile at a red light and allow a window to be broken by an assailant, instead of driving through an empty intersection or onto the sidewalk.

On longer stretches of freeway or rural highway, a car that matches your speed should at least raise your level of concern. It may be a road-weary motorist or it may be a predator. If another driver's actions alarm you, exit at the next ramp and drive to a busy service station or other public facility. If not followed, this is an opportunity to break up your own driving exhaustion. If followed, however, you have a much better idea what you are up against. Before stopping, make at least three turns to determine if you are truly being followed, then call for help. A cellular telephone is mandatory equipment in a car, by my standards. Use it to call 911, giving a full description of your harasser, location and your circumstances.

We have been trained to get out of the car if involved in a minor accident. Predators recognize this training as an opportunity. The rapist causes a fender bender and attacks when you leave the safety of your car to inspect the damage. Remaining in your car is much safer, and you may wait for the police to arrive, or drive to a busy, well-lit area to report the accident from a safe place. Under no conditions should you get out of your car if only you and the other driver are on the scene. I would hesitate to get out of my car if a second motorist stopped to assist, recognizing the risk of criminal teamwork. I would ask the "Good Samaritan" to go call for help, remaining safely inside the car until the police arrived.

Never stop to help what appears to be a stranded motorist. You simply cannot know their disposition or true identity. If you feel you should help, call the police who will respond and help those who are truly stranded. As mentioned earlier, one of the best safety tools you can possess is a wireless phone. It is an excellent way to obtain help if you are involved in a minor accident. If lost or stalled, the cellular phone lets you summon help without leaving the safety of your vehicle.

Do not overlook the value of the cellular phone as a way to call for help without leaving the relative safety of your car.

This same caution holds true for walking situations. Never approach one who calls out for help–assess the situation cautiously from a safe distance and call out that you have heard their cries and are going to summon the police immediately. The plea for help is a ploy of rapists, who may cry out that they have just been assaulted and injured, but grabs the woman who comes to his aid.

If you use bus transportation, try to establish a schedule that lets you use the bus during daylight. If that's not possible, board and disembark at stops that are busy and well-lit. On the bus, be alert, know who is on the bus, what they're doing and how close they are to you. Try to sit in the front near the driver, and make an effort to break through the anonymity of being "just one of the passengers," if the driver seems trustworthy. On the bus, be very wary of strangers who strike up uninvited conversation or try to elicit information about your destination, or where you live or work. Also be aware that personal conversation between friends may be overheard and exploited.

On some public transit coaches the front seats consist of length-ways benches that make it much easier to maneuver in and out of and allow you to watch the occupants of the bus easily and unobtrusively and are situated so no one can sit behind you.

Pepper spray clipped to the car visor keeps an intermediate defensive tool accessible and in view where you will remember to take it along when you leave the car.

When disembarking from public transportation, watch to see who exits with you. If evasive action like crossing a street several times does not dislodge your follower, run to the nearest populated and well-lit area yelling, "Help! Call the police! I'm being followed. Call the police!"

Choose safety

In every situation, the aware woman will ask herself, "Does it feel safe?" She will mentally explore the potential for danger before committing herself to any action. For example, if asked to visit the home of a new male friend, the aware woman will probably respond that she is sorry, she cannot, but may counter with an invitation to get together in a restaurant or other public location. A responsible man will recognize her prudence without taking offense; a predator will act insulted, exhibit hurt feelings or ridicule her caution. Consider this kind of episode a good test to find out if your new friend will respect your intelligence and sensibility.

We must take responsibility for creating our own safe zones. We must not blithely wander into another's control. A full, secure life is possible; we need only take responsibility for our own well being.

---

1 Rich, Curt, *Drive to Survive*, ISBN 0-7603-0525-0, 1998, MBI Publishing Co., 729 Prospect Ave., P O Box 1, Osceola, WI 54020.
2 Scotti, Tony, *Counterambush Driving Skills and Evasion Techniques,* Paladin Press, Gunbarrel Tech Center, 7077 Winchester Circle, Colorado 80301. 800-466-6868, 800-392-2400.

7

The Comfort of Home Safety

Make personal safety your leading priority. This requires an investment in safe living quarters, assuring the road worthiness of your car, and budgeting for self-defense equipment and training. The year I began shooting, my wardrobe came from second-hand stores, because my training and ammunition budget took precedence over new suits and dresses. Devoted parents may pour all their money into their children, yet the survival of one or both parents is paramount to children, even those little ones to whom adults cannot deny the latest toy or game.

One woman with whom I attended several classes argued with instructors about safe housing, saying she was unable to apply any of the suggested safety precautions in her low-priced apartment. She drove a beautiful classic Mercedes, affordable because she skimped on rent. I, too, went through a time when my living quarters were completely unsafe–a cheap basement apartment with un-barred windows. Looking back, I admit that I was spending the additional $100 a month I needed for safer housing, to support a jobless friend. I believed I couldn't spend the additional money on safer housing, and I know a number of other women make the same claim. We need to hard-headedly assess our expenditures to find the resources for safer quarters.

When you look for a new home or apartment, study the security provisions and seek out potential danger spots. Every house and each apartment layout differs. Use your survival awareness to identify potential threats. If renting, the presence or absence of dead-bolt locks and window bars gives you a measure of the owner's commitment to tenant security. Demand bars on ground-level windows or lease an apartment without ground-level access to windows or doors. Most municipal codes require landlords to provide dead-bolt locks on doors, not just keyed doorknobs. If the landlord objects when you ask why these security devices are absent, look for another place to rent!

The superintendent of an apartment building with good security measures will investigate the references and background of those to whom he or she rents, reducing the threat of unsavory neighbors. If you rent, find a secure building, where only residents have access through automatically locking doors, and raise Cain if someone violates that security measure by blocking doors open for visitors or their own convenience.

Home security

Every now and then, a newspaper carries a story about someone who rose in their sleep and discharged a firearm... into themselves. These poor souls are the victims of their own lack of training, or of bad advice from another novice who said, "If you can't get to your gun instantly, it won't be any help if someone breaks into your house at night!" You'll hear no snickering from me as I emphasize this fact: I was a sucker for that advice, and until better educated, I slept with a loaded, unholstered gun on my bed headboard. I was then living in a basement studio apartment with ground-level windows without bars, and I believed the threat great enough to justify the potential for disaster at my own hands.

If you believe a gun must be instantly accessible to protect you inside your home, the home's security provisions, locks, lights and layout, need serious scrutiny.

This is the first principle of home defense: If your home can be breached so easily and rapidly that you must be able to make an instantaneous response to danger, the problem does not hinge on your quick response. The problem lies in how to strengthen the perimeter of safety around your home! If you feel you are unable to provide safe housing, reassess your personal priorities and analyze your commitment to your safety and well-being.

Even in secure housing, a sensible person can increase the perimeter of safety around their home. That's right, security begins well beyond your front door. Burglars and intruders prefer anonymity in which to commit crime. A dwelling that appears to be empty, or is obscured behind a fence or dense foliage is an ideal target.

It is easy to equate a fenced yard with security, yet the common privacy fence serves primarily as a vision barrier and is as much a danger as an asset. Most residential fences can be broken through or leapt over, and once an intruder is concealed behind the fence, he can break into the house without worrying that anyone will report his crime. If deterrence is part of the fence's raison d'être, at a minimum, replace common gate latches with a good lock so an intruder can't walk right in like they belong. A neighbor is more likely to report someone breaking out a board in your fence or jumping over than someone who walks up the drive and opens your gate as would a family member or meter reader.

Think twice before landscaping with a thick hedge or bushes that provide hiding places around the home. Particularly thorny ornamental bushes positioned beneath windows and decks to discourage unauthorized access are, of course, the exception.

An absolute requirement for home safety is bright, well-placed lighting. Home security lighting systems range from gimmicky to great. Consult the experts, yet maintain a skeptical attitude to select the most useful. At a minimum be sure your doorways, sidewalks, garage and halls are well lit. If you park in a garage, either leave a light on when you depart, or install lighting you can activate by remote control before you enter. While living near downtown Seattle, I narrowly avoided a prowler revealed by the light above the door. It was late when I approached the building door. As I drew within 20 feet, I saw a figure slip from the shadows, through the light's beam then stop in the shadows between the building and an adjacent garage. Had I not detected movement, I would have been in easy striking distance while unlocking the door. I don't know if that prowler meant any harm, because I didn't stay around long enough to find out. His furtive actions indicated his presence was not authorized. I hurried to another entrance, shaken by how easily I might have walked into danger had I approached a second later.

Install motion-activated lights around the home's exterior, not forgetting areas where you can't see what has activated the light. Sudden illuminating the less visible parts of home and yard, conveys the impression that an occupant of the home has detected a lurker's presence.

Create the illusion of an occupied home. During daytime hours, drawn shades indicate an empty home nearly as emphatically as windows revealing empty rooms. Instead, hang sheer draperies with sufficient texture and weight to occlude the view from outside, while still allowing daylight into the room. Buy and set timers to unpredictable intervals. For example, one timer might turn on the bathroom light for a few minutes in the middle of each night, as suggested by Tanya Metaksa in her excellent book *Safe, not Sorry.*[1] A TV or radio activated for periods of time, lamps lit then extinguished, all cycling at varied hours of the day while you are absent, can discourage daytime burglaries.

The inside story

The value of a good-quality security alarm should not be under-estimated, yet bear in mind that even the best alarms are merely reactive unless slaved to a loud exterior siren or bells that would alert you, the neighborhood and the burglar of a break in. The value of any alarm system should be measured by the vulnerability of phone lines by which it is serviced, battery back up for power failures, as well as the professionalism of the service notified if the alarm is activated.

Even if you choose to install a security system, a number of secondary and companion safety provisions are necessary. First, consider the locks and keys barring intruders from your home. Re-key or change all locks when you move into a new home, whether as buyer or tenant. It is ridiculously easy to allow access to your home with a key used by or stolen from a previous occupant.

Keys can be easily copied, bringing us to other security issues include separating keys from anything giving

Home security systems provide information about unauthorized entry into your home.

your address or telephone number. If possible, keys should be carried in hand or on your person, not in a purse, which might be stolen. Separate house keys from car keys, which can end up on a mechanic's clip board, in the hands of a valet, and other unsecured places. At work, don't leave your keys unattended on top of your desk, in your coat pocket or other vulnerable spots. Children who carry house keys must be capable of similar responsibilities.

The locks are as important as the keys they fit. Doors and windows need locks of sufficient strength to impede a burglar. Consider how an intruder might gain entrance to your home. All exterior home entrances should have metallic or solid-core doors fitted with dead-bolt locks. Bolts must reach over an inch into the door frame after passing through the strike plate shield. Long strike plate screws need to tap deeply into the door frame studs to secure it to the frame. Exterior doors generally open inward. If they open outward, be sure the hinges are not installed on the outside, where anyone can pop out the pins and lift the entire door off its hinges. A wide-angle peep hole lets you ascertain the identity and number of people outside. Windows need sturdy metal or heavy wood frames, also fitted with locks. Take special care to secure basement and garage windows, where distance from the living area may mask the noise of an intruder breaking in.

While considering locks on doors and windows, don't forget attached garages. Here, the easiest unauthorized entry is from the roll-up door, which may be pushed up or even activated by an automatic garage door

opener set to the factory default setting. If you use a remote garage door opener, program it to operate on your own setting, not that with which it came. In addition, block the garage door roller from being thrust up in the roller track by threading a padlock or a

A properly installed deadbolt lock will extend several inches into the door frame, fitting into a strike plate that is secured in the door frame by long screws to hold it firmly in place.

pin through a hole above the roller, or using some other device like a clamp to keep the door from being opened while you are inside the home. Don't ignore the door between attached garages and your home. It must be sturdy and fitted with a good lock, which cannot be left open for convenience.

Vertical sliding windows, especially in older wood frames, can be made more secure by adding a removable 1"x2" stick the height of the movable window pane. After several break-ins at an old apartment building where I once lived, the police told us that the burglars were inserting a wedge of wood or metal at the base of the window frame, then depressing the wedge to create enough leverage to break out the lock at the top of the old, wooden window frame. There was no noise of shattering glass, only the dull, wooden pop as the lock broke out of the frame. Be wary of doors with glass windows that, if broken, give access to the knob inside and the lock. If you choose not to replace this type of door, at least change the lock to the double-keyed, double cylinder variety to keep a burglar from simply breaking out the small panes of glass and reaching through to turn the deadbolt knob on the inside.

If cursed with a double sliding glass door, better advice than the dowel in the lower track is placing a tension bar (like a chin-up exercise bar) midway between floor and top of the frame. If able, eliminate the sliding door altogether, because even the tension bar does nothing to prevent a burglar from smashing the glass or from lifting the door off its track and removing it altogether.

Finally, none of these precautions are of much worth if doors and windows are left unsecured. After an Edmonds, Washington, woman survived a rape, then got to her gun and held the serial rapist for police, another local woman remarked to television reporters: "I'm so glad they caught him. It's getting warm and I need to be able to leave my sliding patio door open again." In hot weather, intruders often find houses open and waiting for them.

This is not a new problem. Richard Ramirez, known as the Night Stalker, found easy entry to dozens of homes during his 1984 reign of terror. An exceptionally hot California summer in which people found it impossible to keep windows and doors tightly closed and locked gave him the opening he needed. All of his murders, rapes and torture took place inside the victims' homes, with entry made through open or poorly secured windows, sliding glass doors, garages and even pet doors.

While you are awake and alert, open doors and windows require an elevated level of awareness. If you lapse into Condition White—asleep, in the shower or other activities that occupy your awareness–you need to secure doors and windows that are accessible from the ground. Lock up your home before leaving, whether going on a five-minute errand to the store or going to work. An empty house with open windows is quite an invitation to those who would take your possessions or pounce on you when you return.

If I return to an empty house, I pause after opening the car door and again at the front door to gather sensory impressions to see if anything is awry. If you have pets who customarily meet you at the door, their absence or demeanor can be a useful indicator. Stop and listen as you light the house, be aware of and cautiously inspect places where intruders might be concealed. Coat closets can be made safer by storing enough stuff on the floors that there is no room for an intruder to hide without moving some objects out of the closet.

A watch dog can be a valuable addition to home security, primarily as a search partner, an early warning device and for their excellent deterrent effect. Don't put too much trust in a dog's ability to overpower intruders, however. One quiet .22 bullet in the head removes a canine obstacle all too easily. If your pooch faithfully greets you whenever you return home, its absence might be the first warning of danger.

Finally, let me emphasize the importance of not entering a house you believe has been breached by an intruder. House clearing is one of the most dangerous jobs imaginable. Despite the fact that it is your "home turf," intruders have the upper hand because they command the element of surprise and can choose a tactically superior place in which to wait for you. You don't know where they are, if they are armed, or how many have intruded. Even if you immobilize one intruder, will you survive attacks by others backing up the one you stopped?

If you find your home has been broken into, don't enter the house. Go elsewhere and call the professionals, police or sheriff officers who can search with trained dogs and other appropriate equipment while you wait outside in tax-funded safety.

Are you safe inside?

It's easy to feel safe and let down our guard once we're inside the front door. Even with the doors locked and blinds drawn, recognizing a predatory approach, whether over the phone, a mail solicitation or a caller at the door, can save a world of heartbreak.

Never tell anyone at the door or on the phone that you're alone. If a caller insists he must "talk to the man of the house," hang up or stage a fictional exchange in which the "man" refuses to come to the phone. Train family members, especially children, never to tell a caller who is home and who is out, when they'll return and how long they've been gone. Rapists and burglars use the telephone to gather information, as do thieves.

Any unidentified caller at the door should be treated with guarded suspicion. First, remember that you are under no obligation to open the door for anyone. A common home invasion ploy uses a nicely dressed female accomplice, who knocks on the door. Lulled by the idea that the stranger is "just a woman," the occupant opens the door to find the woman plus one or more men who force their way inside. Multiple intruders are common in gang-committed crimes. Be extremely guarded in opening your door to any stranger, and if you choose a gun for self-defense have it on your person, otherwise the hope of fending off this crime is very limited.

Criminals may also disguise themselves as repair or utility workers. Request company identification and verify the identity with the utility company, your landlord or whoever sent the individual before letting them in your home. Leave the worker standing on the porch, door locked, while you get the weapon, if necessary. Once inside, monitor them while they perform their work. Have your firearm or self-defense weapon on

When practical, a large watch dog can provide a degree of intimidation. Even more important, a dog serves as an early warning system, often detecting danger before a human will.

your person. If at any time their words or actions make you feel threatened or uneasy, tell them to leave. If they resist, you may have to escape and call the police from elsewhere.

I repeat, you are under NO obligation to allow into your home anyone with whom you do not feel safe and comfortable. This includes ex-husbands, former boyfriends, distant relations, anyone from your job or casual acquaintances. YOU control the access to your home. Children's visitors must also meet with your approval and children should be trained not to invite *anyone* inside without parental approval.

The bump in the night

There are many concerns if your home is broken into while you are present. Everyone has been wakened from sound sleep by a shattering or bumping noise. You awake and try to determine the source of the noise–is it merely your four-year-old trying to get a drink of water, a pet scratching at the door, or has a burglar entered?

This is one defense scenario in which immediate action is inadvisable. You need the ensuing moments to listen listen carefully for the source of the noise. Your four-year-old will probably call out or act in their usual way, letting you know that rushing out to confront this particular noise, gun in hand, is a very, very poor idea. Even if someone has entered your house, there are many reasons not to seek out and shoot the intruder. Could an innocent person be in your home without your knowledge? Do your teenagers have friends they might allow to come in and sleep off too much beer? Do any friends, relatives or other innocent people have keys to your home? Your best friend may have had a midnight fight with her boyfriend and taken refuge on your couch without waking you. Have you given her a chance to identify herself before she meets you and your gun in the hallway?

If I knew the noises were not caused by family members or guests, and continued movement and noise convinced me that an intruder was inside, I would go to a pre-established tactical HQ, likely in the bedroom, and dial the emergency number. Evan Marshall suggests putting 911 or your police emergency number on speed dial. When you call, give the police dispatcher information along these lines:

"There is an intruder in my home at 100 Center Street. I believe he is on the first floor; I will wait on the second floor. I am a white female, 5'5" and have on a red bathrobe. I am armed with a snub-nosed revolver. I repeat, there is an intruder in my home..."

The unreliability of telecommunications dictates that you state your address first, then describe the situation and give pertinent details. Make the message brief and to the point, then repeat the information. Experts advise you to stay on the line with the emergency dispatcher so you can identify the responding officers, confirming with the dispatcher that the unit has arrived at your address, and perhaps the names of the officers responding to your call. Locked in a safe area of your home, it is wise to refuse entry to anyone you cannot positively identify as a law enforcement officer. Every self-defense situation is unique in itself, and you will have to remain fluid and able to make decisions based on the circumstances. If it becomes necessary to protect yourself or family members from the intruder, you may have to break off communications with the dispatcher or flee the room.

Why offer your personal description and reveal that you are armed? Two reasons. Law enforcement agencies will respond rapidly to a scene where they know at least one firearm is involved. The presence of a deadly weapon tells them this is an explosive situation. The personal description is vital. You may be mistaken for a house breaker in the surprise and confusion as the police arrive and search out the first person who looks threatening.

After calling for help, you have two choices. You can remain silently ensconced in your safe room, taking cover behind a bullet-stopping obstacle, weapon in hand. Pause a moment and listen again for auditory clues to the intruder's location. Contrary to the movies, no one can move through unfamiliar territory without creating rustling or other noises. As an alternative, you may choose to warn the burglar: "Intruders: The police have been called and are on their way. We are armed. Leave the house immediately and we will not harm you!" In either event, do not abandon your room's security unless the safety of children or other dependents is threatened.

Evan Marshall suggests a more direct approach. His version of the challenge is "Get out!" delivered in command voice. He strongly recommends arranging the home so the defender can wait, firearm in hand, at the head of a stairwell or a hall, blocking access to the rest of the family.

The problems with seeking out and confronting a housebreaker are legion. Even though you know your own home layout, the intruder has the advantage of surprise. You simply cannot know where he has hidden or if he has an accomplice protecting him. If you search your own home, you may become the prey and your responses will be in reaction to the intruder's actions. He is running the game and you will likely be at his mercy.

Your safety is greatly enhanced if you can take refuge in a secure area, call for help and wait out the intrusion from a protected position.

I've made several earlier references to a safe room. Simply put, this is a "hardened" area containing emergency equipment like weapons, a wireless phone for outside communication if the intruder cuts your phone lines or a storm has interrupted normal service, flashlights and other necessities. The phone can be the same one you carry in your car or purse. When you come home, go straight to your safe room and place your wallet or purse, keys and wireless phone in the same place each time. This may be the best place for the cell phone's charger, to be sure it will be fully powered if ever needed in an emergency.

Alternate escape routes from the safe room are advisable in the case of arson or other dangers. The only reason to leave your safe room or a place of tactical dominance is to escape or ensure dependents' safety. Call the police, then pad quietly from room to room, gathering up the smaller children. Wake the older children with the instruction to remain exactly where they are and lock them safely in their rooms, unless you believe the intruder may gain access to that child's room before you or the police can intercept them. Other times, the emergency may make it necessary to secure the safety of family members while calling the authorities, and it is in these moments that wireless communication is worth every expensive cent it costs.

In a two-story home, if all the bedrooms are on the upper floor, you may choose to establish a place of strategic dominance at the head of the stairs. This denies a hostile any access to the vulnerable sleeping areas, and the intruder must come through your gunfire before he can reach those in your care.

In "hardening" a safe room, replace the door with a solid-core door with a good dead-bolt lock. In addition, a quick-access gun safe might be an appropriate accessory, as would be a bright flashlight, body armor, and some kind of furnishing that will provide cover and protection from an assailant's gunfire. You might want to include a small supply of first-aid supplies, with emphasis on dressings to staunch blood flow.

Practice fields

How strange it is that we practice musical skills, our tennis game, and public speaking at Toastmasters club, yet rarely practice scenarios to ingrain skills to ensure our own physical survival!

An example exercise is surveying your house or apartment. Starting at your car or front door, enter, looking carefully for all the spots where an assailant might hide. You may decide to install better lighting, move or trim certain bushes, or clear out boxes and debris in your garage that could conceal assailants. Entering your home, check for alcoves or closets where an assailant might hide. Check for fast access to light switches, or the consider changing to remote controlled lighting.

Moving through your home, be aware of lanes of movement–advantages for both you and a burglar. Be aware of heavy furniture that would provide you cover in a gunfight, and conversely, look for places where an assailant might be concealed. You might choose to relocate a large, packed bookshelf to a strategic position where it could provide bullet-stopping cover. Consider rearranging furniture to impede unauthorized entry through a window or sliding glass door. You should be sure the location of

a waterbed or a large, packed chest of drawers provides bullet-stopping cover in your safe room. Crouch or lay down behind the furniture to be sure it is large enough to protect your body.

Families with children should assign bedrooms so the armed adults can protect the dependents. Take the room at the head of the hallway or assign the children to upstairs bedrooms, if the sleeping rooms are located on both first and second floors. Work out a home-defense plan with other adults who share the house and brief youngsters about what to expect in an emergency. This is also a good time to go over escaping fires, gas leaks and other dangers.

A home intruder can hide in surprisingly small places. Try to locate and eliminate these dangers in advance.

Contact local police, fire service, and ambulance or emergency care providers. Determine approximate emergency response times for your neighborhood and formulate your home defense plans around the worst-case possibilities.

Another exercise that can be conducted with a bit more levity, is one suggested by Massad Ayoob in his excellent book, *In the Gravest Extreme*.[2] He recommends playing a game of hide-and-seek with your children. They know all the best hiding places, and he says, any place your four-foot child can hide offers concealment to a motivated, full-size house breaker. Again, you might rearrange the furniture if you find a very risky point from which an intruder might spring on you.

For renters, apartment halls and doorways are excellent places to practice your survival awareness. How many times have you rounded a corner in a public hallway, in the grip of a daydream or a worry, and gasped as you almost collided with a neighbor? Learn not to walk carelessly around blind corners or into laundry rooms or utility rooms. Walk out and around 90° corners, open doors fully and look in before entering. Make the most of these utilitarian moments as practice to sharpen your awareness of clues like noise, movement, smell and shadow, developing skills that may some day alert you to an assailant's presence before you are in his grasp.

Your safety depends on knowing who occupies a public space such as an elevator or laundry room before you commit yourself to entering. Learn, by daily practice, to scan the room, including behind the door you just opened, to ascertain if another person is present. A door that opens against a wall can simply be pushed all the way open to check for anyone hiding behind it.

Information control

Just as you guard access to your home and its occupants, it is prudent to limit publicly available information about yourself. Using initials, instead of your full name on the mailbox, telephone directory or other listings helps protect you from people who target women. Don't use Ms., Mrs., or Miss or any thing else that indicates gender. When asked for a phone number by a sales clerk accepting your check, give a false number, a ruse suggested by Paxton Quigley, author of *Armed and Female*.[3] Even if the clerk seems harmless, a member of the store staff or another shopper may divert that information to harass you. Do not reveal your home address, telephone numbers and especially social security number. If pressured, demand that the sale be hurried along, implying if necessary that the item can be purchased elsewhere.

Business women who need to give clients contact information are safer renting an off-site mail box and phone service. Never list residential telephones or home addresses on business cards or promotional literature that you hand out. Even if you are careful to whom you give your card, you cannot control where it goes after it is out of your hands.

A rich resource for thieves is the information deposited in the garbage can. Paper shredders are quite affordable, or set aside one trash can for "burnables" if you have a fireplace or woodstove in which to destroy credit card slips, offers of credit, or any other paper containing personal data. Be particularly careful what you leave in the trash in a motel room or other place outside the home. A newer risk is shaping up for those who communicate or do business over the Internet. Be extremely guarded in revealing any personal information, and monitor children's use of this new resource for the same exposure.

Earlier we discussed protecting the security of your keys. Along the same line of thought, the information you carry in an easily-snatched purse can lead a committed criminal to your door. One of my friends has solved this problem by carrying identification, licenses, emergency cash, credit cards and even a spare key in a separate folder marketed in stationary stores as business card cases. The case is small enough to carry on your person in a pocket where it is less vulnerable to theft.

Personal security entails a lot of different concerns—physical safety, protecting against harassers, and denying common thieves access to information that can be exploited to your physical or financial harm.

Do the preparations in this chapter sound a little paranoid? Do not mistake a cautious person for a cringing paranoiac. And there is a big difference between a fear-ridden person and one who acknowledges the possibility of danger and practices simple precautions to intercept anyone who would harm them or their family.

---

1 Metaksa, *Safe, not Sorry*, ibid.

2 Ayoob, *In the Gravest Extreme*, ibid.

3 Quigley, Paxton, *Armed and Female*, released in paperback in 1990 by St. Martin's Press, 175 5th Ave., New York, NY 10010.

8

Safety at Work & in Public

Gone are the days when a woman's place was in the home, presumably buffered from the dangers of strangers and other stresses of the outside world. The truth is, women began entering the workplace in noteworthy numbers during World War II. By 1998, almost 60% of all American women worked or sought work outside the home and 47% of all jobs were held by women, according to the Department of Labor.[1]

At the same time, the 1990s were a time of increased awareness of workplace violence. The Department of Justice's National Crime Victimization Survey (NCVS) estimated that 1.5 million simple assaults, 396,000 aggravated assaults, 51,000 rapes and sexual assaults, 84,000 robberies and 1,000 homicides occur yearly in the workplace.[2] Women are the targets of more than half of all non-fatal work-place assaults, and are more likely than men to be attacked by someone they know–a co-worker, repeat customer, patient or domestic partner.

While massacres committed by disgruntled workers captivate the news media, the daily dangers to working women are more prevalent and considerably broader in scope. These daily hazards go largely unreported in the press, being less dramatic than a madman shooting up a factory. Perhaps it is this lack of drama that enables employers to ignore many ongoing workplace dangers. While both state and federal law requires employers to provide a safe workplace, in reality the individual remains the final compliance checkpoint. Because threats to personal safety can never be completely removed, you remain responsible for your own defense at work.

Making choices

Minimizing workplace dangers asks that we acknowledge a wide range of risks and preventive measures. We become comfortable in our jobs and are loath to make changes, even for personal safety. Sometimes, it is easier to address safety issues, whether at work or home, when change is already underway. When considering a new job, give careful consideration to risks the job and location entail. While successfully employed, few people are likely to rock the boat by demanding the correction of workplace hazards, although we often should.

An employer's failure to correct hazards is an excellent motivation to seek a better position elsewhere! During a job search pros and cons weighed against different offers should absolutely consider safety and self-defense issues just as seriously as the salary. Job seekers would do well to investigate the employers' commitment to workplace safety. Start by just keeping your eyes and ears attuned to the environment during your job interview. Is the building entrance easily visible from the street and is the approach free of heavy foliage or other concealment? Are security cameras or concave mirrors installed in and around the building? Are the windows plastered with signs and advertisements behind which a robbery could occur undetected? Are drop safes or time access safes used to secure cash?

Assess the location of the business, and any neighborhoods to which you may be required to travel. Consider the safety of the employee parking area and the walk from it into the workplace. Observe customers and work-

Windows and doors to 24-hour convenience stores should be easy to see through, not covered with advertisements which provide the anonymity the robber or rapist requires.

ers, watching for disrespectful or threatening language, racial or sexual insults or inappropriate physical contact.

Finally, the type of work sought influences the statistical chance that you will be the target of workplace violence. Which workers are least protected?

The NCVS shows retail sales workers in the highest risk category, with 330,000 attacked each year, followed by an average of 234,200 police officers victimized. The popular idea that professionals are safer is fallacious: between 1980-90 27 pharmacists, 26 physicians, 18 registered nurses were murdered at work and in 1994, 179 retail supervisors and 49 restaurant or hotel managers were killed.[3]

At elevated risk are employees working between 9 p.m. to 6 a.m. In retail settings, clerks who work alone are particularly endangered, with hazards magnified by environmental perils including a remote location, poor lighting, obscured windows, the absence of escape routes, and duties including stocking merchandise from, or dumping trash in, areas outside the relative protection of the well-lit or occupied portions of the store.

Other dangers include work like sales or home health services that takes you into clients' homes. Particularly risky are the initial contact, and conditions including substance abuse or mental illness in the client or others sharing the dwelling. If you believe the dangers are greater than you can reasonably defend against, you may need to ask for protections like working in pairs or requesting an escort.

Understanding how and under what circumstances people are injured at work helps us focus on appropriate self-defense training and tools. In no way is shooting skill alone sufficient. Disarming skills against both gun and knife are highly recommended, as well as unarmed defenses to escape grabs, parry a blow, slip or defuse the power of a punch, and even verbal defenses.

Responses to harassment

One in four workers interviewed told a Northwestern National Life company survey that they had been attacked, threatened or harassed in the previous year. Hard statistics from the same study showed that 2 million actually were attacked, 6.3 million threatened, and 16.1 million harassed in a one year span.[4] Makes going to work sound pretty grim, doesn't it?

The old adage that "words can never hurt me" is not completely true. In the workplace, verbal harassment and veiled threats are not only illegal, but contribute to physical symptoms of stress, anxiety and decreased work performance. Editor of the Assault Prevention Information Network, Judith Weiss, a Texas-based self-defense trainer gives a cogent description of worker harassment and the challenge of choosing an appropriate response. She has written:

"Mini-rapes–the verbal and physical intrusions that women routinely put up with–may be a simple attempt to demean and demoralize us, or may be a test to see whether we are compliant or easily manipulated (and therefore a likely rape victim). About 70% of assaults on women are by people we know (dates, co-workers, spouses, neighbors, family members) and occur where we live, work and socialize...We do want to discourage or interrupt a verbal or physical intrusion, but if the perpetrator is not actually threatening bodily harm, it would be inappropriate (and probably illegal) to wound or kill him...Verbal assertiveness and simple evasive techniques (like a release from a wrist grab) may be enough for pest control."[5]

Assertive deterrence by verbal and physical deflection, should be part of every woman's working skills. As discussed in earlier chapters, predators prefer easy prey, and are less likely to harass the woman who early and actively resists bullying or exploitation. Sadly, there are so many easier targets on whom the harasser may prey.

Abuse in the workplace must be reported, even if the employer refuses to take the complaints seriously. Physically resisting a fellow-worker's attacks will be more defensible if you can show you tried every other means available to you before the conflict escalated.

Even then, the amount of force used to stop undesired contact, groping, grabs, or more serious assault must be in proportion to the offense. In the following chapter, we discuss vital intermediate defenses and physical skills that have a very real application in fending off creeps, gropers and worse.

Co-workers' problems

In addition to worker-on-worker harassment, remain aware of fellow workers' backgrounds. Listening to your co-workers can alert you to personal conflicts that may migrate into the workplace. A 1994 study showed that of women killed on the job, 17% were domestic violence homicides that had carried over to the workplace.[6]

If you worry someone you work with may become violent or be the target of aggression, you will need to choose the appropriate degree of intervention. At a minimum, being aware and monitoring workplace "time bombs" will give you an enormous advantage over most workers who are completely surprised when violence erupts and they are caught in the crossfire. Early recognition of behavioral cues, as well as learning techniques to prevent or diffuse volatile situations, is a useful first step that may prevent more serious dangers.

Give wide berth to clients or co-workers displaying danger signals identified by researchers as violence precursors. Early-warning signals include verbal threats against employer, supervisor or co-workers; trouble accepting authority; obsessions about grudges; real or imagined romances or other troubled co-worker relationships; social withdrawal; legal, financial or marital problems; inability to accept criticism or accept responsibility for problems; substance abuse; recently disciplined or passed over for promotion; history of violent behavior; manifestations of despair or depression, paranoia, suspicions or jealousy; and mood swings.[7]

Unless personally attacked, escape from a dangerous situation lets you call for help instead of become a hostage or a victim. The layout of the work area can aid or interfere with your ability to scan for danger, as well as hinder escape during an attack. If you can, arrange your workplace for maximum visibility, especially of public entrances. When arranging your own personal work area, resist the urge to turn your back to the world, as

"Testing" or harassing touches require physical resistance, effective in circumstances where introducing deadly force into the situation would be quite wrong.

many do to improve concentration. Your chair should face the entrance into your personal space. In areas of elevated risk, seriously consider a deep or angled reception counter that offers greater protection. If that is not possible, re-arrange generic workplace furnishings to limit physical accessibility. Most importantly, know various escape routes, and be sure that back doors or other alternative routes are not blocked by trash, storage boxes or other detritus. A keyed deadbolt is not an appropriate lock for an emergency exit, of course, but especially in small businesses these kinds of oversights often go unnoticed until an emergency.

More and more often, possession of a variety of defensive tools is restricted in the workplace, as management struggles to understand and prevent violence. If prohibited from carrying a self-defense gun, pepper spray, knife or other weapon at work, you owe it to yourself to ratchet up your alertness, hone your unarmed skills and increase escape route awareness even more. A quick glance at your desk top will reveal items that can be improvised as weapons. Remember, though, if you can strike a blow with a tool or furnishing, so can an assailant.

Entrepreneurs and employees who *are* able to possess handguns and other weapons for defense at work may feel safe with the gun locked in the desk drawer. While a firearm anywhere on the premises is better than none at all, I think this is a false sense of security, especially for women who are at greater risk of physical harm. Concealing a handgun beneath business attire is challenging, yet one that can be accomplished. Carry devices like Kramer Handgun Leather's Confidant® holster undershirt and elastic belly bands, like those marketed by Gould and Goodrich provide deep concealment that keeps the gun on your person.[8] It is available when you go to the supply room, greet a client, and perform other duties that take you away from your desk.

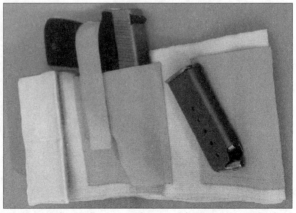

Professional women have one of the more difficult dress codes to balance against sensibility and safety. Instead of one-piece dresses, skirted suits or pants suits

The small, flat Kahr Arms Mk9 pistol fits into the work-place dress code when worn discretely in a belly-band carry device beneath a full-cut dress blouse or textured sweater.

will more easily conceal a small, defensive handgun. For freedom of movement that facilitates defense or escape, consider pleated or fuller skirts. Instead of spike heels, acceptable low-heeled alternatives include dressy versions of the classic loafer or modifications of the ballet slipper silhouette. Accessories like neck scarves are not without risk, as are chains or jewelry that will not break away with a brisk tug. Flashy or expensive jewelry may also target you for a spur-of-the moment robbery.

Tough times all over

In a study focused on health care worker's dangers, the National Security Institute accurately diagnosed one cause of dangers. "In the shrinking job market, employees feel they must prove themselves and devote more and more time to their careers. Employers struggle to keep companies productive and successful. Both employers and employees have need to be reminded that a safe, secure work environment enables both to achieve their goals."[9]

Be aware of personal work habits that increase your risk, including staying late at work, going in to work early or on weekends when the building is deserted, and failing to report harassment to management for fear it will effect your chances for promotion. All represent very real dangers, and you will gain little if you become unable to work due to death, injury or stress.

1 U.S. Department of Labor, Women's Bureau, *20 Facts on Women Workers,* April 1999.
2 Warchol, Greg (1998), *Workplace Violence, 1992-96.* National Crime Victimization Survey (Report No. NCJ-168634).
3 National Institute for Occupational Safety & Health, 1995, Bureau of Labor Statistics, 1995 and *Guidelines for Workplace Violence Prevention Programs,* National Safety Institute, 1995.
4 Northwestern National Life, July 1993.
5 Judith Weiss, Assault Prevention Information Network, *ibid.*
6 Toscano G, Windau J {1994}. *The changing character of fatal work injuries.* Monthly Labor Review 117 (10):17-28.
7 *Fatal Injuries to Workers in the United States,* 1980 [1989: A Decade of Surveillance (Jenkins et al, 1993).
8 Kramer Handgun Leather, P O Box 112154, Tacoma, WA 98411 or Gould & Goodrich, P O Box 1479, Lillington, NC 27546.
9 *Guidelines for Workplace Violence Prevention Programs,* National Safety Institute, 1995.

9

Intermediate Defenses

"I was asleep. He was on me so fast I didn't have time to do anything. Besides, he had a knife," confided the first.

"He had my arms pinned down. I couldn't have used a gun even if I had one. All I could see was the Bible on the headboard of my bed, so I concentrated on it to keep my sanity while he raped me," another said later.

I was at a women's exhibition promoting self-defense and firearms classes with an aggressive sign that asked, "Could You Stop a Rapist?" Relating their stories, both women desperately needed to convince me–and themselves–that nothing could have prevented the rape they endured. Both spoke quietly for a few minutes, with obvious effort to dismiss the possibility that anything might have allowed them to escape. While I never question the decisions made by a sexual assault survivor, the visits cast a pall over my day. I felt sad that neither had detected the rapist entering the house or been able to fight back. I was deeply troubled that neither would consider preparing for the possibility of further danger.

Since you've made it this far in the book, you know that I earnestly advocate crime avoidance over fighting, and escape over shooting. Safe housing, safe public behavior, and awareness of danger when you're at home, work, in your car or in public, are among the first survival lessons I want to emphasize. Next, we need to realize that the gun is merely a safety rescue tool. Alone, a gun cannot save us unless we are mentally prepared to fight back, and know how to escape an assailant's restraint to gain the time to reach the weapon. Finally, the gun is inappropriate against a minor threat: even displaying a gun is justified only in situations where innocent life is in immediate danger. How much better it would be to avoid or deter the predator before suffering rape or other injury.

When prevention alone is not enough, understanding how physical force is exerted helps us frame appropriate responses and can motivate even the inactive women into defensive training.

The weapons you always possess

Unarmed escapes and defenses should be mandatory training for all girls as they grow up. A girl's or woman's size or stature should be little detriment if the teacher is innovative and the martial art selected is suitable for women's self-defense. For example, Aikido techniques work on principles of leverage, so do not depend on weight or size to work against a larger assailant, a factor we can safely predict when discussing women's self-defense.

Women need a repertoire of basic defensive skills they can learn in a manageable length of time, perhaps one to two months, with simple, powerful techniques that can be regularly reviewed with friends or partners. These include basic blocks and parrys to deflect physical attack, responses to an armed attack and uses of less-than-lethal weapons. Some students will find physical training and practice relaxing and empowering and will continue formal classes. While that is a wonderful experience, it is unfair to deny defensive skills to students who cannot or will not commit years to the discipline.

Simply learning new ways to use your body and spirit is the door that opens self-defense studies for some. More than posture, stance is the way you stand to distribute weight and maintain better balance. Breaking habits like standing with knees locked, feet close together or on a line from which balance is easily broken are all part of developing a strong stance that is relaxed yet ready, in tune with the "condition yellow" discussed in Chapter 5.

Stance and body awareness are the definitive factors in individuals who possess command presence. This awareness claims and usually receives a respectful allowance of personal space. When crowded from behind, either as a "test" or simply by a rude, invasive oaf, strong stance and body awareness makes it natural to simply turn sideways, enlarging your personal space without saying so much as a word of rebuke. As balance and stance become natural, chances decrease that you will be caught off-balance. If you are, simply drop one leg back ten or twelve inches, bend your knees and you have regained your balance. From this stance, you are powerful and poised and can deliver strikes, kicks or simply sprint away.

Another elementary aspect of physical defense training is developing response speed. Attacks happen so quickly there simply is not time to fall back and devise a strategy. If you expect to escape, a harsh, rapidly-executed defense will be required. Most people wait too long to fight back, whether simply moving off the line of force, discharging pepper spray, or drawing their defensive handgun. Some deny that the attack is truly happening to them, others search in their handbag for the can of pepper spray they dropped in months ago, and still others are caught in what John Farnam calls "mental fibrillation" trying to decide what to do.

self-defense training, as well as continued practice and mental rehearsal, are all good preventive medicine for mental fibrillation.

In seeking physical defense instruction, be clear about what you need. A lot of traditional martial arts have been diluted by tournaments and rules and have lost sight of the defensive necessity from which they evolved. If a self-defense instructor boasts of tournament wins, or shows off elaborate, choreographed sequences and flamboyant high kicks and spins, keep shopping. A street fight doesn't recognize belts or trophies. It is survived by returning simple, vicious physical responses that can be implemented on irregular ground, in darkness or disorientation, and other unfavorable circumstances.

Simple and vicious

In hand-to-hand defense, the defender must disable the assailant's ability to breathe or see, or impede movement by damaging limbs and extremities. "Disrupt wind, vision, or limbs," advises Phil Messina, founder of Modern Warrior.[1] When you evaluate a defensive art or weapon, ask if it accomplishes at least two of these objectives.

A hard palm-heel smash is a disorienting blow that allows the small person to drive power all the way up from the ground.

Defense training is often scenario-specific. Women are advised to kick the assailant in the groin or jab him in the eyes. Both strikes are fine if the assailant does not block the groin kick or reflexively deflect the jab to his eyes. Protecting eyes and groin are natural human reflexes that can prevent a counter-attack from connecting. A kick to the groin may not disable an assailant, and if it does not connect accurately, it may further enrage an already violent attacker.

In unarmed combat, I'm a strong believer in low kicks to break joints, injure limbs and disrupt balance. Unlike men, women's power is centered in the lower body and legs. A smashing kick to the side of the assailant's knee can break or disable the limb sufficiently for you to escape an attack from side or front. Even a kick and downward shin scrape can surprise someone making a rear grab enough for you to break free.

Women can deliver a disorienting palm-heel smash to an assailant's face if they are grabbed from the front. Bending the knees and dropping the hips, then slamming all your power up into the palm-heel smash turbo-charges the blow.

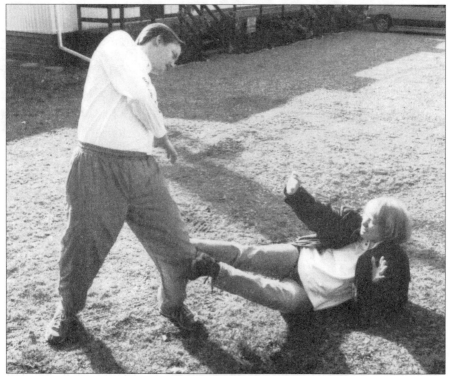

Even on the ground, maintaining evasive mobility and delivering well-aimed kicks can prevent an assailant from getting his hands on his intended prey.

If you are knocked to the ground, orient your head away from the assailant by spinning on your back like an upended turtle. Use your legs to kick and trap the assailant's legs. A strong leg trap can put the assailant on the ground while you roll to your feet to escape or draw a gun. Finally, you may not have time to stand or find yourself unable to get up. When deciding where to carry a canister of defense spray or a handgun, be sure you can reach it quickly from a variety of disadvantageous positions.

While every instructor has some favorite empty hand skills, a book isn't the place to learn unarmed defense techniques. Words are inexact at best and at worst written descriptions of physical techniques are horribly subject to misinterpretation. You can't learn fighting from a book anymore than a written manual can prepare you to pass the road portion of the driver's licensing test.

Find a martial arts instructor willing to work with you on stance and speed, recovery skills to get back on your feet, choke-hold escapes, ground-fighting techniques, improvised impact weapons, and weapon retention and disarming. Seek out empty hand techniques you can perform naturally and reflexively to buy the seconds necessary to escape or draw a firearm.

Intermediate weaponry

An intermediate (non-lethal) weapon is meant to deflect an assault before it turns lethal, or to gain time and distance to draw and use a gun. The greatest value of non-lethal weaponry may be the legality of open carry. Devices like the Kubotan, mid-sized pepper spray canisters and other tools are legal to carry openly in the hand in many areas. Thus, the immediate availability is a strong selling point for carrying intermediate defensive tools, even if you legally possess a defensive firearm, as well.

The intermediate defensive tool is not an appropriate response to a lethal force attack. On the other hand, using a gun or other deadly force is justified only when murder or crippling injury is imminent. Must I wait until I know I'm going to be killed to use some degree of force to stop someone who is hassling me? No! I need to react quickly to employ non-lethal or intermediate force to deflect or escape before the situation becomes deadly.

Finally, in a gun-phobic society, we are encountering more and more places where the law prohibits firearms possession. Setting aside the issue of constitutionality, we should discuss intermediate weapons to carry from your car into the courtroom, from the parking lot into the post office, through other restricted areas, and for an increasing number of readers, in your place of employment.

Aerosol defense

Pepper spray, an aerosol deterrent that has all but replaced Mace®, is becoming the most commonly carried self-defense chemical. Pepper spray is based on Oleoresin Capsicum (OC), found in red peppers like chilis and habaneros. OC, compared to earlier chemical restraint agents, can boast greater proven effectiveness against drug influenced, intoxicated, deranged, and enraged individuals, as demonstrated repeatedly in police service. It is also used as grizzly bear deterrent, and is effective against dogs. Only strictly trained attack dogs have been shown to withstand an application of pepper spray.

Between 1987 and 1989, the Federal Bureau of Investigation made extensive studies and tests of pepper sprays. In one report, the FBI showed that virtually 100% of 59 people sprayed suffered some inflammation of mucous membranes and upper respiratory systems. Inhaling the spray caused coughing, shortness of breath, gasping and gagging. Eyes closed involuntarily as the OC contacted sensitive tissue. Skin inflammation is common, ranging from redness to acute burning. Perspiring or fair-skinned people suffered greater skin discomfort.

FBI results confirmed a principle also apparent in police reports about OC: success depended on discharging enough OC at the target. The FBI suggested at least one three-second burst or three one-second bursts but field experience has shown that people in a stressful situation do little but spray and move away. Not surprisingly, the FBI tests showed the OC is more effective in enclosed areas, and my experience has shown that the user is very likely to suffer cross-contamination if discharging OC indoors. Be aware that wind will disperse OC if it is sprayed outdoors. Indoors or out-side, you need to leave the area after discharging OC into the air, to avoid secondary contamination. The private citizen has this luxury; law enforce-ment officers may not.

Varied reports, including personal experience, show that coughing and respiratory discomfort after OC exposure usually diminishes in fifteen to twenty minutes in fresh, uncontaminated air. Skin irritation may well linger for half an hour or more, burning even after the oily agent is washed away. The best antidote for OC contamination is soap and water to remove it from skin, and plenty of running water in which to bathe the eyes. Police often carry Sudecon wipes, but in my experience training people to use OC, the wipes do not remove as much of the irritant as does a generous application of soap and water. Generally, the effects of contact with OC spray will disappear in 30 to 45 minutes, if the agent is removed.

Interestingly, during the FBI's evaluation, none of their spray test subjects required medical attention. However, a 1993 study by the U.S. Army declared OC "capable of producing mutantagenic and carcinogenic effects...cardio-vascular and pulmonary toxicity, neurotoxicity, as well as human fatalities." In police custody fatalities have occurred after OC was used on drug-intoxicated subjects and offenders with bronchial conditions or severe asthma. While pepper spray is thought to have contributed to these deaths, the literature is divided on how much it is to blame.

Private citizens who discharge OC in self-defense should retreat, then call 911 to report the incident and request assistance for the person sprayed. After any act of self-defense, report the incident to protect against liability stemming from charges that you initiated the assault, and to establish a record of the attack in case you must later prove a pattern of harassment. The sprayed assailant may need protection from hazards like automobiles in the street. Engaging bystanders to stop traffic if the sprayed assailant wanders into the street would be a reasonable, responsible effort. The assailant may need help while recovering from the effects of the pepper spray. None of these responsibilities fall to you, but are the duties of police or paramedics.

Pepper spray sounds like a good solution to many self-defense problems. However, it is like any other defensive method: it can fail, especially if the user is untrained or unfamiliar with the delivery system.

Best tool for the job

When and why do aerosol defenses fail? The answers are many and varied, and should be thoroughly covered in a user's course taught by a manufacturer-certified or law-enforcement certified trainer. In the private sector, success of an aerosol defense requires that the substance sufficiently distract or disable an assailant so the intended prey can escape or initiate a more forceful means of defense.

OC spray is marketed in varying intensities, ranging from 2% OC in a base carrier to 17% concentrations. However the important measurement is stated in Scoville Heat Units, which should be in the 2 million unit range for best results. In selecting an OC spray for intermediate defense, I would advise more concern about the delivery system than concentrations. Defense spray manufacturers market several delivery systems: an aerosol fog that comes out of the container in a cone-shaped cloud, cans that deliver a thin, solid stream, and foam containing OC.

For civilian self-defense, I firmly recommend the cone-shaped aerosol fog. Your goal is escape, facilitated by temporarily disabling the assailant.

The stream delivery system affects only the area it contacts, and is harder to deliver to the eyes, nose or mouth, since it is only a thin stream. The foam carrier may linger on skin, but has limited effect on respiration and can be blocked from eye contact. The cone-shaped cloud, however, billows out from the container and is impossible to keep out of the nose and lungs and settles on the skin to cause irritation, as well.

Against experienced subjects holding their breath or shielding their eyes, lay down a fog of OC through which they must come to reach you, then move away laterally when they enter the OC. For example, you are crossing a supermarket parking lot when a deranged person rushes at you, fists clenched, face distorted. "Get back! Don't come any closer," you yell in a commanding voice. The OC spray is in your hand, and you have it up and ready to spray. Your non-dominant arm is fully extended to deflect the assailant and protect the spray canister. If they don't obey your command,

you fog the space between you.

After breathing or contacting the mist, the assailant may crouch defensively, and in a natural instinctive motion, bring the hands to the face and double over protectively. While they are distracted, choose the nearest escape–return to the store or get into your car. Call 911 as soon as possible to report the attempted assault and your use of the chemical defense.

If you discharge the OC you carry, replace the canister after the incident to be sure you have a sufficient quantity if you

Applying even the relatively simple pepper spray gains effectiveness with proper tactics.

ever need it again. In all likelihood, your perception of the time lapsed and amount of spray expelled will be distorted by the fight-or-flight experience. When you buy a new canister, give it a brief test spray to be sure the nozzle is functional. You should continue to test the canister every four to six months to be sure the aerosol propellant has not escaped or the nozzle become clogged. Plan to replace OC spray units on a yearly basis. Although the OC remains potent, it is useless inside a defective canister.

Few weapons can instantaneously stop an assault. OC is no different. Though the results are good enough to justify carrying OC, tests and my own experience show that a fully contaminated person is capable of aggression after contacting the aerosol fog. In fact, when we certify police cadets to carry OC, exercises require them to complete a given task, like a foot pursuit or handcuffing after being sprayed with the irritant. In more advanced training experiments, we have sprayed an officer with OC, then, under very tight safety constraints had him hold an eye open, draw his gun and accurately shoot several targets. With determination, both drills can be accomplished. Students find that the pain and discomfort sets in with a vengeance after the task is completed. Trust me, I know.

Knowing now that humans can fight despite the effects of pepper spray, add movement to your defense plans. If you discharge OC to avoid being stabbed, hit or otherwise assaulted, you need to move on an angled path away from the attacker. If you merely back up, the attacker, continuing their forward momentum, can run right over you. Always disengage and run for safety. Don't mistakenly believe that OC is the magic formula that will take an assailant to his knees.

Pepper spray sounds like a wonderful defense tool, doesn't it? I certainly like having it among my defenses, but please do not make the mistake of believing it is more effective than it really is.

We possess and learn to use aerosol restraint sprays, empty hand techniques, and other intermediate weapons to buy the time needed to escape or reach a gun. A spray will not perform well in high wind or at great distances. It takes longer to affect a person wearing a baseball cap and wraparound sunglasses, if it is effective at all. Don't rely entirely on the spray!

Legal concerns

At press time, only nine states restrict purchase, carry and use of OC sprays. Many incorrectly classify the aerosol agent as a "tear gas" which technically is a lachrimater agent (induces tears), while OC is an irritant agent. Restrictions range from age limits for purchase to a licensing requirement. A few states strictly prohibit possessing OC. Violations can result in charges ranging from misdemeanors to felony charges. Before carrying OC spray, especially if you bought it outside the area in which you wish to carry it, call a local law enforcement agency, the attorney general or municipal attorney and inquire about laws covering its use and possession.

As of this writing, OC sprays are illegal on commercial airlines, and your canister will be confiscated if detected when you attempt to take it through security with carry-on baggage. More severe penalties are allowed by law, yet are rarely imposed. Cabin pressure changes could result in canister leakage, a problem for which you do not want to be responsible. A ruling released near publication of this book allowed commercial airline passengers to check in their baggage up to four ounces of no greater than 2% aerosol defense agent.

Laws and regulations change too frequently to report with any accuracy in this book. Please be responsible for yourself and research the law before obtaining any sort of defensive tool.

"What is that stick on your key chain?"

The great value of any intermediate weapon is the ability to carry it openly and ready for use, in your hand. During the women's exposition I spoke of at the beginning of this chapter, a few women came up and smugly showed me the small OC canister in their handbag. "That's good," I encouraged, "but you ought to start carrying it in your hand. Don't fool yourself into thinking you can dredge it out of the bottom of your bag when you see trouble."

The most natural intermediate weapon to carry continuously is the mini-baton. It attaches to key rings, and at 5 $^1/_2$" long by $^5/_8$" diameter, fits naturally into the hand. The first mini-baton was developed in the 1970s by Takayuki Kubota for California businessmen needing a defensive art. Looking for items the businessmen carried regularly, he developed a defense system using the expensive writing pens all the gentlemen used. The pen was later replaced with the grooved metal or plastic mini-baton we know today as the Kubotan.

The Monadnock Company produces a similar mini-baton called the "Persuader." Of identical dimensions to the Kubotan, instead of grooves the Persuader has ridges that dig into nerve and bone during certain techniques. The ridged Persuader is less likely to slip off a pressure point than is the grooved version.

Neither variety of mini-baton is of much value without appropriate training. Mini-baton escape techniques are based on nerve and pressure points. Pressed or jabbed into specific physical locations, the baton causes sharp pain, distracting the assailant. As he loosens his grip or hesitates momentarily, the defender escapes. Other control techniques employ pain compliance. Applied properly to the wrist, the mini-baton can effectively disengage an assailant who is grabbing the front of your clothing; continued pressure can drive him to the ground. Grabs from behind are countered by driving the end of the baton into the delicate bones on the back of the hand or into selected points on the arm.

Because leverage and pain compliance are at the heart of mini-baton techniques, size disparity is only a limited disadvantage to the petite mini-baton user. However, in teaching Persuader techniques, the Fire-arms Academy of Seattle staff has en-countered a few students with very high pain tolerances, who exhibit little response to the pain compliance techniques. It is reasonable to expect that as many as one in fifteen people can endure this level of pain, so you must be prepared to switch to another tactic if the technique, properly applied, fails to elicit an immediate response. Remain fluid: if the pain compliance approach doesn't work, quickly switch to a destructive technique.

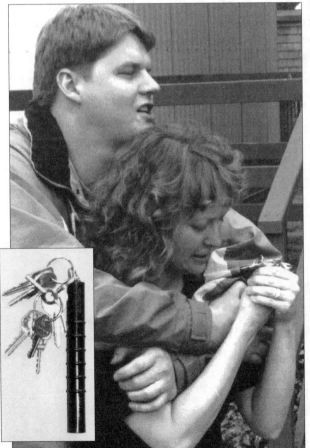

Used to defeat a rear grab, the mini-baton (left, inset) is driven into the hand's metacarpals creating such pain that a release will generally follow.

Mini-baton training also includes jabs and flaying with the keys on the end of the baton that can inflict more pain and actual physical injury, depending on the location of the strike. Classified as capable of causing great physical injury or even as deadly force, this type of strike may cause loss of vision or result in other permanent disability. In a fight for your life, however, you are justified in inflicting this kind of harm if no other reasonable alternative exists.

Just as we recognize the uses and shortcomings of pepper spray and other alternative defenses, the mini-baton is not the answer to every kind of attack. It is extremely valuable, however, for the legality of carrying it in-hand nearly everywhere. The secured areas of airports and aboard airliners are the most common places that prohibit possession of a mini-baton. Most other locations, like post offices, courthouses and schools, allow possession of this small easily-carried defensive tool while prohibiting more effective forms of self-defense. It is in these locales that the mini-baton is worth well more than its weight in gold.

Facing the blade

A long impact weapon is superior to the short mini baton if facing a knife or other contact weapon. Impact weapon training, transferred to an expandable baton or aluminum-shafted flashlight offers some help against this terrifying danger. With society skittish about defensive weapons, we are greatly restricted in tools which we can openly carry immediately available in hand. No such restrictions are placed on a 3- or 4-cell flashlight like the Mag-light, however. No one looks twice at a woman crossing a parking lot casually carrying a flashlight, yet this utili-

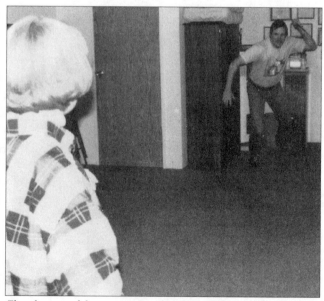

The danger of being overrun by an assailant with a contact weapon increases greatly when the intended victim is forced to back pedal while trying to get their gun out.

tarian instrument can be employed quite effectively by one who understands impact weapons and their use. The aluminum shaft of a simple C-cell Maglight can become an agile, improvised baton that is capable of injurious strikes, yet no one is worried by its benign presence!

Until you understand just how fast a deadly assault can be acted out, you may be puzzled by all the emphasis on having a defensive tool already in hand. In 1983, research by Dennis Tueller of the Salt Lake City Police Department showed conclusively that an attacker can dash across 21 feet in less than the two seconds it takes a skilled handgunner to draw a pistol and fire two accurate shots (that cannot be expected to take immediate effect). The Tueller study taught us several additional lessons: to maintain an extreme distance from anyone who could pose a cutting or bludgeoning threat, the importance of moving off the line of force established by a charging attacker, and the absolute and deadly danger of knives and other contact weapons.

Distance equals survival in a knife fight. Defenses that increase distance between you and the knife-wielding assailant can give you time to draw a gun or escape. A four-cell aluminum flashlight or an expandable baton extends your reach twelve to twenty inches, distancing you from the knife and giving you a striking weapon with which to disable the offender.

Courses in baton use or stick fighting ingrain skills that can put any

improvised weapon to effective use. Don't bypass training and go right to the security guard supply store to buy a baton, which may not even be legal for possession by the private citizen in your area. Impact weapons can be grabbed and turned against you viciously if you poke ineffectively at an assailant or even if you make a good strike, then fail to move quickly out of a vulnerable position. Integral to

The risk of a disarm attempt is very real when the assailant closes to within close proximity.

this skill is footwork to keep you in position to inflict injury, while moving out of the way of retaliatory strikes, slashes or kicks.

Calibre Press has produced a video entitled *Surviving Edged Weapons* that is must-see viewing for anyone at risk from knife-armed assailants.[2] If the scenes depicted on that classic piece of video don't convince you to seek further training, consider the following. Stabbing survivors frequently report that they were quite unaware of the knife, or other weapon, until they saw their own blood. Any blade can do incredible injury in the hands of even an untrained person, making it a truly fearsome threat.

Contact, puncture and slashing attacks are suffered from a variety of utility tools–not just knives. Screwdrivers and other weapons of opportunity are often used with deadly results, and can be obtained and possessed by felons with no threat of prosecution. Likewise box cutters are legal, available and common tools on many job sites.

While counter-intuitive, a rapid and violent defensive reaction is one of the most effective responses to a knife threat. Called "getting inside," a hasty rush inside to control the attacker's arms is an effective option to disarm an assailant using a contact weapon. Realistically, moving inside and blocking the arm's arc of motion offers greater control than dodging thrusts and being forced backward, where losing balance is a real hazard.

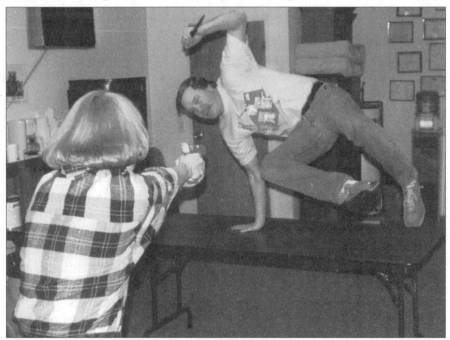

When possible, move to place intervening obstacles between attacker and intended victim, earning sufficient time to escape or draw a concealed handgun.

A forced retreat is extremely dangerous, for the attacker has all the advantages of forward momentum's speed and balance. No one can move back as dynamically as they can press forward, putting the retreating victim at a dangerous disadvantage–one that may cost her life. From the stronger inside position, the trained practitioner can trap the hand or arm to disarm the attacker and counter strike with her own elbow strikes, head butts, eye gouges or leg traps.

Think through what you would and could do if threatened with a knife. Keep your defenses simple and immediate. The goal is to disable the assailant, break free and run for safety. If attacked with a knife or other gouging, stabbing or cutting instrument, the odds say injury is likely. If the crime attempted is simple robbery, by far the wisest course of action is throwing your purse or wallet to the robber and running away if at all possible. This is yet another reason to be careful what information is inside your purse or wallet that could lead a thief to your home. Cash should be kept separate from driver's license and proof of automobile insurance or other identifying paperwork, and keys should absolutely be in a pocket or on your person, not in your handbag. These plans are food for thought, and are ideas you can implement immediately to increase your security.

Lies and dangerous scams

In a society that does not seem to trust women with deadly force, we are often given ineffective, dangerous tools for our defense.

"#1 Police Recommended Safety Device." Funny, I read that claim on an ad for a stun gun, and less than a week later, was told by a high-decibel personal alarm saleswoman that their device was the #1 police recommended safety device! The truth is that neither is adequate defense in an attack. The stun gun, despite advertisements bragging about 75,000-volt shocks, works only if both terminals are held against the attacker for seven to ten seconds, until the muscles go into spasm. No one, not even a small person, will compliantly stand still while you press the stun gun's electrified prongs against them. A struggle will break the contact before the muscle spasm can be induced. Why are women being told to use non-lethal gimmicks against rape and lethal assault?

High-decibel noisemakers are frequently touted as deterrents to assault. The high-pitched siren "will drive him away and bring help," say the promoters. These devices sound much like car alarms. The screech of a car alarm is considered more of a nuisance than a deterrent. If the owner is in hearing range, they can run to the car to quiet the alarm, but no one else, police or otherwise, hurry to the squeal of a car alarm. Do not believe noisemaker claims that a siren will summon help. It will not.

I do endorse the motion-sensing noisemakers as budget alarm systems, if you can adjust the device so it responds only to gross movement, like the opening of a door or window. Not everyone can afford to pay a major company to install and monitor an alarm system, yet all of us need ways to be sure our doors and windows won't be pried open as we sleep, allowing an intruder in our homes while we are vulnerable. Attach the noisemaker to your sliding patio door or to windows that don't have adequate locks, and trust it only to alert you if someone enters your home without your knowledge.

Tools are only as good as your training

Any self-defense device is only as effective as the training you receive in its use. Even the simple OC spray is more effective when combined with patterns of movement and other good defense tactics. Equally important is the legal defense you muster by presenting training certificates in both non-lethal and firearms defensive techniques. Your training certificates show the prosecutor, judge and jury that you carefully studied appropriate ways to stop varying levels of criminal assault. You can testify that your training was the basis for the method with which you choose to defend self and family.

Legitimate instructors of the mini-baton, oleoresin capsicum, stick fighting, or hand-to-hand defenses must inform you that intermediate force is not sufficient against a deadly force attack. Use intermediate defenses to stop harassment before a lethal assault begins, yet always be prepared to answer lethal force with your own firearm if that is the kind of attack you face.

1 Modern Warrior, 711 N. Wellwood Ave., Lindenhurst, NY 11757.
2 *Surviving Edged Weapons*, Calibre Press, Inc., 800-323-0037.

Even a small assailant can knock away and hold off the stun gun's prongs, breaking the contact well before the seven to ten seconds of contact required to send muscles into spasm.

10

Rape Prevention & Survival

In our effort to prevent and avoid sexual assault, we need to learn the hunting patterns of sexual predators, using this information to heighten our defenses during windows of vulnerability thus identified. If we are to stop sexual assault, we need to understand what motivates the rapist, ways these predators gain control over their victims, and what can be done to survive if sexually assaulted. If unable to prevent or terminate the assault, survivors need to know what to do after a rape to regain their own safety, deal with the physical and emotional aftermath, and to prosecute and incarcerate a criminal who will certainly repeat his offense.

While we train and take care to prevent sexual violence, it would be foolish for even accomplished martial artists and pistol shooting champions to conclude that we are invulnerable! This chapter incorporates sexual assault information presented in newsletters and brochures made available by the American Women's Self-defense Association,[1] an organization to which I proudly belong, as well as data and details from a variety of women's advocacy organizations, women's counselors, law enforcement sources and more.

Understanding the crime of rape

The rapist is driven to control women, either in an expression of power or of anger. Some need to degrade their victim, others are sated by the terror and anguish their acts cause. For others, the ultimate control of life or death is the key to their satisfaction. In an effort to apprehend rapists, law enforcement psychologists have suggested four different profiles that define most sexual predators. Over 40% are estimated to be power-assertive types, typified by the perpetrator of date rape, who attempts to get a woman vulnerably alone and uses violence to gain submission. More spontaneous is the anger-retaliatory rapist, who acts out sexual violence to punish and degrade women, subduing his victim through explosive and unexpected violence. This criminal's warning signs include substance abuse, an explosive temper and an impulsive or ungoverned personality. Authorities believe this type is responsible for a third of the rapes committed.

One-fifth of rapists are thought to fit the power-reassurance model, indicated by low self-confidence and passivity in day-to-day life. Victim selection may start with stalking or peeking in windows. Entering through unsecured windows or doors, exerting minimal physical force, the intruder is likely to make verbal threats regarding a weapon the victim is not actually shown. This man may act out a fantasy that he is with a lover.

The smallest percentage of rapists fit the description of the anger-excitation category. This minority are sexually satisfied by inflicting pain, and may hold a victim for torture beyond the initial attack. An intelligent and organized criminal, he has rehearsed and planned his crime well in advance, using his charisma to mislead those around him.

Rape is a repeat offender's crime. Five and a half years in jail is the average sentence served by convicted rapists. Parole, conditional release or partial supervision puts a lot of rapists back into society even earlier. In 1994, it was estimated that 60% of the 234,000 men serving sentences for rape were in programs outside prison walls.

We are too often blinded to the presence of these men by our own stereotypes, presuming that we "know" how a rapist looks or acts. Statistics reveal that women often know their attacker and have chosen to trust him. During his more stable days, Ted Bundy worked as a phone volunteer in a women's rape crisis center, thus becoming the title character in one of Ann Rule's excellent crime paperbacks. The Bundy volume is labeled *The Stranger Beside Me*, because Rule and Bundy volunteered for the same organization at the same time, and even this veteran criminologist was unaware of his capacity for evil.

Women cannot assume safety with acquaintances from work, from social or church contacts, or from even within their own families. The Biden report states "Strangers are not the most dangerous sources of violence against women. The numbers of women attacked by those they loved far outweighed the number of women attacked by strangers."[2]

Too many women have obtained a court order restraining an intimate male offender from further contact, only to find that restraining order useful only in further legal action, and of little value in assuring her physical safety. If a spouse, boyfriend or acquaintance harasses or assaults you, your immediate defense is your own responsibility. The police simply cannot arrive in time to stop a determined attacker.

Restraining orders are, however, vital in obtaining cooperation from police and the courts in pressing charges against an abuser. The survivor needs to report the contact to police and keep scrupulously truthful records of restraining order violations, listing dates, times, and descriptions of the incident. Write down your exchange with the abuser and keep a diary of witnesses who can corroborate your account.

Police also use restraining orders as a tool to interrupt the psychological control an abusive mate uses to draw the repeat victim back into his control. More than one abused wife has been freed from on-going mindgames when the husband violated a no-contact order and landed back in jail for a month or so. Sometimes that is enough time for the woman to establish a new, safer life elsewhere.

Violation of trust

Over 60% of women who report that they have been raped were attacked by someone they knew–one-fifth of the time by a husband or boyfriend.[3] Warning signs–even in men who seem very ordinary–include indications that they place little value on what you say or wish. Not listening to your words, interrupting, talking while you are speaking, or ignoring what you say are all signs that should not be disregarded. Doing what he wants despite your explicit request is a huge red flag, even if it is only a choice of restaurants, radio station or other minor issues.

Listen to the jokes, vocabulary and conversations of the men with whom you associate. Notice how they speak of former wives or girl friends. Expressions of hostility toward women, demeaning views about women, or beliefs that women exist to serve men, are all harbingers of trouble. Be wary of people who invade your personal space, and when you push them away play mind games to make you feel guilty, prudish or otherwise embarrass you into allowing the invasion. You are being tested for submissiveness, suggests Assault Prevention Information Network organizer Judith Weiss.[4]

> *If at any time one participant says "no," "stop," or in any other way indicates unwillingness to participate, continued sexual activity becomes the* **CRIME of RAPE.** *It is that simple.*

In dating situations, possessiveness or jealousy is not endearing–it is cause for concern! And finally, heavy drinking or other substance abuse can unpredictably reduce normal barriers to assaultive, sexually aggressive behavior.

Social activities are important to active, healthy women. In today's world, however, with date rapes frighteningly common, you must exercise caution and common sense at a bar, a party or other gathering. If you go to the rest room or elsewhere, safeguard your beverage or do not drink from it when you return. Know where your drink came from. Ask for the unopened bottle or can, watch the bartender mix it or offer at a private gathering to serve yourself. Rohypnol and other sedative/hypnotic drugs have rocketed through the U.S. Consumed with alcohol, these substances produce disinhibition and amnesia, which is no doubt the reason for its popularity as the "date rape drug."

An epidemic for women aged 15 to 24, date rape may follow mutually desired contact that exceeds the woman's wishes. Intoxication by either or both parties contributes, but ultimately date rape is caused by the assailant's contempt for his date's rights and wishes. When this disregard is physically acted out, a crime has been committed.

One of the most difficult aspects of rape by an acquaintance is self-accusation that the violence was the victim's own fault. The survivor suffers the loss of ability to trust others as well as her own judgment. As a result, rape by an acquaintance, especially in the course of a date, is rarely reported and prosecuted. Although physically and psychologically traumatized, some date rape survivors do not identify their trauma as rape, and thus do not seek help from women's counselors skilled in assisting in rape recovery.

Rape is defined as non-consensual sexual acts completed through violence or threat, or enacted when the victim is physically unable to consent. It is that simple. If the woman says "no," "stop," or in any other way indicates her unwillingness to participate, the sexual activity **is** non-consensual. It is that simple. If the aggressor forces intercourse on the woman against her wishes, he commits the crime of rape. Too often responsibility is placed on the victim, who feels unable to stop the sexual activity for fear of immediate physical harm or later reprisal. Blaming the survivor is an ages-old dodge, one you can short-circuit by recognizing and rejecting it.

Rape prevention

Your determination and mindset, as much as your training will keep you alive if you are sexually assaulted. Rape prevention training should include physical fighting methods, weapons skills and panic control. Your training will help you keep a level head, because it has prepared you to choose the right response without a lot of wasted thought. Expect to feel the fear, yet remember that you have been trained and know how to protect yourself. Use your mind to interrupt the panic.

Don't expect to be saved by pleading, stalling, reasoning or crying. Remember that this predator rapes as a means to control and degrade his victim. Establish your unwillingness to be his victim. Take the first opportunity to resist and escape when you find a window of opportunity. Use your own body or any object available–a bedside lamp, the corner of a hardbound book, a bottle picked up from the street–to smash an attacker's face, nose, eyes, Adam's apple, knee or groin.

Although a knife is not at your throat, non-consentual intercourse IS an attack against your life because the rapist communicates he will use any force necessary to overcome your resistance.

Look for a way to fight back and escape immediately instead of "hoping" for a chance later. Any defensive plan, vigorously enacted promises more success than thinking of the perfect plan after it is too late. Many women escape abduction by running and screaming before the predator has them fully under control. Statistics show that a combination of forceful verbal commands and physical resistance provides the greatest chance of stopping a sexual assault. Be prepared to back up verbal resistance with physical violence whether or not you possess a gun.

Rape is a deadly force attack. Sometimes the rapist uses verbal threats and the intimidation of his greater physical size and strength to force the victim's compliance. Although a knife may not be at your throat, non-consensual intercourse is still an attack on your life because the rapist implies that he will use any degree of force necessary to overcome your resistance. Too often men trivialize the severity of rape by arguing that no one was ever killed by a penis or mockingly suggest that victims should "lay back and enjoy it." This cruel stupidity discourages women from fighting back and often from prosecuting rapists, because it clearly communicates that society does not recognize the severity of the violence a rapist inflicts against his victim. Deadly force is completely justified against a rapist because it is his threats of death or crippling injury that cause the victim to submit to non-consensual intercourse.

You may face an unarmed assailant who uses his greater strength and size to coerce and gain submission. Assailants threatened or applied force without a gun in nearly 90% of the violent crimes against women between 1973 and 1983.[3] Survivors of unarmed rape may struggle with a heavy burden of self-doubt and recrimination, and suffer questions from others who wonder why she submitted to an unarmed man. Even the police may seem to question the survivor's claim, and in the courtroom the rapist's defense attorney may argue that being unarmed indicated the criminal's benign intent. Self-defense experts and counselors who deal with sexual violence survivors are needed to overcome these lies, showing that the threat of harm forced the victim's compliance. If able, the survivor should take pains to preserve physical evidence that reveals force used against her. This will mean cooperating with police detectives and medical personnel in allowing photography to record injuries and efforts to collect evidence.

Understand, also, that you are capable of resisting an rapist, whether armed or not. Knives are frequently used in rape attacks, however prior training can help you survive against a knife as discussed in the previous chapter. Remember you may be cut and may bleed, but use this knowledge to avoid panic and keep fighting to gain your freedom. With proper training, you can disarm a gun-carrying assailant. As often as not, an audacious, unexpectedly violent counter-attack so surprises the assailant that his plan is derailed when the survivor is not terrified into submission.

Early, dynamic resistance can short-circuit life-threatening danger during and after the rape. Don't allow yourself to be tied up or otherwise restrained, nor put into a vehicle. The majority of victims who are restrained are murdered during the assault. It is better to fight for your life while you can actively resist, than to trust your survival to the predator later.

For decades, women have been warned not to resist rape, counseled by men and police officials who understood neither the effects of rape on the victim, nor the rapist's motivation. Refuse to believe anyone who

Rape prevention training should include disarming skills with which to resist an assailant with a gun. The first step is a parry to get out of the line of fire.

does not value your life and survival enough to allow you to use forceful defensive tactics and effective weapons to preserve your life.

A leading argument against putting up a fight was the imagined danger to the intended victim. Citing National Crime Victim Survey data researcher Don Kates reports, *"The gun-armed resister was actually much less likely to be injured* than the non-resister . . . Only 12 to 17 percent of gun-armed resisters were injured. *Those who submitted to the felons' demands were twice as likely to be injured* (gratuitously [after the rape or incident])."[5] (Emphasis author's.) Kates goes on to report that resistance *without* a gun is much more likely to result in injury to the intended victim, as one would expect. However, I would never conclude that submission is preferable to suffering injury while fighting off assault in any way possible. Data drawn from crime statistics cannot consider the post-assault trauma stemming from the absolute loss of control the non-resister suffers.

No one can teach you specific sets of movements to stop a rapist since each attack is unique. Learn principles of physical defense, and if attacked, fight back immediately and assertively. Inflict the most damage you can with the tools you have, even if that is only your empty hands.

If you are raped

Avoid panic during the attack. Never give up. If the rapist prevails, try to remain aware of his actions and alert to escape possibilities that may open up during the assault. Never conclude that you are defeated. With increasing frequency, rapists kill their victims to avoid identification and arrest or for their own satisfaction. Do not consider the attack over until the rapist is truly gone. When he is gone, get to a safe place or if the attack

After getting the gun's muzzle pointed elsewhere, disarmer isolates and uses leverage against the assailant's hand and arm, breaking the gun free toward his thumb, the weakest point.

has taken place in your home, secure the house when he has departed. In addition to summoning law enforcement and medical aid, call a trusted friend or family member who can come to support and watch over you.

If attacked by a stranger, memorize details about his height and weight, if only by comparing height to a door frame or sign post. Notice clothing he wears and look for distinctive physical characteristics like a muscular or thin physique, his complexion tone, scars, tattoos or blemishes, hair and eye color. If he drives a car, try to determine make, model, color and license number and state, or at least some of these details. If you can't determine the make of the car, try to remember the emblem on the car well enough to sketch it for an investigator. If attacked outside your home, leave your fingerprints everywhere you possibly can, drop personal items

Early, pre-emptive resistance is essential against an assailant who attempts to restrain, tie up or force his potential victim to get in a vehicle. Anything becomes a weapon in such a situation, including the common aluminum-shafted flashlight.

that can be identified as yours, including buttons, jewelry, gloves or cosmetic cases bearing your fingerprints.

Disagreeable as it sounds, sexual assault investigators hope that rape survivors will avoid bathing, and changing or washing clothing after an attack, to preserve the maximum evidence for prosecution of the crime. Avoid cleaning your nails or applying medication, they request. For example, we are taught that in cases of oral rape, evidence has been destroyed by as simple an act as drinking water or brushing teeth. Your body holds important evidence that is needed to prosecute the attacker.

Without survivors' reports of rapes and attempted rapes, police are hard pressed to prevent continued sexual assaults. Your cooperation and report allow the authorities to help you and to stop the rapist before he attacks another woman. While it may seem unbearable to face outside scrutiny at this time, reporting opens the door to help and healing. Because one of the great injuries suffered by the rape survivor is a loss of personal volition, I encourage you to use the legal process as a way to regain control, even strike back at the assailant. By contributing to his arrest and prosecution, you may find yourself renewing your ability to choose the direction your life takes, to regain your own power, and in so doing contribute to the community effort to stop the rapist's crimes.

A thorough investigation of the crime and the place it happened must be conducted. The investigators need to discuss the assault in detail and may ask questions that seem offensive or senseless, yet are important in preparation to arrest and prosecute the rapist.

A friend can accompany you during the investigation and go with you to a hospital for examination and treatment. You may want to take along a change of clothing as what you were wearing during the assault may be held as important evidence. If you prefer to interact with a female police officer, ask the investigators if one is available or request a women's advocate who is familiar with the post-assault process and can guide you through it as gently as possible. An advocate is unencumbered by the emotional response a family member or close friend may feel, and she knows how the system works. In short, an advocate is a valuable member of your recovery team and you should not hesitate to ask the police to call this professional. Many cities have rape crisis centers that provide women's advocates and can later recommend a counselor and help you find legal advice.

Rape recovery is an arduous and often lengthy process, one facilitated by professional assistance which entails monetary expense, too. Without reporting the sexual assault, the victim is not eligible for Crime Victims' Compensation programs that can help defray medical expenses, the cost of counseling and psychotherapy, and in some instances financial losses related to the trauma of the rape.

Don't be dissuaded from pressing criminal charges by anyone, including the rapist, your family or others with influence over you. Rapists frequently threaten retribution if you report the assault, and family members, employers or land lords may pressure you for silence if they fear embarrassment or social or financial loss. Your testimony, often joining with the testimony of other victims, can stop the rapist. Your testimony reduces the chance that the rapist will do the same violence to someone else.

Physical and emotional recovery

Sexual assault survivors face a challenging recovery process that should not be undertaken alone. Professional rape recovery counselors recognize and can guide survivors through the following symptoms, and will provide comfort when friends and family members, mired in their own problems, are unable to respond supportively. Survivors should remember to take advantage of counseling, support groups and the care of their friends and families, not only in the first months of recovery, but throughout the entire process, no matter how long it takes.

Rape survivors wonder "Why me?" and all too often follow up that query with a heavy load of self-blame. Losing trust in one's own decisions, a sense of powerlessness and concluding that to be female is to be vulnerable are all psychological results of rape.

Recovery moves through stages of trauma, denial and resolution.

The first could be characterized by fear: fear of being alone, which may continue for some time, and is usually especially acute directly after the attack; fear of retaliation; fear of men, all men. Fear meshes with emotions of anger, feelings of helplessness, guilt, pain, degradation or anxiety. Physical manifestations are classic Post Traumatic Stress Disorder (PTSD)

> *The survivor can never be held responsible or blamed for the actions of another person–especially those of the rapist.*

problems, in addition to conditions directly linked to the rape, like sexually-transmitted diseases and physical injury.

Denial can consume a long time, during which some survivors work manically to regain control of their lives and well-being. It is an uphill climb, however, because the trauma of the rape has not yet been confronted. Sometimes, unresolved issues manifest themselves in poor concentration, inability to respond in an emergency, trouble maintaining relationships, irritability, sleep and eating disorders, and other symptoms that indicate PTSD (See Chapter 4).

PTSD sufferers endure vivid and disturbing memories–reliving the violence in flashbacks or nightmares, emotional numbness and isolation, hyper-vigilance and excessively sensitive startle responses, feelings of betrayal and anger, trouble building trust, as well as physiological symptoms like back aches, headaches, chronic pain syndrome, appetite disturbance and subsequently poor nutrition. Healthy sexual enjoyment can be tainted by the rape for periods lasting from six months to years and years after the assault. Alcohol or drug addiction afflicts many PTSD victims, yet temporarily numbing memories or emotions can rebound with a vengeance when the crutch is removed. Depression, ranging from occasional to continual, can also last for quite a long time. Not surprisingly, those who are able to talk to a counselor or trusted friends suffer depression less severely and in shorter duration.

In recovery, the survivor comes to understand that although she is responsible for her own actions, she can never be held responsible or blamed for the actions of another person–especially those of the rapist. The attack is not her fault, and regardless of the circumstances around and preceding the attack, the rapist's actions remain beyond excuse.

Recovery takes time and requires a safe environment and a non-judgmental atmosphere that allows the survivor to work through the anxieties, emotions and physical symptoms. It is a complex and multi-faceted problem, one that should not be faced without professional help and the love of friends and family.

---

1 American Women's Self-defense Association, 713 N. Wellwood Ave., Lindenhurst, NY 11757.

2 *Violence Against Women: A Week in the Life of America, ibid.*, p. 7.

3 *Violence by Intimates*, Bureau of Justice Statistics Factbook, U.S. Department of Justice, NCJ-167237 March 1998.

4 Judith Weiss, Assault Prevention Information Network, ibid.

5 Kates, Don B., *Guns, Murder and the Constitution*, 1991.

11

Staying Safe

As young girls we are taught behaviors that discourage taking responsibility for our own well-being, even after we're fully grown women. We learn to depend on others to protect us, and we're programmed not to hurt any living thing, even when we are endangered. By the time we're teenagers, we'd rather be harmed or die than break the taboo on aggression. Female role models are delicately thin with toothpick arms and legs that illustrate anything but strength. It is extremely difficult to remain unaffected by the barrage of print and broadcast media portraying these fragile women as the model of desirability, success and beauty.

Equally depressing are society's unspoken rules about femininity. Aggressive women are called bitches, and early on female children are taught that they will receive the most praise and approbation when filling a role of service and support. Is it any wonder that getting our girls to seek positions of leadership and responsibility is an uphill fight? Should we be surprised when teen-aged girls, as well as grown women, behave foolishly?

Women demonstrate feminine irresponsibility in the desire to remain child-like and carefree—the Peter Pan mindset. Carelessness is like a drug, it allows euphoria and those hooked on it have a hard time recognizing the reality of this risky world. I remember the carelessness of my twenties, drinking with my friends and taking stupid chances. By way of confession, let me say that it is a credit to the friends looking out for me that I came through those reckless years unscathed. I gratefully remember friends extricating me from of barroom situations, walking me home and making other protective gestures.

Popular female role models are delicately thin with toothpick arms and legs that illustrate anything but strength.

In the last decade, society has changed the way it judges social behavior. A lot of us used to go out drinking, then drive ourselves home. Today, few challenge the severe societal disapproval that interdicts such behavior. Why can't we likewise accept that it is dangerous to be in Condition White in public places, the same way we acknowledge the danger of driving under the influence of alcohol? If you party, appoint a designated "caretaker." If you use intoxicants, take along someone who will remain sober and assure that you return home safely. Promise to honor that person's judgment, the same way you would surrender car keys to a designated driver.

Doing God's job?

One of the most puzzling dilemmas about self-defense and personal responsibility is that faced by devout Christians. With doctrine assigning the survival of each individual fully to God's hands, some say, "It must have been God's will" when women are raped, abused or killed. Because scripture says "He sees the sparrow fall," many believe God will decide if they should enjoy safety or become a victim.

Possession of a means of self-defense is seen by some as a failure of faith. God is in charge of his children's safety and trying to augment His power is disrespectful, some argue. If this is your belief, will you to enact it to its fullest degree? Throw out the fire extinguishers, cancel your automobile and home insurance, get rid of your car's spare tire and remove the locks from doors and windows. That kind of risk is equivalent to refusing to provide a means of physical defense for oneself and family.

It is dangerous to base entire beliefs on just one or two scriptural citations, if truthfully seeking the intent of any doctrine. Balance is found in vignettes like the apostle's report of the Last Supper in the New Testament book of Luke Chapter 22, where Christ prepares His disciples for the trials preceding His crucifixion. "But now, let him who has a purse take it, and likewise a bag. And let him who has no sword sell his mantle and buy one," directs the Saviour.[1]

According to gun rights advocate Jeffrey R. Snyder, as little as two centuries ago, the message from the Christian pulpit was that submission to violent attack showed contempt for God's greatest gift: precious human life.[2] What a sad contrast to recent events, when in 1999 the church played a major, political role in defeating legislation to license concealed weapon carry in the state of Missouri.

Please hear this: It's OK to defend innocent life. Clear up any confusion by understanding that it's acceptable even dutiful to fight for your life, although few philosophies will endorse killing in defense of your material possessions. Up to this point in this book, we have emphasized avoiding trouble and intermediate defenses to deflect dangers *before* they become deadly. Both are necessary components of a sensible survivor's mindset. There is more, however. In coming chapters, we will discuss employing deadly force with firearms to defend against unavoidable dangers.

While sport shooting and marksmanship training can be very enjoyable, no one relishes the idea of facing deadly danger and having to lethal force to stop a threat to innocent life. The ability to defend against rape, crippling injury or death, however, is a better alternative than victimization. I have come to recognize the peace of mind and freedom from the morbid fear of attack and abuse as a great blessing. Perhaps a good scripture for the dojo or gun range might be found in the Old Testament book of Psalms, where David writes: "Blessed be the Lord, my Rock, who trains my hands for war, my fingers for battle."[3] The Psalmist voices, far better than I could, my own gratitude for the skills and ability to defend myself.

First, accept responsibility

Thought this was going to be a book all about guns, didn't you? Well, we'll get into that next, however it is terribly important that gun owners be sufficiently mature to handle the responsibility of immediate access to the power of life and death. Your daily decisions about how you live reveal your attitude toward life and death! First, address the delusions and mental blocks that put you in danger, then learn the skills and finally obtain the tools with which to protect yourself.

Taking this level of personal responsibility is really about caring enough for yourself to assure your own survival. If you don't care enough about yourself, maybe you care enough about those who love you–a child your death would orphan, a spouse your death would widow, a parent left alone in old age. Your awareness and self-responsibility can spare these cherished people the anguish of dealing with a loved one's horrible death.

Finally, if you don't care enough about those who love you, can you find it in yourself to care enough about the world we are creating for those who follow us? Will it be a world where assault and victimization is a quasi-acceptable thing, like forgery or embezzlement, or will it be shaped by women who have stood up and said no more–then taken the steps to make it a safer world?

Moving beyond the mental, spiritual and emotional aspects of self-defense, lets next discuss the appropriate firearms, skills and tactics of the task.

---

1   The Holy Bible, New Testament, Luke 22:36.

2   Jeffrey R. Snyder, *A Nation of Cowards*, published in the Fall 1993 issue of *The Public Interest*.

3   The Holy Bible, Old Testament, Psalm 144:1.

12

Safe Gun Habits to Live By

"I was told the gun is unloaded, so I don't have to be careful with it." Have you ever heard these words?

Uncounted firearms tragedies are "explained" by people who believed the gun they held was not loaded. You can prevent enormous tragedy if you always treat every gun as if it is loaded...even if you just put it down or if someone tells you, "It's OK, it's not loaded."

The sages of the firearms fraternity have correctly noted that gun safety is a state of mind. Although firearms of all types are enjoyed in a variety of shooting sports and recreation, a gun must never be considered capable of anything less than lethal results. Strict adherence to a few sensible safety rules will prevent the vast majority of negligent or unintentional firearms discharges. These are taught in many of the world's leading firearms training schools as the Four Universal Gun Safety Rules and begin with "TREAT ALL GUNS AS IF THEY ARE ALWAYS LOADED." The first step in gun safety is understanding that a firearm can never be handled as if it is not dangerous.

At the gun store or shooting range, check any gun you are handed to determine that it is indeed unloaded. You can also ask a knowledgeable gun store clerk or an experienced shooter to show you how to safely unload your revolver or a semi-automatic.

Maintaining safe muzzle direction, check by sight and by feel to assure that the gun is unloaded.

Learn to check for ammunition in the gun by both sight and feel. Some semi-automatic pistols have chambers that are obscured by the slide even when locked open. It is likewise easy to miss a cartridge in the chamber of a bolt action rifle if checking visually. A round of ammunition may be in the chamber, ready to fire if the trigger is pulled. By probing with a finger, you can detect the presence of a cartridge you cannot see. Training yourself to verify an empty gun by sight and feel increases understanding of the gun you intend to use under the stress of a self-defense emergency, sometimes in darkness or other unfavorable conditions.

Next, safe gun handling demands that you NEVER POINT THE GUN AT ANYTHING YOU WOULD NOT SHOOT. The second rule applies equally to loaded and unloaded guns. Always know at what and whom the gun muzzle will point. Determine a safe muzzle direction *before* picking up the weapon, that way you won't cross yourself or someone else with the muzzle while you look for a safe place to point it. And remember, a visual obstruction, like a sheet rock wall, will not stop bullets. Avoid handling firearms off the range unless you are safely practicing dry fire, cleaning the gun, or securing it for the night. Don't show off the gun like a toy or curiosity. Treat your personal protection weapon as a very private item, even more personal than lingerie or cosmetics.

Always practice gun safety habits

Treat every gun as if it is loaded; and never point a gun at anything you are not willing to shoot. These are the first rules of safe gun handling. The third rule, KEEP YOUR FINGER OUTSIDE THE TRIGGER GUARD UNTIL YOUR SIGHTS ARE ON TARGET is equally important.

Suppose you hear noises in the kitchen some night. Gun in hand, you go downstairs to investigate. As you approach,

Learning to keep the finger off the trigger until the sights are on target and the decision to shoot is made requires careful attention until the habit is well-formed.

the noises continue. You are convinced you will soon face an unknown intruder. In the grip of this stress and fear, anything unexpected will startle you. If startled, your muscles will contract as part of the body's natural fight-or-flight response. When the fingers gripping the handgun convulse, the trigger finger also contracts. It can do nothing else; the hand's fingers respond as one unit.

If the finger rests on the trigger, the trigger will be pulled. On a single-action semi-auto, this pretty much guarantees that an unintentional shot will be fired. A revolver or double action semi-auto is only slightly less likely to be fired during the startle response.

In more ordinary day-to-day circumstances, keeping the finger off the trigger will prevent almost all the negligent gun discharges that occur. High quality guns of modern design don't just discharge by themselves. Someone has to put pressure on the trigger. Never break the safety rules because you think the gun is unloaded. Your actions are the basis for habits that will be repeated under circumstances that are not safe.

At the start of this chapter, I suggested that gun safety is a state of mind, a set of habits that govern our actions when handling firearms. It follows that any harm inflicted–intentionally or unintentionally–is *not* the fault of the mechanical device we call a gun, rather of the individual in possession of the firearm. Responsible gun owners need to make firearms safety their own personal crusade, for with the individual rests the future of gun ownership in the United States.

Safe shooting locations

The danger of shooting in many of the informal public shooting areas is ironic. Across the nation, in timber land, gravel pits and other remote areas, the public is allowed to discharge firearms. The danger of shooting in remote, isolated areas comes from thieves and marauders who recognize the vulnerability of small groups or the lone shooter. The solitary individual is lulled into complacency by friendly conversation with a couple of strangers who purport to be fellow gun enthusiasts, coming to share the shooting area. When our good-gal's guard is down, the predator restrains her and steals the firearms. Women are at further risk of sexual attack, having been disarmed by the criminals.

Personal safety sometimes costs a little more. Spend the $50 to join a local rifle and pistol club, or pay $10 to rent a lane at an indoor gun club where a range safety officer is present at all times. Shooting in isolated areas is a dangerous activity, not only because of thieves, also because of unsupervised, hazardous gun handling by "weekend warriors."

Informal outdoor shooting areas also pose great peril to hikers, dirt bikers or wandering children who may come over your backstop. When you fire your gun, you must know that your target is safe to shoot at, as well as being certain what is behind that target. KNOW THAT YOUR TARGET IS SAFE TO SHOOT AND THAT IT IS SAFE TO SHOOT INTO THE AREA BEYOND. I believe this safety rule is probably the strongest argument against shooting in the woods or at a gravel pit. You must **know** the terminal resting place of each bullet you fire. On a formal range, bullet traps or earthen berms provide backstops to stop the bullet.

Handgun cartridges expel bullets that can travel from 1 to $1\frac{1}{2}$ miles; unimpeded rifle rounds come to rest from $1\frac{1}{2}$ to $2\frac{3}{4}$ miles from the point at which they were fired. Do not discharge a gun if you do not know where the bullet will land. You must know that the area between your muzzle and the bullet's terminal resting spot is empty of people or property that could be harmed.

Even if you shoot at an indoor range, take responsibility to keep the area safe while you are there. Don't be afraid to correct unsafe gun handling by others or notify the range safety officer of hazards. If you complain that guns have been pointed at you and the offense continues uncorrected, leave the range. People become over-stimulated while shooting, and just because they claim the weapon is unloaded is no guarantee that they haven't removed the magazine, but forgotten to eject the round from the chamber. Do not accept this or any other explanation as a valid reason to violate the safe muzzle direction rule.

Protect your senses

On a firing range you must protect your hearing and vision, both of which may be damaged by gunfire. Repeated exposure to gunshots has robbed a lot of shooters of their hearing. The 263rd volume of the Journal of the American

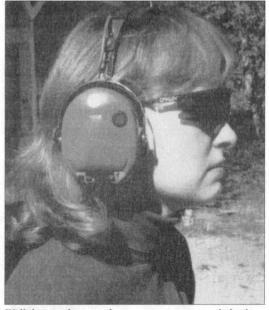

Well-designed eye and ear protection is needed whenever you are on the range, not just when you are shooting. Be sure to wear it properly to avoid unrecoverable loss of hearing or vision.

Medical Association reported that "Sounds that are sufficiently loud to damage sensitive inner-ear structures can produce hearing loss that is not reversible by any presently available medical or surgical treatment."[1]

The journal includes gun fire in the list of "acoustic trauma" that can cause irreparable harm that even hearing aids can't always help. In addition to permanent hearing loss, symptoms of damage include tinnitus, a constant noise that interferes with communication and disrupts sleep.

At a minimum, use the foam protectors inserted deeply into the ear canal to block the noise when you go to the range. Good quality ear muffs are the better choice, since they block more of the noise. Muffs also cover the sound-conducting bones around the ear that transmit damagingly loud concussions. A lot of beginning shooters display an exaggerated flinching reaction when shooting their handgun. There are several reasons for the flinch, which we'll discuss later. One aspect is anticipation of the painfully loud noise. That's avoidable with a $20 to $30 purchase of industrial hearing protection ear muffs.

Equally important is tightly-fitting, wrap-around eye protection. Shooting a semi-automatic, or shooting beside someone with a semi-automatic, you quickly realize that the bullet isn't the only object expelled from the gun. The hot metal case is very uncomfortable if it falls between the lens of safety glasses and lodges on the shooter's cheek. Be sure your safety glasses fit tightly at the eye brow and extend to your temples.

Flying brass cartridge cases are a common danger. Less common, yet posing a much greater threat of injury, is the possibility that an ammunition cartridge may be defective and blow apart the revolver or semi-automatic pistol. If this happens, debris are thrown in every direction. In other instances, a semi-auto itself malfunctions, and an unlocked breach at the moment the cartridge is detonated allows parts of the brass case to break out and fly in all directions like a little grenade. Both are sobering accidents, and can blind unprotected eyes.

The industrial-strength safety glasses, with their all-important side shields, are not very attractive, but the fashion glasses shown offer almost no protection.

Buy safety glasses designed as protection against industrial accidents, not just sunglasses or fashionable prescription eye wear. The polycarbonate material needs to meet or exceed the ANSI Z 87.1

Industrial Standards for impact resistance. Do not trust your drugstore sunglasses or fashionable prescription eyewear to do the job!

Neither eyesight nor hearing are recoverable when lost. A small investment of $30 or $40 is all it takes to obtain rudimentary safety goggles and ear muffs. Put eye and ear safety above the stylishness or comfort of using lesser levels of protection.

Finally, just owning safety gear is not enough. The ear muffs and protective safety glasses must be put on before entering the shooting range and remain in place until leaving the range. Although you may not be actually shooting, your eyes and ears can be damaged by the noise and bullets of others who are shooting.

No, I'm not suggesting you'll be shot, when I say "bullets." Any experienced shooter has felt the problem of "bounce backs." While good ranges are designed and maintained to prevent part or all of the expended bullet from ricocheting or bouncing back toward shooters, inevitably some do. A tiny shred of metal bullet jacket lodged in a cheek or chin is uncomfortable, yet recoverable. If striking an eye, instead, the injury is agonizing and removal requires a trip to the doctor.

Other times, the entire bullet strikes a stone in the backstop, part of a metallic target holder or other object and bounces back. While its return velocity is considerably slower, a bounce back can break skin and will certainly bruise. If it hits an eye, the damage can be devastating. In one case, a woman wore her eye and ear protection in accordance with club rules. Her glasses prescription was incorrect for the distance to her front sight, however, so she slipped the spectacles down on her nose as she shot. As bad luck would dictate, a round she fired hit low on the metallic table holding the targets. The bounce back struck one of her eyes, in which she subsequently lost the vision. Safety gear is only effective if worn and worn properly.

Invisible hazards

A less apparent shooting hazard is the lead particulate matter generated when ammunition is discharged. Lead poisoning is a well-recognized risk, although if queried, most Americans would respond that lead poisoning results from old paint, ancient water pipes and water heaters or years ago when lead was a fuel additive, from car exhaust.

Firearms and shooting aficionados need to protect themselves against lead contamination and take steps to avoid being poisoned. With a few limited exceptions, firing a cartridge of ammunition releases lead into the air in two ways. If the projectile is a bare lead bullet or had exposed lead portions, lead shavings are created when the bullet is discharged. Even if the bullet is fully encased in copper, nylon or another covering, lead is expelled during the firing process, because the primer contains lead styphnate. When it is detonated a cloud of molecular lead compounds is released. Lead is present in the air as a gas when firearms are discharged, and settles on horizontal surfaces like the floor, shooting benches, window sills, and even the hair, clothing and skin of shooters present on the range.

If you pick up empty cartridge cases from the floor—either in pursuit of range cleanliness or to reload the cases—take special care with hygiene. Put the brass into a sealable plastic bag, and wash carefully as soon as the job is done.

While lead can be absorbed through the skin, quantities more likely to create toxicity are taken in through breathing the dust or vapor, and by ingestion. If you think the latter is unlikely, observe yourself for the next hour to see how often your hands touch your lips or mouth. During range time, make a conscious effort to keep hands and objects away from the mouth, and when you leave the firing line, wash your hands and face around your mouth without delay. Do it immediately, before you unconsciously touch your face or eat, drink or smoke. At the same time, take a tissue and vigorously blow your nose to discharge the dust and particles cap-

Nose blowing and a good wipe around the nose and mouth remove lead particles before they can be ingested.

tured by the small nose hairs. This natural filter has done its job, now do your part to expel the lead, before you sniff or swallow, ingesting the lead.

Lead contamination symptoms

Lead toxicity is not always correctly diagnosed because the symptoms are varied and are frequently mistaken for more common medical conditions. Shooters should inform their physicians that they may be at risk for lead toxicity, although they may face the disapproval of the anti-gun medical establishment. While this list is in no way all-inclusive, lead poisoning results in loss of memory, difficulty concentrating, insomnia and fatigue, irritability and aggressiveness, depression, headaches, elevated blood pressure, loss of sexual interest, bleeding gums, digestive problems, joint pains, menstrual irregularity, fertility problems and other ills. Neurological symptoms like hand twitching can show up, with other central nervous system problems possible.

The test for lead poisoning is not difficult. Blood is drawn and sent to a laboratory for analysis. Pollution can cause limited blood lead levels, but physicians consider lead levels above 40 micrograms per deciliter of blood risky, and 60 mcg/dl is defined as lead poisoning in adults, although considerably less can cause some of the above symptoms. Lead is not naturally present in the blood stream, unlike copper, zinc and other metals. There is literally no acceptable blood lead level, only degrees of toxicity.

Prevention requires good hygiene, including washing and nose blowing as discussed earlier. Like many shooting professionals, 99% of the ammunition I shoot is loaded with full metal jacket bullets. This eliminates a lot of the lead particulate in air and on surfaces. I think avid shooters who are on the range more than once a week are crazy if they continue to shoot unjacketed lead bullets. An additional preventive measure is under development by Remington, Federal and other ammunition companies to refine lead free primers.

Additional hygienic concerns include tracking in lead particles on shoes and clothing worn in the range. This is of particular concern if children are in the home. Because children are more sensitive to lead, the Center for Disease Control puts their danger levels between 20 mcg/dl to 25 mcg/dl. In addition, toddlers spend more time on the rugs and floors onto which you may track lead residue. Lead poisoning can be prevented; it requires awareness when you are exposed, determination to wash up and taking other precautions during and after range time, even when it is inconvenient.

Women of child bearing age owe it to themselves to be particularly careful about lead contamination, as lead can be stored in the bones to later be mobilized by a variety of physical conditions including pregnancy and lactation.[2] Research by the Reproductive Toxicology Center of Columbia Hospital for Women Medical Center cites studies that give a severe warning about lead exposure in pregnant women. "Lead can be readily transferred across the placenta to the fetus."[3] Stillbirth and miscarriages are common problems associated with lead poisoning.

A contentious topic

The question of firing range safety for pregnant women and their unborn children is one fraught with highly emotional opinions. I am certain that in response to this section a number of women will report that they shot regularly while pregnant and little Johnnie or darling Susie has come into the world quite unharmed. From a less anecdotal viewpoint, however, I believe there is compelling reason to avoid live gunfire during pregnancy. Lead toxicity and the potential for birth defects is alone very compelling reason to stay away from live fire during pregnancy and breast-feeding.

Some have hypothesized that the potential for hearing loss is further reason to give up shooting during pregnancy. Liquid is an astounding medium for sound transmission with sound waves traveling four times faster in water than in air. Thus the amniotic fluid in which the fetus rests cannot be expected to muffle gunshots or other loud noises, and may magnify sound instead. On the other hand, medical studies reported in Vol. 78 of Obstetrics & Gynecology suggest that the liquid environment and the fluid filling the fetus' developing hearing organs may reduce "the risk of mechanical trauma."

Studies of the impact of noise on unborn children have more often focused on environmental noise like that found around major airports and in industrial settings. In 1989 T.V.N. Persuad of the University of Manitoba wrote "exposure to noise represents a major health hazard, largely due to elevated catecholamine levels (epinephrine and norepinephrine produced by the mother) which produce vasoconstriction and hypoxia" in unborn infants. Fetal response to noise stimulation includes movement and cardioacceleration.

For the expectant mother, the wide selection of air guns marketed allows continued marksmanship and defensive firearms practice. Plinking practice with these quieter, cleaner tools keeps the draw and fire motions quick and smooth, as well as maintaining the skills of quick sight picture acquisition and smooth, surprise trigger break, all skills that transfer quite well to the conventional firearm the expectant mother may be carrying for the defense of herself and her unborn child.

Assure ammunition and gun are same caliber

Be careful that the ammunition you buy is the correct caliber for your firearm. The gun's construction is strong enough to withstand the pressures of the round it is designed to fire. Some ammunition-gun misfits are more readily apparent. The powerful .357 Magnum cartridge is identical in diameter to the .38 Special cartridge. It cannot be fired in a .38 Special caliber handgun, however, because it is slightly longer, preventing the .38's cylinder from closing. Likewise, smaller cartridges will fit in the chamber of a larger caliber gun, and dangers include malfunctions that happen when the case doesn't eject from a semi auto, as well as bursting the cartridge's case wall as it expands when the powder is burning.

You can be certain you've purchased the correct ammunition, if the caliber shown on the box corresponds with the caliber stamped into the frame or barrel of your handgun. If you're not sure you have the right caliber of ammunition, ask a knowledgeable gun store clerk for advice.

If you own several handguns of different calibers, only fire one at a time when you're at the range. For example, set out the .380 ACP and its ammunition. When you're done firing the little gun, bring out the 9mm semi-auto. Don't have both guns and both calibers of ammunition on the bench at the same time.

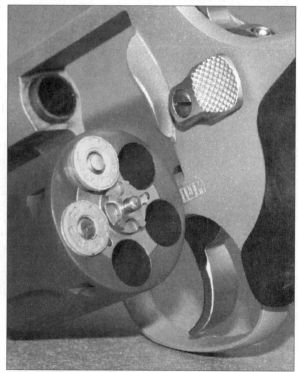

.357 Magnum ammunition (top) is slightly longer, so cannot fit into a .38 Special revolver. Other ammunition misfits, however, are not so readily detected.

Danger at more than the muzzle

The four universal gun safety rules outline essential gun safety that must be habituated and practiced whenever guns are used. There are additional dangers about which we should speak, although the likelihood of injury from the following is much less likely than from breaking any of the four rules.

By learning and practicing gun safety, we acknowledge that handling guns can be a dangerous activity. Without a clear understanding of the mechanical function of your firearm, there are additional risks. For example, when a revolver is discharged, some of the gasses created by the burning powder escape between the front face of the cylinder and the forcing cone and can burn close-by skin. While burns from the gas and punctures from lead shaved off the bullet as it goes through the forcing cone are minor compared to a gunshot wound, the revolver shooter should be aware of the hazard. The hands belong on the grip panels. If practicing one-handed shooting, the unoccupied hand should be held far away from the gun, preferably anchored somewhere on the body.

Handling just ammunition alone is relatively safe. The cartridge's function is to expel the bullet from the mouth of the cartridge case into a gun barrel, where the gas pressures are harnessed behind the bullet. A primer can spark and ignite gunpowder outside the of gun. Without the chamber walls to contain the pressures created by the burning powder, the bullet doesn't go anywhere, so the hazard is not from gunshot wounds. Instead, extreme pressures rupture the sides of the metallic cartridge case in a tiny

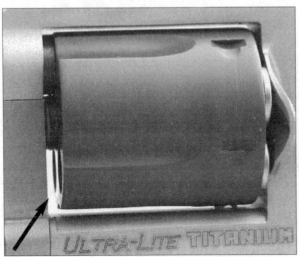

grenade effect. Now, it requires intentional effort to dent something so small as a centerfire cartridge primer, although curious children have managed to do so over the years. Ammunition, as well as guns, should be kept away from unsupervised youngsters until they are responsible enough to be trusted and to understand the hazards.

Hot gas and bullet shavings escape at the gap between the forcing cone and the cylinder face of the revolver.

Beyond detonating a cartridge outside a gun's chamber, there is an important lesson to learn about semi-automatic pistol manipulation. Some years ago during an IPSC (International Practical Shooting Confederation) match I saw a participant come off the range with blood flowing from the palm of his left hand. Several years later, an identical injury occurred on our own range during another IPSC match.

What had happened? Both shooters had completed the course of fire and were directed by the range officer to "unload and show clear," the IPSC procedure for unloading a gun before holstering. In the latter case, the shooter tried to rack the slide, but the live cartridge was lodged tightly in the chamber. He said later that after fighting several times to cycle the slide, he moved his hand further down the slide to obtain better grip and more leverage. He gave one last, mighty tug and the extractor jerked the live cartridge from the chamber, forcefully ramming the primer of the cartridge into the auto-pistol's ejector with enough power to spark the primer. The powder burned and with the cartridge outside the walls of the chamber, the pressures ruptured the case walls. Little shreds of the metallic case blew out like shrapnel and punctured the competitor's hand. Fortunately, neither episode resulted in permanent injury, although there have been other incidents in which the "shrapnel" from the case walls have caused permanent nerve damage.

Is this danger attributable to the semi-automatic pistol? In part, perhaps, although it is as likely that improperly manufactured ammunition

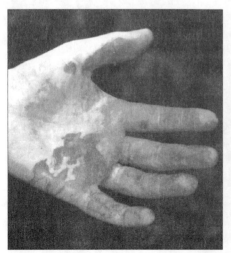 

In this case (left) the wounding was only superficial, however a cartridge accidentally detonated is capable of incredible tissue devastation. Safe semi-automatic manipulation (right) requires the shooter to grasp the slide well behind the ejection port.

may be slightly too large, and thus lodge tightly inside the chamber. At most fault was the technique used to unload the semi-automatic handgun. The semi-automatic is not in itself any more dangerous or difficult to manipulate than the revolver, however when using one, care must be exercised to keep any part of the hand well away from the ejection port.

During unloading, instead of allowing the hand to grasp far forward on the slide, grip the slide at the rear serration in the same motion one would use to shoot a slingshot. Gripped thus, if the worst possible happens, the hand is well out of the blast zone.

Living with snakes

Guns can be dangerous! You'll get no argument from me, but we must also recognize that a number of other useful inventions, including automobiles, chain saws, matches, even knives or scissors are dangerous, too.

Much has been written and voiced about "dangerous guns." Our society has literally become phobic about a small mechanical device–the firearm. If fear and emotion could be set aside, we would be forced to acknowledge that a firearm is an inert assemblage of mechanical parts designed to perform one function. Without emotion, we would recognize that function as accurately discharging bullets for a variety of purposes, ranging from warfare to hunting, competitive shooting to self-defense. Similarly, a larger mechanical device, the automobile, serves a useful function,

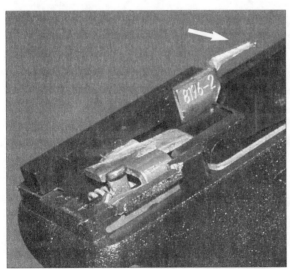

yet is grossly subject to misuses that cost thousands of lives. Amazingly, society does not loath cars!

Practically every aspect of this physical existence is fraught with danger. We harness tools and other elements to offset some of these hazards. In so doing, we tacitly agree to adhere to rules of general safety, as elemental as containing fire so it doesn't burn unchecked. The gun has its own such

The semi automatic design entails the slight risk that a cartridge's primer may be rammed into the ejector (seen in the upper right of the picture) during unloading.

rules of safety. If you choose to own any firearm, it is your responsibility to learn, practice and make these safety tenets a habit.

1 *Noise and Hearing Loss–Consensus Conference*, JAMA, June 20, 1990, Vol. 263, No. 23.
2 *Lead in bone: Implications for toxicology during pregnancy and lactation*, Silbergeld E., Environ Health Perspect 91: 63-70, 1991.
3 *Transfer of lead to the human feotus* from Moneral Metabolism in Pediatrics, Barltrop D and Burland WL, eds., Blackwell Scientific Publ., Oxford, 1969, pp 135-151.

13

Basic Training

While there may exist a few naturally talented shooters, accurate shooting skill is not a genetic ability. Marksmanship is the application of a specific set of psycho-motor skills that adults can learn and maintain. For example, a skilled, trained shooter manipulates the trigger with a finger that is acting in disassociation from the other muscles of the hand. In comparison, the untrained shooter's trigger finger convulses as the hands tighten on the gun in anticipation of the shots and recoil. That inadvertent motion on the trigger pulls the shot off center.

Trigger control and sight alignment are partners in the primary skills of pure marksmanship. Beyond these skills are concerns specific to the application of marksmanship to the self-defense emergency. The self-

Handgun training, like this women's only class, is both fun and rewarding. New skills are developed and often friendships formed that participants long value.

defense shooter needs to know shots can be consistently accurate, avoiding misses that endanger innocent bystanders.

The question of how much marksmanship training is enough varies from individual to individual. I believe anyone who carries a handgun for defense needs to study and practice tactical drills that require making split-second decisions, as well as practicing accurate shot placement. These skills far exceed being able to place five shots at your leisure in the X ring of a paper target!

A male friend or lover may not be the best choice to teach you to shoot. A man can become a decent marksman without adopting a technically correct shooting stance, because the mass and strength in his upper body better overpowers the recoil. The female physique typically has much less upper body mass and musculature to absorb the handgun's recoil. Conversely, a woman's legs are her stronger limbs and she can position her body to take advantage of this strength. Women's smaller, thinner hands grip the gun and manipulate the trigger differently. Despite his good intentions, even a master of tactical skills, a policeman or member of the armed forces, cannot intuit the female body's response to firing a handgun nor is he likely to understand the emotional component of what, to him, is merely a physical skill.

The intimidating task of learning to defend oneself with a deadly weapon is a job better approached without the emotional baggage of a male-female relationship. At this point, you need a respected teacher, not a beloved friend. self-defense issues that have nothing to do with shooting ability also need to be addressed. Women will have different concerns, and, to a limited degree, different parameters governing their use of deadly force. A classroom format that allows you to learn with other women or with women as well as men, should encourage discussion of female-specific issues in self-defense and in shooting.

Finally, there is the difficult issue of male and female styles of communication. Women learn by gathering a great deal of information, while men prefer to be given the bare basics, then learn by hands-on application. When these styles collide, a husband or father will often express "Why does she question *everything* I say? Why can't she just *do* what I tell her?" With equal frustration, the female student may respond "How can I do anything right until I understand it? Why won't he explain it to me?" When these conflicts surface, it is time to find professional instruction that does not have the baggage of family or marriage relationships!

Take time to find a training course that is sensitive to women's concerns about self-defense. Check the phone directory for a list of firearms or handgun instructors, or start by visiting the gun shops and commercial shooting ranges in your area. Ask for names of people in the area who offer beginning defensive handgun instruction.

After compiling a list of likely candidates, contact these instructors and ask for a résumé of their credentials. Ask about their philosophy of women's self-defense, with whom they trained, the length of their experience as an instructor, if they participate in competitive shooting events, and explore their attitude toward women. Get to know the mindset of your potential instructor. Ask if they discuss local firearms laws and use of deadly force, in addition to live fire instruction. Ask for a brief written course description for their beginning shooting classes. An excellent starting place is a handgun safety seminar or an introduction to handguns. An inexpensive one-day or evening course gives you a chance to decide if you like the instructor's teaching style and to learn about other courses. That, however, is only the beginning.

The considerably different musculature of this male shooter makes the modified Weaver stance his method of choice, while the author enjoys better results in the Isosceles position.

What to look for

A basic defensive firearms course should include an awful lot more than learning to shoot accurately. Is the world's best target-shooter prepared to save their own life if they are not truly convinced of their right to use the firearm to stop a violent assault?

When I teach beginners, I answer a lot of questions about appropriate use of deadly force–is it OK to shoot someone who is running out of your house with your jewelry and television? If you can't find an instructor who includes material on the use of deadly force in their curriculum, obtain and read Massad Ayoob's book *In the Gravest Extreme* as recommended earlier. At the very least educate yourself about your responsibility as an armed citizen by logging on to your state's law website via computer or visit the law library at your county courthouse to read up on your area's firearms and self-defense law. Finally, the National Rifle Association's basic firearms classes include instruction by local law enforcement, attorneys or prosecutors to expose gun owners to this vital legal information. Call their headquarters for the number of an instructor near you.[1]

Next, I believe a basic handgun course should provide beginning students with appropriate training guns and ammunition, allowing hands-on experience before they even buy a gun. First-time shooters learn the fundamentals of marksmanship most easily with the "friendly" .22 LR caliber revolver and semi-automatic. After becoming safe and proficient with a training gun, the student can move on to a caliber that is big enough for self-defense. A lot of beginners can avoid purchasing a gun that's not right for them by joining a friendly, low-key class with the handguns and ammunition already supplied. They learn to shoot, have the chance to ask lots of questions about handguns and defensive ammunition, concealed carry, safety, maintenance and cleaning of the weapons, all before dealing with the expense and intricacies of their first gun purchase.

Professional training is a responsibility you should fulfill before adopting the gun for self-defense. If you absolutely cannot find competent training in your area, arrangements can be made for qualified instructors to come to your area or you can travel to one of the nationally-recognized defensive shooting schools footnoted below.[2]

When beginning training is complete and those questions answered, the student is able to present herself knowledgeably at a gun counter and fend off the patronizing suggestions that the little lady needs a pretty little gun–maybe this .25 caliber Raven here in the bottom shelf. The educated woman can respond that she would prefer to see, perhaps, that nice Glock, Heckler & Koch or Taurus.

Next, buying a gun and ammunition for self-defense.

1 National Rifle Association, 703-267-1000.
2 Lethal Force Institute, P O Box 122, Concord, NH 03301 800-624-9049; John and Vicki Farnam's Defense Training International, 749 S Lemay, Ste. A3-337, Ft. Collins, CO 80524 970-482-2520; Thunder Ranch, HCR 1, Box 52, Mt. Home, TX 78058 210-640-3138. If you are interested in hosting a course by the author in your area, call The Firearms Academy of Seattle, 360-978-6100.

14

All About Ammunition

Reduced to the most basic terms, the heart of any self-defense firearm is the cartridge of ammunition with which it is loaded. While sales hype and the human affinity for the mechanical glamorizes the pistol itself, in reality, whether used in target practice or self-defense, the handgun is nothing more than the platform to launch bullets, which actually cause the terminal effect.

While I appreciate the pleasures of well-made firearms of many varieties, let us begin our firearms education at the heart of the matter: the ammunition.

Handgun ammunition comes in so many varieties that the beginning shooter often feels overwhelmed by the task of selecting ammunition for self-defense. It often falls to a clerk in the gun store to recommend ammunition to the first-time gun buyer. The men who worked at a now-defunct Seattle-area gun range are probably still snickering about the woman who asked for a box of Federal Hydra-Shoks by requesting the "cartridge that causes a great hydrostatic shock if it is fired into a body." The clerk grinned and replied, "Lady, that describes most of the ammunition behind this counter."

We all must start somewhere! You see, that woman was me.

Selecting a defensive handgun caliber is an exercise in compromise, because in reality handguns are the least powerful of common defensive

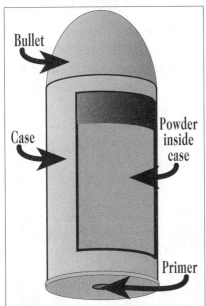

Components of a cartridge of centerfire ammunition.

weaponry. If available, a carbine or shotgun would serve far better in most defense emergencies, yet the larger guns are rarely accessible beyond home, ranch or business locations. The handgun is favored for convenience, mobility and legal concealed carry, not for superior ballistics. When choosing a handgun for home or self-defense, caliber is one of the first variables addressed, for confined to its limited power, we earnestly pursue the maximum effect possible.

Ammunition selection is a task complicated by the new shooter's ignorance of terms and vocabulary with which to communicate their needs, concerns and desires. Let us, then, conduct a little vocabulary session.

Ammunition terminology

Ballistics: The science that deals with the motion of projectiles.

Cartridge: One unit of ammunition, comprised of a bullet, a case, a primer and gunpowder also called propellant. You will also hear the word "round" or "load" used informally to describe a cartridge of ammunition or a variety of ammunition.

Caliber: The diameter of the bullet at its base, measured in 100ths or 1000ths of an inch. Thus, a .22 caliber bullet is $^{22}/_{100}$ths of an inch in diameter, a .45 caliber bullet is $^{452}/_{1000}$ths of an inch in diameter. Bullet diameter is also measured in millimeters. The European-born 9mm ammunition is a good example of bullet caliber expressed in metric units, as is 5.56x45 rifle ammunition, called by Americans .223 Rem.

Bullet: The projectile seated in the top of the case that is fired out of the gun barrel. Bullets come in a multitude of shapes for various uses. The most common are hollowpoint, roundnose and truncated cone, either lead or jacketed, plus lead semi-wadcutters and full wadcutters. Bullet weights also vary by intended use.

Caliber generally refers to the bullet's diameter.

Hollowpoint, with expanded bullet of same caliber.

Wadcutter ammunition.

Bullet weight: Bullets are described first by caliber (diameter), then by weight. Bullet weight is measured in units called grains: 7000 grains equal one pound. It is common to hear discussion of a .45 caliber 185–grain hollowpoint bullet, referring to a bullet weighing 185 grains that measures $452/1000$th inch in diameter at the base.

Wadcutter: A bullet that is a cylinder of lead, some with flat ends on both top and bottom, others with a cavity hollowed out at the base. The bullet is seated flush with the top of the case, and is used in revolvers for target shooting.

Semi-wadcutter: A bullet that resembles the wadcutter (hence its name) that tapers to a small, flat top and when loaded extends above the case mouth. It is used in both revolvers and semi-automatic handguns as target and practice ammunition.

Roundnose: Also a practice ammunition valued for its reliable feeding in semi-automatic handguns. It consists of a round-nosed bullet, either jacketed or lead, and is less expensive than hollowpoint bullets. This is sometimes also colloquially referred to as "ball" ammunition.

Hollowpoint: Hollowpoints resemble a semi-wadcutter or roundnose bullet with a deep well cut into top of the slug. The hollowed out section allows the lead bullet to expand to a mushroom-like shape when it encounters tissue or a similar medium. The expansion increases the size of the projectile, causing a larger wound channel and more tissue disruption for quicker physical incapacitation. This is *the* bullet you should carry for self-defense unless prevented from so doing by law. Not only can hollowpoints bring about quicker physical incapacitation, they are designed to stop inside the body of the assailant, dramatically reducing the danger that your bullet will go all the way through the assailant's body then hit an innocent bystander. This danger has been repeatedly documented by the NYPD,

Semi-wadcutter ammunition.

Round-nose ammunition, often called "ball," has varying shapes.

Unloaded primers (left, enlarged for detail) and primer seated in case.

which was for years mandated to carry only solid, non-expanding bullets and cite numerous cases of wounding a second person with a bullet that passed through the offender at whom it was fired.

FMJ: Full metal jacketed ammunition consists of a lead projectile fully encased in a copper jacket. This ammunition is free of the lubricant found on lead ammunition since the copper jacket slips easily through the gun's barrel when fired. Since there is no lubricant, it produces considerably less smoke when fired, and because the lead bullet is enclosed in the jacket, reduces lead exposure. Semi-jacketed bullets leave the tip bare to aid in hollow-point expansion, especially at lower velocities.

Case: The metal cylinder and base that holds the gunpowder, bullet and primer. Cases are generally made of brass, but also steel and one-use disposable aluminum. While the strength of the case is important, it is the firearm's chamber that supports the case wall and keeps the case from rupturing while the burning powder is building up pressure to push the bullet out of the top of the case.

Primer: A small "cap" seated in an indentation in the base of the case which, when struck by the handgun's firing pin, sparks to ignite the gunpowder inside the case. The primer's function could be compared to an automobile spark plug.

Powder: Also called propellant. Gunpowder, when ignited by the primer, burns rapidly, building pressure inside the case until it forces the bullet out the barrel of the gun. The proportion of powder to airspace in the case, as well as its chemical composition, influences the pressures that build up while the powder burns and the velocity with which that pressure pushes the bullet through the gun barrel and out the muzzle.

ACP, S&W, Luger and Parabellum: These are caliber designations that give credit to the inventor of the particular caliber ammunition in question. Example: .380 or .45 Auto Colt Pistol; .40 Smith & Wesson, and 9mm Luger or 9mm Para-

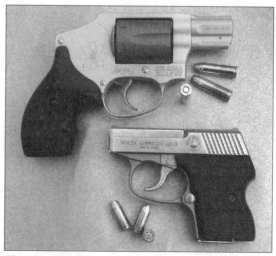

The .32 H&R Magnum (top) is a revolver cartridge, while the .32 ACP fits the semi-auto on which it sits Both are .32 caliber, but the case length is different.

bellum. 9mm *Luger* and 9mm *Parabellum* are exactly the same size, and both can be fired through any 9mm Parabellum or Luger handgun. However, 9mm *Kurz*, 9mm *Corto*, and 9mm *Short* are multi-lingual terms used to describe *.380 ACP* ammunition chambered for a .380 ACP semi-auto pistol, and they *do* differ from 9mm Parabellum or 9mm Luger in overall length. Similarly, .32 H&R Magnum rounds are for .32 caliber revolvers and are radically different from .32 ACP auto cartridges.

Velocity: The speed at which the bullet travels is measured in feet per second. Thus, on boxes of "high performance" ammunition, you may find a declaration of how fast the bullet will travel. For instance on a high velocity .45 ACP caliber, the bullet weight may be stated as "185 grains," followed by "1150 fps," indicating that when fired from a 5-inch long barrel, the bullet was ripping along at 1150 feet per second when it left the muzzle.

Velocity is determined by how much pressure builds up in the case as the gunpowder burns, the weight of the bullet and of the length of the barrel of the handgun. Smaller, lighter bullets travel faster, and according to some opinion, higher velocities cause greater shock and tissue disruption in an assailant, bringing faster incapacitation.

+P or +P+, Subsonic and Magnum: Subsonic ammunition expels the bullet at speeds under 1000 feet per second. +P indicates ammunition designed to generate higher pressures than standard ammunition and +P+ is a very high pressure load. Magnum ammunition, best known in the .357 and .44 Magnum calibers, have additional powder to build enormous pressures before the bullet is expelled. Thus, a .357 Magnum cartridge may have a bullet velocity from 1350 to 1450 feet per second.

What is stopping power?

Since humans began to study ballistics, theories about what makes ammunition effective have proliferated. Included in these theories are the Relative Incapacitation Index, the FBI Multimedia Wound Value, and many others. These and other theories of stopping power continue to be hotly debated in the gun press to this day. The unabridged versions make great reading for insomniacs, and frankly, unless you are a data cruncher, most of these theories are harder than heck to digest. The topic is crucial, however, as we seek the most effective ammunition for our self-defense firearms.

Let's begin by defining the terms that are loosely bandied around in this debate. The most ill-defined phrase, yet one with which we must contend, is "Stopping Power." Much bewilderment has been created by different missions in which stopping power is needed. For example, a military outfit's stopping power must diminish the enemy's numbers and ability to fight, and can be accomplished over hours and days. However, when private citizens or police officers need stopping power, the force to end criminal assault immediately is urgently needed. Upon this latter topic, we might do well to replace the phrase "stopping power" with "rapid incapacitation." In a self-defense emergency even a brief incapacitation may be enough to allow the armed citizen to escape or to assert control.

Incapacitation in a gun fight occurs if the central nervous system is damaged or if bleeding diminishes blood pressure and decreases blood flow to the brain. Sometimes, I tell students that they need to disrupt "electrical or plumbing," that is, the nervous or circulatory systems. Location of the gunshot wound plays a vital role, as does, to a lesser degree, the energy of the bullet. A great debate rages whether permanent wounding is the method by which incapacitation occurs, or whether the effect of the temporary wound channel (or stretch cavity) occurring during the bullet's passage through tissue and the concurrent shock effect is the factor causing physical shut-down.

In addition, the individual shot is affected in varying degrees by the pain of the wound and their psychological response to being shot. These factors differ greatly from one circumstance to another, and while they are factors in intimidation, they are exceedingly difficult to quantify.

Author visits with Evan Marshall at a firearms industry convention, the Shooting, Hunting Outdoors Trade Show some years ago.

While I don't expect to solve the debate, I respect the compilation of results occurring during and after real-life shootings, many involving police officers. These are collected by Evan Marshall, and contained in two volumes he co-authored with engineer Ed Sanow. If wishing to study more,

> A single round of handgun ammunition, no matter how large, is a poor gamble to accomplish incapacitation.

obtain *Handgun Stopping Power: The Definitive Study* and *Street Stoppers, The Latest Handgun Stopping Power Street Results* from Paladin Press.[1] For information from the opposite side of the argument, contact the International Wound Ballistics Association, which leans toward the value of the permanent wound channel.[2]

We use the terms "muzzle velocity" and "terminal velocity" to describe projectile speed at the beginning and the end of the bullet's flight. A handgun cartridge's self-defense potential, however, relies heavily on the energy the bullet actually delivers, and that requires much more than pure speed, which brings us to the term "momentum."

Momentum is quantified as the bullet's mass in pounds (7000 grains to a pound) multiplied by its velocity (in feet per second). When restricted to non-hollowpoint bullets, momentum is second only to shot placement as the crucial factor in handgun ammunition performance. Additional equations quantify the actual foot pounds of energy delivered by discharged ammunition, determined by multiplying the mass of the bullet times .5 the square of its velocity. Both "momentum" and "energy" are ways to describe the power of a cartridge of ammunition, but equations alone are not sufficient data upon which to make a choice about ammunition for self-defense. However, without the design characteristics of the hollowpoint or expanding bullet, the projectile can go and go and go-through the primary target and beyond without transferring all the energy into the target.

Bullet performance

This brings us to bullet design. In addition to bullet weight and velocity, shape, design, and even material composition of the projectile governs how it behaves when it strikes a consistent medium. Fortunately, at least as of this writing, most readers have the choice of hollowpoint bullets. hollowpoints, the subject of much misinformation, have existed since the 1800s, though only coming into common use since the late 1960s and '70s.

About that time, ammunition manufacturers combined the idea of high velocity handgun cartridges with the hollowpoint bullet, showing that hollowpoints would expand more reliably if their velocity exceeded 1000 feet per second. hollowpoint expansion prevents over-penetration and forces the bullet to expend its energy inside the target, with none wasted beyond. In this single development, handgun ammunition technology took a gigantic step forward, to the great benefit of smaller calibers like the 9mm Parabellum.

Continuing advances in bullet design came from Tom Burczynski, inventor of the HydraShok projectile and other hollowpoint bullets in which he used specific shapes, configurations and materials to further enhance expansion.

In the years between 1982 and 1999, the Illinois State Police loaded their 9mm pistols with +P+ Winchester cartridges using a 115-grain jacketed hollowpoint bullet. While Winchester did not sell this product to the civilian market, we can learn from the success of this ammunition concept. Given what we understand about bullet design and weight, velocities and energy transfer, we know we cannot expect *every* 9mm cartridge to perform as have the ultra-fast 9s carried by the ISP. Pursuing similar power, we would need to shop for 9mm ammunition using a light bullet with muzzle velocities in the 1300 feet per second range. Ammunition meeting these specifications is available commercially from several manufacturers.

High velocity jacketed hollowpoints increase the likelihood of rapid incapacitation with smaller calibers like the .38 Special and 9mm parabellum. The effect on .357 Magnum, .40 S&W and .45 ACP is to supercharge already decent handgun calibers by increasing *velocity* in the momentum equation.

Not one of the stopping power theoreticians can truthfully predict shooting results with 100% reliability. For one thing, although we evaluate ammunition in ordnance type gelatin, in real life, body construction varies from lean to obese, and bullets may strike solid bone. Other considerations include barriers ranging from bare skin to a heavy leather jacket, and incapacitation is further hindered by physiological factors including drug use and adrenaline or psychological conditions like dementia.

Making a choice

If the mission is defending self and family, stopping power will rely on shot placement, bullet design and momentum. Using this guideline, few self-defense instructors will recommend cartridges in calibers below .380 ACP, because the projectile lacks sufficient mass to do its part in the momentum equation. Handgun cartridges cannot produce pressures sufficient to compensate with pure velocity, as does rifle ammunition.

Can we agree that beyond shot placement, stopping power largely depends on bullet momentum coupled with the hollowpoint's expansion into a larger frontal profile? To exploit all available energy, we can next conclude that larger calibers should cause quicker incapacitation. However, incapacitation results from damage to the circulatory or nervous system, taking us back to the importance of accurate shot placement. A peripheral wound to a muscle group like the upper arm or thigh, even with a .357 Magnum,

> *Not one of the conflicting stopping power theories can truthfully predict shooting results with 100% reliability.*

will not incapacitate a criminal as well, if at all, as gunshots to the central torso where the heart and spine are located.

The handgun and caliber you choose should be sufficiently controllable that you can learn to accurately deliver quick, multiple shots. Otherwise, you simply have a tool, without the skills to make it work. Like driving a high-performance automobile with minimal skill, inadequate training makes handgun possession a real liability.

Perceptive readers have already noted that although we have argued the defense potential and short-comings of smaller calibers, nothing has been said about the very large handgun calibers like .41 Magnum, .44 Magnum, and .50 AE. Discussing incapacitation, we identified the need to disrupt circulatory or nervous system function. A single round of handgun ammunition, no matter how large, is a poor gamble to accomplish that goal. Multiple shots greatly increase the odds of incapacitation. The large magnum calibers produce such profound recoil that the recovery time to realign sights between shots is considerable and follow-up shots very slow.

The magnums and 10mm recoil viciously and will slow your shot-to-shot times. A good test of your ability to use a handgun in self-defense is the "5 in 5 at 5" test I use in my gun reviews. Position a five-inch circle target at five yards. Load the gun. If you don't have a shot timer, have a friend time you, saying, "go," and at the end of five seconds, yelling, "stop!" If you have fired five rounds inside the five-inch radius in five seconds at the practical self-defense distance of five yards, you have found a gun you can use effectively for self-defense. The individual's variables include strength and skill; the mechanical variables are recoil impulse and ergonomic pistol design.

In addition to producing punishing recoil, the very large handgun calibers require a larger framed gun, and this alone disqualifies them for the many who will legally carry a concealed pistol. Reasonable self-defense caliber choices, when partnered with modern hollowpoint ammunition, include the .380 ACP, .38 Special, 9mm Parabellum, .357 Magnum or it's semi-automatic counterpart .357 SIG, .40 S&W, .44 Special and .45 ACP. Each caliber listed is served by numerous models and brands of handguns, and various ammunition labels, as well.

No magic bullet

There is no magic bullet. Accurate shot placement is of utmost importance. The most viable target is the center of the chest at armpit level. This increases the chances of a heart, lung or spinal cord hit. In addition, a center-of-mass aim point is quickest and most reliable for the adrenaline-filled defender. Additional discussion of shot placement is included in *Tactics*, Chapter 19. Students of armed self-defense must learn to shoot until the threat ceases. Unless the spinal cord is severed or the brain's medulla oblongata hit, the assailant may be capable of continued hostilities after taking several handgun bullets. You must be capable of repeated, accurate shots to the center of the assailant's chest.

Misses don't count in a gunfight, and in the end, your life is the prize.

---

1   Marshall, Evan, and Sanow, Ed, *Street S*ⴰ*ppers, The Latest Handgun Stopping Power Street Results* and *Handgun Stopping Power: The Definitive Study.* Paladin Press, Gunbarrel Tech Center, 7077 Winchester Circle, Colorado 80301, 800-466-6868, 800-392-2400.

2   International Wound Ballistics Association, P O Box 701, El Segundo, CA 90245, (310) 640-6065.

15

Annie, Get Your Gun

Shopping for a handgun entails a lot more than finding a firearm that feels right in your hand. Though we will discuss guns that fit some hands better than others, the first-time gun owner must deal with other considerations, too.

Years ago, when I asked Massad Ayoob what guns he recommends to women, he said my question was a lot like asking a carpenter if you should buy a hammer or a saw for a building project. "What do you need to do with the tool?" he asked. A gun for home defense can be considerably larger than a gun for concealed carry. A person who can afford just one gun may have to consider its concealability beneath clothes for both hot and cold weather. Someone who can afford a summer gun and a winter gun, or a

A good grasp of handgun vocabulary makes it much easier to communicate your needs and wishes to the gun store clerk and to learn from his or her suggestions.

carry gun and a competition gun, must look for guns that locate features like the safety lever and magazine release in similar locations.

I asked the same question of retired cop and fellow gun-writer Charles Petty, and thought he summed it up best when he said, "The best handgun is the one you have with you when you need it." He went on to add that, due to the importance of shot placement, an individual's best self-defense handgun choice is one with which they can hit accurately every time they shoot.

Gun vocabulary

Before heading out to the gun store, it helps to have a grasp of the terminology you will encounter. As illustrated, handguns are broken down into two basic categories: revolvers and semi-automatic pistols.

The double action revolver is the simpler of the two. Take a look at the diagram (see next page) so the terms are more meaningful. Modern double action revolvers fire when the trigger is pulled, simultaneously compressing the mainspring and cocking the hammer. At the same time, the trigger pull moves the cylinder to line up a chamber (and cartridge if it is loaded) with the firing pin. At the end of the trigger pull the hammer is released and falls forward to strike the firing pin, which in turn hits the primer.

On some revolvers the firing pin is integral to the hammer, and strikes the cartridge as described above. On other brands of revolvers, the hammer is flat and strikes a transfer bar which carries the impact to a spring loaded firing pin. The blow overcomes the firing pin spring and the firing pin jolts forward to hit the cartridge primer. In either case, when the

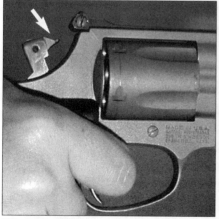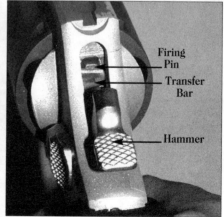

The revolver shown to the upper left uses the design in which the firing pin (indicated by arrow) is integral to the hammer. On the right, the transfer bar of a Taurus revolver is rising into the position from which it transfers the hammer blow to the firing pin.

primer is hit, the impact sparks the primer compound, and the spark ignites the gunpowder.

Most handguns must be cocked to fire. A cocked hammer is one that has been drawn back so there is some distance between it and the firing pin. Inside the gun, drawing back the hammer lines up two parts, the hammer hook and the shelf of the sear. When they engage, the hammer will sit

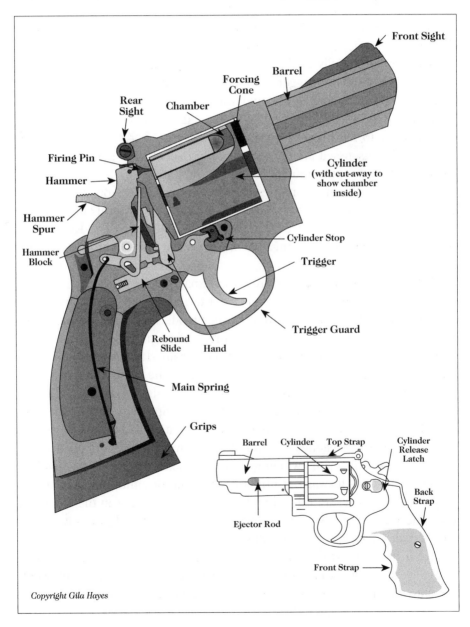

Copyright Gila Hayes

in the cocked position until light pressure on the trigger releases the sear from the hook and lets the hammer slam forward.

On the double action revolver, cocking can be accomplished two ways—the shooter can manually pull the hammer back or the hammer can be cocked and released by continuous pressure on the trigger. When the trigger is pressed through the final $\frac{1}{16}$th inch or so of the trigger pull, the hammer is released and slams forward.

The semi-automatic handgun cocks the hammer one of two ways depending if its design is double-action or single-action. The double action semi-automatic initially cocks the hammer the same way as the revolver, with a long pull of the trigger compressing the mainspring. Trigger pressure compresses the mainspring and draws the hammer back into a cocked position, then the end of the pull disconnects the sear from the hammer and allows it to fall forward onto the firing pin. After the first shot, the slide's cycle (discussed later) automatically re-cocks the gun, making the subsequent trigger pulls much shorter and lighter.

Single action semi-automatics must be cocked to fire, too, and the trigger cannot accomplish that task. The single action semi-automatic is cocked when the slide is cycled to chamber ammunition. Every shot through the single action semi-auto fires with the same light pressure and short trigger pull.

When the semi-automatic fires, the expanding gas generated by the burning gunpowder pushes the bullet out of the cartridge case and down the barrel as is the process with any other modern firearm. As the bullet leaves the semi-automatic's barrel, the pressure propels the slide rearward, so it pushes down and cocks the hammer again. The extractor, a small hook set in the slide at the ejection port, catches the rim of the now-empty cartridge case and jerks it out of the chamber. While traveling briefly rearward, the empty case strikes the ejector and is flipped out of the ejection port that is cut in the slide of every semi-automatic.

When the slide reaches the end of its rearward travel, it is pushed forward by the recoil spring, which was compressed when the slide recoiled. As the slide slams forward, it lifts a fresh round of ammunition from the magazine and places it in the chamber. When the round is in the chamber, the slide locks with the barrel (called "in battery") and is ready to fire another round if the trigger is pulled again.

After firing, most semi-automatics will be cocked. The safety lever of single action semi-automatics should be moved to the "on" position when the shooter brings the sights off target. A double action semi-automatic should be decocked–mechanically lowering the hammer safely and placing the trigger in the far-forward double-action position. The double action semi-automatic can be carried with just the long trigger pull to keep the

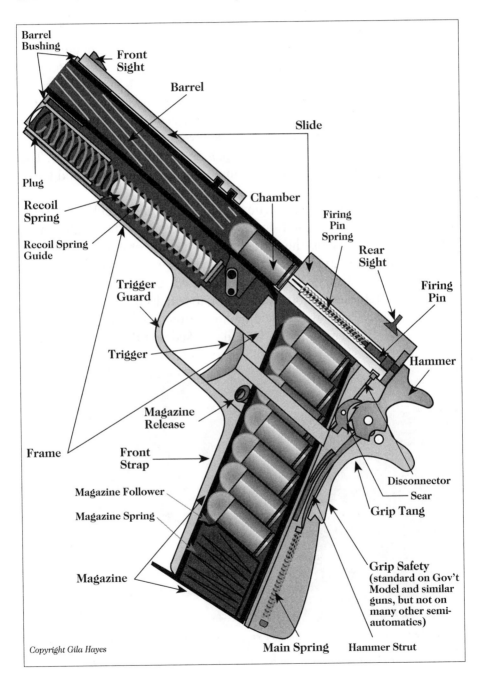

Copyright Gila Hayes

gun from being unintentionally or prematurely fired. This carry mode is NO different than that of the double action revolver, considered one of the safest handguns made. Most double action semi-automatics also have a manual safety that can be engaged, locking the trigger or hammer (gun designs differ) for further safety.

Both revolvers and semi-automatics have a further division: double action guns, single action guns, and guns that operate double action only. In the most accurate, technical sense, double action is a term used to describe a firearm that can be fired two ways—by manually cocking the hammer or by trigger cocking as earlier described. With a double action, or trigger cocking gun, the trigger is pulled from its most forward position all the way to the rear, often as far as half an inch, sometimes more. The trigger movement draws back the hammer, preparing it to fall and strike the firing pin.

To manually cock a double action gun, the hammer is held beneath the shooter's thumb and pressed down until it catches in the single action notch. As the thumb pulls the hammer back, the trigger moves to the rear, leaving only a short trigger pull, often about one-eighth inch, from which the gun will fire with very little pressure on the trigger.

Many modern semi-automatic pistols feature a decocking lever that lets the owner safely lower the cocked hammer from single action to double action mode. The semi-auto will be slide-cocked and the trigger in single action after the slide has cycled, either from manually chambering a

The bobbed hammer Ruger SP101 won't snag when drawn from beneath concealing garments. Nonetheless, the hammer's rearward travel is visible, as pressure on the trigger moves it to a cocked position. This is an example of shooting a revolver "double action."

round, or after firing. Unless actually shooting, a double action trigger pull that requires a concerted effort to fire the gun (12 to 15 pounds of pressure) is safer, so the hammer needs to be decocked whenever the gun is no longer aimed into the target.

Years ago, during my first months of teaching women's handgun classes, a new gun owner reported on the first morning of class that her new gun was defective because when she depressed what she believed was the safety lever "the gun would fire!" With consternation, my assistant and I listened carefully as she explained why she was certain this was the case. Experimenting with the *unloaded* gun the night before class, our student found that when she pressed down on what turned out to serve as both manual safety and decocking lever, the hammer fell forward, just as she had observed during live fire with other handguns.

When sold her new semi-automatic pistol, she was not introduced to the decocking feature, so naturally feared if it lowered the hammer it would also discharge the gun. A wonderful feature of women's only gun classes is the ability to clear up such mechanical misunderstandings–and other topics–without embarrassment or further confusion!

Examples of semi-automatics that can be manually decocked include the Rugers, Smith & Wessons, the Walther PPK, and Beretta and Taurus

semi-autos and Heckler & Koch's USP line. A few guns, like the HK USPs, and others can be carried either decocked only, decocked and put on-safe, or placed on-safe in single action.

Other semi-automatic pistols have single action only triggers with no other option available. The trigger is short and requires only three to six pounds pressure to discharge the gun. The hammer must be cocked for the gun to fire, either by racking the slide to cham-

Smith & Wesson's Model 3953 is one of the nicest double action only semi-automatics ever made. To use informal gun lingo, both the 3953 and the bobbed hammer Ruger SP101 shown several pages back are "double action only" guns, since both must be cocked using the trigger, as no hammer is available to manually cock.

ber the round or by the slide's rearward movement during the firing cycle. When loaded and cocked, these guns' safeties must be applied, usually by flicking a frame-mounted lever up. Examples of single action handguns include the Colt, Springfield and Kimber Government Model 1911-style guns and their clones, as well as the Firestar semi-autos and Browning Hi Power handguns.

The industry added to traditional gun terminology when it coined the expression "double action only." While double action is used to describe a gun fired through trigger cocking, a Double Action Only (DAO) firearm is one that has NO provision for manual cocking—like a revolver with a bobbed or shrouded hammer. DAO revolvers include the Smith & Wesson Centennial lines, as well as revolvers with bobbed hammers, including Taurus' excellent M85CH and Ruger's SP101 bobbed hammer variation. Double Action Only semi-autos are designed to return the trigger to the long, far-forward position after each shot and are represented by Smith & Wesson's 3953, by Beretta's Model 92D, the CZ 100 and by Ruger's P89 DAO, to name only a few.

The term "double action only" is inaccurately applied to semi-automatic pistols that are the striker-fired, as are the Glock line, Kahr handguns and others. These pistols have no hammer, so the striker is held under spring pressure until movement of the trigger moves a plunger that blocks the striker, freeing it to go forward and hit the primer.

Beretta Model 86, with the tip-up barrel, remains one of the nicest .380 ACPs on the market.

Stopping power: how big is big enough?

Before discussing defensive gun choices, it must be reiterated that no firearm or ammunition is guaranteed to stop an assailant. Individuals have differing capacities to withstand gunshot wounds. self-defense may require a number of shots to stop an assailant, especially if he is enraged, insane or using drugs. Acknowledging that there is no magic gun or bullet, let's discuss the best choices available.

What follows is a breakdown of different styles and sizes of guns that the shopper may want to check out in her search for a self-defense gun. Manufacturers are selected on perceived "staying power," an assumption that they will continue to provide quality handguns and service in the foreseeable future (a risky prediction in the Year 2000's political and business climate). This discussion of guns can by no means be comprehensive, yet is intended to provide first-time buyers the terminology, features and considerations they need to understand before buying a handgun.

When considering a handgun for self-defense, a minimum caliber should be the .38 Special revolver loaded with at least +P ammunition. (See *Ammunition*, Chapter 14). Many believe the .380 ACP ammunition is powerful enough to stop an assailant, and indeed, stories are told in which the round performed admirably. Yet, a confrontation with an assailant is dangerous enough without the disadvantage of a gun selected for small size and light recoil, but lacking the power to quickly stop a deadly assault.

At one time, people chose the .380 ACP, because it was the only handgun small enough for easy concealment. Today, several manufacturers sell 9mm handguns that are literally as small as most .380s. Before compromising on a .380 ACP pistol, at least try the 9mm Kahr Mk9 handgun or the 9mm Smith & Wesson's Chief's Special. The .380 ACP cartridge has a small, light bullet that needs to be loaded to higher velocities to increase the likelihood it will stop an assailant, and even then is not very powerful.

Guns that chamber ammunition smaller than .380 ACP are not sufficiently powerful for reliable use in self-defense. Historically, .22 LR or .25 ACP caliber guns have failed to stop assaults decisively. The bullet doesn't transfer enough energy to do much damage in body tissue. Probably the best hope for someone armed with a .25 caliber handgun is to try to penetrate to the brain's medulla oblongata, yet these kinds of shots are very difficult, if not impossible, in dynamic self-defense situations. .22 LR ammunition may possibly be more effective than the .25, but the little bullets have a troubling tendency to zip through tissue making only a small wound channel and causing only slow bleeding unless striking the spinal chord or brain's medulla.

People DO die from small-caliber wounds, although death usually occurs later from blood loss or much later from untreated infection. In self-defense, the intent is to use a weapon of sufficient caliber to stop an assault decisively before you are injured. As a self-defense shooter, your goal is not the death of the assailant, rather to put an immediate stop to the assault.

The .380 ACP semi-automatic should be considered by people who suffer reduced hand strength, who will practice and train to become extremely accurate with their gun. After one of our training courses, a student who suffers from degenerative arthritis chose a Beretta Model 86 .380 caliber semi-automatic. This gun's barrel tips up so the shooter can chamber the first round without having to manually cycle the slide, making it an excellent choice for people with physical conditions that diminish strength. He has continued to practice and take classes, to ensure beyond a shadow of a doubt that he can deliver rapid, accurate fire in self-defense.

In other useful roles, the .380 ACP semi-automatic is often carried as a back-up gun worn on the ankle or in a pocket holster as a second gun, insurance against malfunction or failure by a primary gun of larger caliber.

After stopping power, the most important consideration in gun selection is the amount of time you are willing to commit to training and maintenance. If you have little time to train, you will be better served by the revolver. If you are interested in shooting and can budget time for good training, frequent practice, and regular maintenance you can benefit from the semi-automatic's ease of shooting and ergonomic design.

Effective handgun selection requires truthful answers to several more questions. Does the buyer have sufficient upper body strength to work the slide of a semi-automatic gun? Willowy bodies with slender fingers may find the slide of many semi-autos very difficult to manipulate. Remember, you have to manually cycle the slide for a lot more than just unloading the gun. The slide has to be drawn back to chamber the first round, to clear malfunctions, and to disassemble and clean the weapon after shooting practice. If it sounds like too much work, consider the user-friendly revolver.

In double action, the high capacity SIG Sauer doesn't fit these hands well enough to assure good marksmanship, as only the tip of the index finger contacts the trigger. This shooter would do better with SIG Arms' P239, and should consider the manufacturer's short trigger option.

I like it, but does it fit?

The buyer next needs to assure the proper fit of the gun in her hand. Could you drive a car with a non-adjustable seat that left you unable to fully depress the clutch? That question is no more absurd than suggesting that someone can shoot well with a gun that is too large for her hand. The index finger's distal joint needs to reach the *center* of the trigger when the grip tang is centered in the hand's web. It's nearly impossible to shoot a double action gun accurately with only the tip of the finger touching the trigger.

Don't be fooled by gun salesmen who say, "scoot your hand down on the grips," or "just move your hand around until your finger reaches the trigger." The grip tang NEEDS to be seated in the web of the hand so the trigger finger can make a natural, straight back pull for accurate shooting. A fit that lets the grip tang ride against the thumb's base knuckle will transfer the recoil into the bony joint with every shot fired, resulting in poor recoil control, shooting discomfort, and eventual joint injury.

After assuring that the gun's back strap-to-trigger dimension fits your hand, there are design features that render some guns easier to shoot than others. The relationship of the bore (barrel) to the shooter's wrist can make a gun easy to fire accurately, or can add hours of training to overcome the gun's upward recoil.

Handgun designs that closely align the barrel with the wrist and arm transfer the recoil directly into the shooter's palm and web of the hand, fleshy areas that can absorb the impact painlessly. Because the low barrel aligns with skeletal support of the wrist and arm, the muzzle rises less during shooting. With increased recoil control, the shooter can quickly get the sights back on target for rapid consecutive shots—an important consideration in self-defense against multiple assailants or a single assailant who is not stopped by the first bullet.

The smaller shooter's hand fits the small grip of the Kahr K9 pistol for a stronger grasp and ability to place the index finger's first joint properly across the trigger.

In addition, the low bore axis takes advantage of the human ability to raise the arm and accurately point the index finger at the center of an object, and as a result, the sights are nearly lined up when you point the gun at the target, due to the good ergonomic relationship of the gun to the hand and arm.

Examples of low bore axis semi-automatics include Kahr Arms, Glock and the Heckler & Koch P7 line of handguns. The Smith and Wesson Centennial revolver has an unusually high back strap that results in a de facto low bore axis for an extremely pointable .357 Magnum, .38 Special or .32 ACP caliber revolver.

If I can only have one, which should I choose?

Most first-time gun owners buy their weapon thinking it will be the only handgun they'll ever own. Later, many shooters find they need to refine their selection after experience introduces them to better fitting or functioning guns; others graduate from a gun purchased for in-house defense to a smaller gun that they can carry with them everywhere. If, at the outset, the buyer is looking for an all-around gun, the more compact handguns will be the natural choice.

A number of .38 Special revolvers fit that description. Good choices include the Smith & Wesson Centennial line, which features a completely shrouded hammer, or the bobbed hammer Taurus Model 85CH, one of the finest budget priced revolvers available. Both are good revolver choices for concealment beneath clothing that could catch on the hammer when drawing the gun.

Traditionally, revolver sizes have been identified as "J-Frames" when referring to the compact, five-shot wheelguns like the Model 36 or 640 Smith & Wessons; as "K-frames" when mentioning six-

Proper handgun fit in center of palm's web is essential to accurate shooting and the shooter's well-being as shown here on Kahr Arms' K9.

shot S&W revolvers of slightly greater size, with larger sizes identified by subsequent letters. While this is Smith & Wesson nomenclature, shooters and gun collectors tend to use the term "J-Frame" to refer to five-shot revolvers, or "K-Frame" to identify the larger six-shot, mid-sized revolvers.

Revolvers with exposed hammers can be entrusted to a gunsmith to bob the hammer, with results similar to the Taurus M85CH. I would consider the Ruger SP101 for such an operation. Because the .357 Magnum is chambered in the same SP101 frame as the .38 Special, I would purchase this heavy-hitting .357, then practice primarily with lighter .38 Special ammunition. Since the .357 Magnum case is only slightly longer than the .38 Special's, a .357 Magnum revolver can fire .38 Special ammunition for reduced recoil or for economical practice. As illustrated on page 112, a .38 Special revolver cannot fire .357 Magnum ammunition.

When money is really, really tight, budget revolvers are generally a safer choice than cheap semi-automatics, because of the simpler design of the revolver. In 2000, a perfectly fine off-brand .38 Special revolver was marketed for around $300–considerably less than the $500 price on the smoother and more widely-recognized Smith & Wessons and Rugers. Used revolvers should be even more affordable. Novice buyers can check for damage, like a bulged barrel or excessive play in a locked cylinder, and visually check for cracks and wear on the frame and top strap. There's simply less to go wrong on a used revolver than on a second-hand semi-automatic.

Revolver selection requires the buyer to think about concealability, frame size, fit in the hand, and probably about after-market replacement grips. The small five-shot revolvers fit small hands better and are more comfortable to conceal. Holstered inside the waistband, the revolver's round cylinder can be uncomfortable. Six shot revolvers, allowing room for that extra cartridge, poke a larger cylinder into the wearer's tummy or hip.

A revolver's back strap-to-trigger dimension can be adjusted by replacing the factory-installed grips with after-market grips or different grips may be chosen to increase or decrease the circumference of the grips and to fill in the void between the back of the trigger guard and the front strap. Large rubbery grips provide more material to absorb the recoil and make it easier to maintain a strong hold under recoil.

Semi-automatic features give the buyer nearly endless choices in capacity, trigger action, size and location of safeties, slide locks and magazine releases, but fewer choices of how the gun fits in your hand. Many semi-automatic grips are integral to the frame and cannot be changed, so the original fit of the weapon is crucial. The polymer framed Glock pistol is an example of a gun that needs to fit right the first time, since the grip is comprised of the same molded polymer as the frame. Of course, for several hundred dollars that grip can be reduced by one of several gunsmiths specializing in this after-market alteration.

Small or weak-handed people will find certain semi-automatic pistols easier to shoot effectively. Several compact semi-autos that are easy to carry, conceal and shoot include the 9mm Kahr K-9 pistol, Smith & Wesson's 3913 or 3953, a 9mm with 8-round capacity magazines; and Heckler & Koch's P7M8, a unique 9mm with 8+1 round capacity.

Women often appreciate the short trigger reach of the high-capacity Glock handguns, and ladies with really small hands are very enthusiastic about the small pistols in Kahr Arms' product line. Caliber choices include 9mm, .40 S&W and, in the Glock, the addition of .45 ACP caliber.

The Glocks, like a lot of guns introduced in the 1980s and 1990s, use a "double-stack" magazine. Instead of positioning the bullets one atop another, as in a single-stack, low capacity magazine, the bullets are staggered zigzag. A double-stack magazine results in a slightly wider grip that will effect the gun's fit in your hand and make the gun a little harder to conceal under clothing. The Kahr pistol, using a single stack magazine is much smaller in grip size and ammunition capacity.

Compared to high-capacity semi-autos, the HK P7M8 and S&W 3913 or Chief's Special 9mm are extremely flat and easy to tuck in the waistband. With the federal government restricting new magazine capacity to 10 rounds, the advantage of high capacity handguns over their smaller, more easily concealed six- or 8-round counterparts is all but obliterated. In any case, I don't believe high capacity is as important as concealability in handgun choice for the armed citizen, for whom accuracy with several initial rounds is far more important than 12 to 17 cartridges in one magazine.

Glock Model 23 (left) with its double stack magazine. Also shown is the grip reduction made by Burns Custom Pistols (right).[1]

Right between the 9mm and the big-bore .45 ACP caliber is the relatively new .40 caliber. Developed by Smith & Wesson, this caliber of ammunition is correctly referred to as .40 S&W, to give credit to the developer, although handguns in this caliber are sold by all the major manufacturers. Ballistically, the .40 has shown stopping power at least as good as the 9mm, and it is estimated that +P .40 ammunition should approach the optimum results of the .357 Magnum based on documented shootings by police. Examples of .40 caliber handguns include the Glock Models 22 and 23, Smith & Wesson Models 4013 and 411, Heckler & Koch USP, Kahr K40 Covert, Ruger P91, several models of SIG Arms pistols and others including the Witness and Firestar.

When my female students shoot guns provided for live-fire demonstration, they are excited to discover they can manage the .45 ACPs recoil. With the development of high performance .45 hollowpoint ammunition, the venerable .45 has become an excellent self-defense handgun. Reacting to the call for lighter, faster bullets, several major manufacturers load a 185-grain .45 caliber bullet that leaves the barrel at around 1150 feet per second.

Good choices for concealable .45s include SIG Arms P245, Smith & Wesson's Model CS45, Kimber's Ultra Carry, Colt's Lightweight Commander, Officer's Model or the even smaller Defender, and Springfield's Ultra

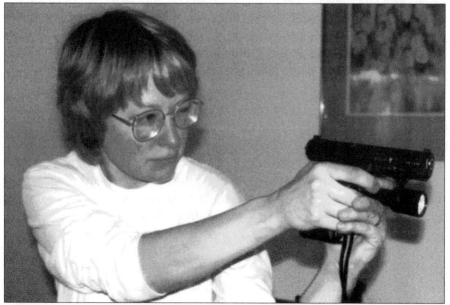

Heckler & Koch's P7M8 has a very low bore axis, making it easy to aim and shoot. It also fits small hands well.

Compact .45. A full-sized .45 with a 4 $^1/_2$ inch or 5 inch barrel will be a better choice for competitive shooting, training or to serve solely as a home-defense gun since the compact .45s recoil viciously.

An individual's ability to shoot well with a particular handgun and caliber is influenced by upper body strength plus hand size and strength in relation to the caliber and dimensions of the gun. Buying a gun recommended by a large number of men may yield a man-sized gun, but one you can't shoot effectively. A fit of machismo when buying a gun is dangerous!

While the gun's fit in your hand can be determined in the sterile atmosphere of a gun store, your reaction to the gun's recoil can be judged only during shooting. Fortunately, good training can help shooters of any physique learn to handle even heavy-hitting calibers accurately. Even then, there is a cut-off after which the time between shots is too long for reliable self-defense, because too much time elapses while the shooter overcomes recoil and re-acquires the sight picture to make another accurate shot.

Most indoor gun ranges rent a variety of the popular model handguns. This is an excellent way for new shooters to gauge their own reaction to the recoil of calibers .38 Special, 9mm, .357 SIG, .40 S&W and .45 ACP caliber guns and ammunition, before investing several hundred dollars or more. After choosing a suitable self-defense caliber, the most important decision is the shooter's willingness to practice with the handgun. A gun that causes a lot of discomfort during shooting is a gun that will not be shot very much. Weapon unfamiliarity is a recipe for disaster in self-defense situations.

Reliability comes first

Many different factors affect handgun reliability. Nonetheless, before one adopts a handgun for self-defense, the reliability of that weapon must be ascertained. Beginning shooters can broadly assume that revolvers are more reliable than semi-automatics, in the sense that less can malfunction in the revolver's simpler design.

Those who favor the semi-automatic owe it to themselves to make an even more intensive study of the handgun they are considering buying. Look for reviews in gun magazines, especially seeking out information on reliability, gun malfunctions, and brands of ammunition tested in the weapon. A semi-automatic's reliability, while first a question of design and production standards, is also greatly affected by cleaning and maintenance, and by the particular model's ability to feed specific kinds of ammunition. A self-defense handgun must cycle high performance hollowpoint ammunition 100% of the time.

After purchasing a self-defense handgun, the buyer must test that weapon with the ammunition they plan to carry. Semi-automatic owners need to fire about 200 rounds of their defense ammunition through their handgun to guarantee flawless feeding of the ammunition into the chamber and reliable ejection of the empty case after the round is fired. If the testing produces multiple malfunctions, repeat the process with a different ammunition, until you have found hollowpoint ammunition that always functions in your self-defense gun.

While this sounds expensive, in reality a well-designed semi-automatic loaded with high quality ammunition will nearly always function properly. The testing will, in all likelihood go smoothly, and if it does not, problems should show up within the first 50 rounds, so the ammunition can be switched before 200 rounds of expensive ammunition has been wasted. If nothing cycles reliably in the gun, you may need to visit the gunsmith for a bit of fine-tuning or trade it in on one that works flawlessly.

Revolver shooters should also test and occasionally practice with their defense ammunition to remain accustomed to its recoil and to be sure the firing pin strikes the primers with sufficient impact to fire the round.

Many serviceable handguns are marketed. The buyer's responsibility is to select one with which they can safely train and practice. The gun needs to be concealable (if the owner intends to carry it outside the home) and must have adequate safety features to assure it will not be unintentionally discharged. Very low budget semi-autos often lack firing pin blocks to prevent the hammer from striking the firing pin unless the trigger is pulled. These guns may discharge if an impact bounces the firing pin forward to strike the ammunition. Read up on the gun you intend to purchase, and ask the gun store clerk about the internal safeties in the model you are considering. If this is the only kind of gun you can afford, you are better off buying a less expensive used revolver.

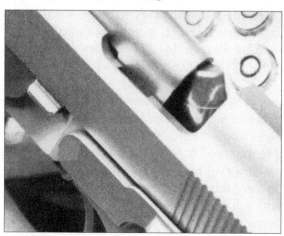

A semi-automatic handgun must fire, eject and chamber the ammunition you intend to carry for self-defense 100% of the time. A feed failure is shown here. The bullet should have traveled horizontally into the chamber, but has jumped from the magazine vertically and now protrudes from the ejection port, jamming the handgun.

These are serious questions. One of the easiest ways to find the answers is to postpone a handgun purchase until after you have completed at least a basic handgun training course. Your basic training should put you in touch with qualified professionals who can help you solve puzzles unanswered by the course curriculum. Study first, buy later.

Getting to know your gun

Cleaning your handgun is an excellent way to understand how it works. A gun isn't like a car that you can turn over to a mechanic every 3,000 miles for an oil change and safety check. A gun is an emergency rescue tool for which you bear an intense responsibility. If it malfunctions, you must understand how to correct the problem immediately and get back in the gun fight. A thorough understanding of its operation is crucial.

Initially, you'll need to ask the clerk selling you the gun to take a few uninterrupted minutes to show you how to take the gun apart and clean it. You have just plunked at least several hundred dollars down on the counter. Don't be shy about asking for this small service before you walk out the door with your new gun. Another reference resource is the owner's manual, which usually includes a section on cleaning the weapon.

In addition, magazines which review guns sometimes include a description of how that gun is disassembled for cleaning. A small handbook *The Professional's Guide to Handgun Cleaning,*[2] is published by The Firearms Academy of Seattle, as is this book. Throughout my career writing about guns, I have also made extensive use of the National Rifle Association's *The NRA Guide to Pistols and Revolvers* and their *Firearms Assembly*[3] for shotguns and rifles, too. I have gone so far as to put photocopied pages from this straight forward source of disassembly and reassembly directions in my cleaning kit, while learning the inner workings of my Remington shotguns and AR-15 rifle.

When I bought my first gun, the clerk assembled a list of cleaning supplies, which I purchased on his recommendation. I went home and for the next month or so cleaned my revolver after each practice session without realizing the cylinder could be removed for a more convenient and thorough cleaning. My first basic shooting class included instruction in gun cleaning, and I was thrilled to learn the easy, correct way to clean that gun. The lesson? Find a teacher who will work with your gun cleaning questions and demonstrate that skill in the course curriculum.

1 Glock grip reduction, Burns Custom Pistols, 700 NW Gilman, Issaquah, WA 98027, 425-391-3202.

2 *The Professional's Guide to Handgun Cleaning*, The Firearms Academy of Seattle, Inc. P.O. Box 400, Onalaska, WA 98570.

3 National Rifle Association *Firearms Assembly: The NRA Guide to Rifles and Shotguns Revised and Expanded*, and *The NRA Guide to Pistols and Revolvers*, NRA Publications, 11250 Waples Mill Rd., Fairfax, VA 22030, 800-672-3888.

16

Shooting Skills

Earlier we discussed obtaining basic handgun training and understanding appropriate use of deadly force. During different chapters, we have emphasized the importance of accurate shot placement. Marksmanship skills are just the beginning; your training needs to include learning to shoot accurately and rapidly despite the distractions and stress of a self-defense emergency.

Remember, you cannot learn to shoot or safely use a gun by reading a book. You must find qualified instructors who will help you give physical form to the concepts we have discussed here. In basic handgun class you should have learned about gun safety, sight picture, follow-through and trigger control. To reiterate anything you may have forgotten or did not completely understand, here is an overview of the basics.

Sight picture

The handgun has two sighting devices to help you align the muzzle on your target. The front sight is generally a blade with serrations, a dot or colored insert to help you see it clearly. The rear sight is shaped like a shallow "U" and may have two dots or a bright outline around the notch to mark the edges in poor light. If the front sight is perfectly centered in the notch of the rear sight and the tops of both sights are perfectly aligned at the moment the gun discharges, *the bullet will hit the part of the target covered by the front sight.* This arrangement is called "combat sights" and is common on most service pistols. Target pistols, guns designed purely for sporting pursuits, may use a slightly different arrangement regulated so the bullet impacts right above the front sight at a specified distance.

As we aim the gun at the target we see three objects: the rear sight, the front sight and the target beyond. All three in alignment is called the "sight picture." If we focus our vision on the rear sight, anything beyond it is blurry. If we see the target clearly, both sights will be too fuzzy to keep them lined up accurately. Like a simple camera, our eyes can focus on only one visual plane at a time. We must concentrate on only the front sight to be sure our sights remain aligned, with the front sight covering the place we wish the bullet to strike.

On paper targets, or facing an assailant, it is natural to want to look at the object we intend to shoot. That is a problem because focusing on the target allows the front sight to wander all over the place and inevitably causes inaccuracy. Allow the target to go slightly blurry. Focus your vision on the front sight as if it holds your life and your future.

Trigger squeeze

A smooth, consistent pressure on the trigger is the key to accurate shooting. Jerking or convulsing on the trigger moves the sights out of alignment, allowing the shot to go wild. Experienced drivers *press* the car brake pedal smoothly until they bring the vehicle to a stop. On a smaller scale, that same smooth control is what you want from your trigger finger.

Physical skills are best learned slowly. Mastery is the result of precise performance of the actions required, first at a slow pace, then with increas-

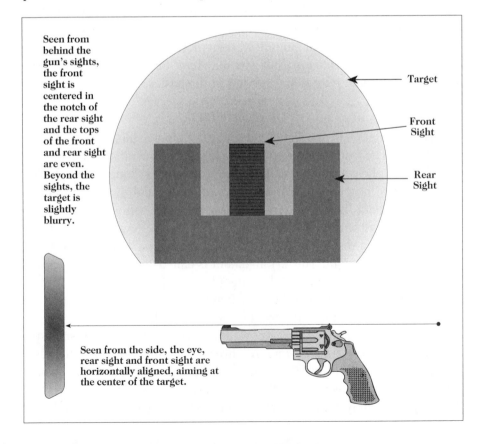

Seen from behind the gun's sights, the front sight is centered in the notch of the rear sight and the tops of the front and rear sight are even. Beyond the sights, the target is slightly blurry.

Target

Front Sight

Rear Sight

Seen from the side, the eye, rear sight and front sight are horizontally aligned, aiming at the center of the target.

ing speed as the motion is refined. Thus, a deliberate four second trigger squeeze starts with up to three seconds of smooth controlled pressure on the trigger. At some point between two and four seconds, the gun fires (sometimes described as the shot breaking) although the skilled shooter does not try to predict exactly when it will discharge. The remaining time is dedicated to follow-through: bringing the gun back on target, lining up the sights perfectly, assessing the situation to see if you need to shoot again and only then releasing the trigger. The same consistent trigger press, surprise hammer fall and subsequent shot break, and follow through can be compressed to well under a second per shot as your skills grow. Consistent, smooth trigger pressure without anticipation of the moment the shot will break are key components to effective trigger manipulation at any speed.

Make it a surprise

Why should we be surprised when the gun goes off? Obviously, if the finger is pressing the trigger, we should expect the gun to fire. The surprise I'm talking about is not being so focused on the act of pulling the trigger that I can predict the exact instant in which the gun will fire.

Again, why? Were you surprised by the noise and jolt in your hand the first time you fired a handgun? I think we all were. Our bodies said, "That's threatening, let's find a way to avoid it next time." Even though our minds know we can survive this aversive stimulus, the body will instinctively try to protect itself. If you know exactly when the gun is going to fire, your body will flinch as it tries to escape the recoil and noise. The flinch or jerking movement pulls the gun off target and the bullet goes astray. However, *if you do not know precisely when the gun is going to fire, you cannot flinch.* Let each shot break as a surprise.

Like bowling or golf, follow through is critical to accurate shot placement. Follow through with a firearm consists of re-aligning the sights after they were disrupted by the recoil of the shot. The sights are re-aligned on target BEFORE the trigger is released. Even if a second shot is not needed (in competition, for example) the discipline

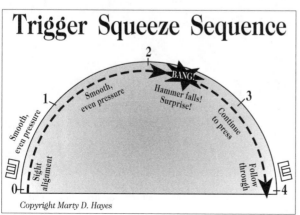

Trigger Squeeze Sequence

Copyright Marty D. Hayes

of a complete follow through keeps the shooter from raising her head to look at the target while the shot goes off. When the shooter peeks at the target, sight alignment is lost at the critical moment the gun fires, sacrificing accuracy. In self-defense, follow through prepares the handgun and the shooter to make an accurate second shot if the threat remains.

Stance builds power

Still having some misses? Check your stance and your grip. Because a handgun recoils with each shot fired, a rock-firm grip is needed to maintain control and to keep the sight picture precise for consecutive shots. The dominant hand grasps the gun grip panels with the hand's web pressed firmly into the grip tang at the top of the back strap. Grasping the gun low on the grips allows the muzzle to rise unnecessarily during recoil. For maximum control, hold as high on the grips as you can, with the fleshy web of your hand blocking the gun's rearward recoil. The support hand wraps completely around the firing hand, like a fist encircling another tight fist. Support-hand fingers press atop the firing hand knuckles, and the non-firing hand's thumb sits right on top of the firing hand's thumbnail and locks down, pushing the thumbs in against the gun. Always remember to keep the index finger outside the trigger guard when the gun's sights are off target or you have decided not to shoot.

A good shooting grip needs the support of strong, balanced footing in the same way a house needs a good foundation to withstand strong winds. The Isosceles stance is inherently the strongest and fastest to assume, although those with more powerful hands and arms may also shoot well from the complex Weaver or Chapman stances. The Isosceles stance is based on shoulder-width feet, with arms and wrists simply locked straight out for fast, accurate firing.

The basis of any shooting stance is foot position. Feet must be placed an immodest shoulder width apart for balance and stabili-

A strong wrap-around grip demonstrated on the .40 caliber Glock 23. The web of the hand pressed up into the grip tang for maximum recoil control.

ty. Women students, especially those of mature ages, find this the most unnatural part of shooting. Women have excellent hand-eye coordination and can manipulate the little safety levers and magazine release buttons well, yet standing with their legs wide for balance is disconcerting, going against all their socialization. It feels bad. People trained in a martial art are comfortable in a wide stance, knowing they're vulnerable to knock-down attacks if they keep their feet together. Before aiming the gun, check that your feet are at least as wide as your shoulders and are not aligned as if walking a tightrope (see diagram).

Starting from the feet up, the feet are at least shoulder width apart and toes point toward the target. Not only is this a natural stance, it accommodates movement, which is essential in a real-life emergency. The leg on the firing-hand side is placed to the rear with a very slight bend at the knee.

The non-dominant side leg is forward and flexes at the knee to act as a shock absorber against the gun's recoil. Flex both knees, because locked joints create a pivot point from which recoil or a blow will steal your balance.

The hips face the target straight on, with the derrière tucked

The aggressive Isosceles stance is a fast and stable shooting platform. The above inset illustrates the wide, squared-off foot position that lends this technique its strength. As shown, if facing North, the right-handed shooter's right foot is back in the SE quadrant, their left foot is forward in the NW quarter. Lefties are opposite.

forward. The shoulders likewise face the target squarely. Arms are locked straight out, punching the gun toward the target. The head may tuck down into the shoulders a little, a natural response to this aggressive, body-forward posture.

If the assailant runs away, but you aren't sure the entire area is safe, you may need to escape, get out of the immediate area or go to call for help. In the wake of a deadly force threat, you will want the gun readily available, yet protected from a gun grab, should a hidden assailant be waiting. This danger precludes stalking around with the gun in a fully-extended shooting stance, a position in which the extended gun also obscures your danger scan. Instead, maintain your strong, two-handed grip on the decocked or on-safe gun, and tuck your elbows back against your ribs, trigger finger indexed on the frame of the gun, well away from the trigger guard. In this ready position, which we will call the "civilian ready," (illustrated below) the gun's muzzle is perpendicular to your torso, out of reach of an assailant who may try to disarm you, while keeping it instantly ready to punch out into a shooting stance.

Held with both hands, close to the solar plexus, the gun is in the strongest retention position possible. When hand and arm strength is required, it is difficult to exert power at arms' length. For example, to open a sealed jar, we hunker down and concentrate our strength at the center of the body.

The Hollywood high ready, with the gun pointing up, is only a cinematic technique to include the gun in the film frame with the actor's face. It has no tactical advantage, and if you live in a multi-story home, "movie high ready" endangers those above you. The low ready, used in law enforcement is specifically designed to allow armed partners to search together without pointing their guns at one another (see illustration on next page). It is not particularly applicable to the armed individual, because it does little to insure against a gun grab.

Author recommends the "civilian ready" for better gun-grab resistance.

Gun handling skills

After you have mastered basic sight picture, grip, and stance, you need to refine skills to keep the gun loaded and firing during combat or competition. Safe speed reloads are important, as is the ability to correct any malfunction of the weapon. You should have one primary, reload technique–a speed reload. Don't allow yourself to ingrain sloppy reloading habits while shooting for fun or during slow fire practice. The motions you make during fun and practice ar.e those you will repeat under stress.

Jim Cirillo, who survived a number of gunfights during his stint with the New York City Police Department Stake Out Squad, cites several incidents in which officers repeated gun handling sequences that had been unintentionally incorporated in their formal training. Some years ago, he relates, the officers were trained to shoot a course of fire then unload their empty brass cases into a can provided for that purpose. They were then to reload and shoot again. The officers were sent to the training range with 100 rounds in their pockets and were not sent to the training line with speed loaders or dump pouches. Reports from on-duty shootings told of policemen who emptied their revolver at the assailant, turned and looked for the brass can while still under attack.

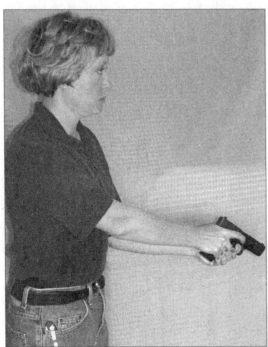

In an armed confrontation, the useless empties must be discarded as quickly as possible, new ammunition inserted and the gun brought back up on target in a matter of seconds. In the comfort of your living room, you may be tempted to say, "of course, I already knew that." But on the range, do you catch your revolver's empty cases tidily in your hand? Do you carefully withdraw your $60 semi-auto magazine before it can fall to the ground and become scratched? Every practice reload should be treated as if it is training for a life-threatening confrontation–it is.

The police low ready shown above allows officers to work in teams without pointing guns at one another.

Speed reloads with the semi-auto can be practiced at home, with the gun's slide and barrel removed and magazines inserted only into the frame. Take the gun apart, then practice over a bed or couch to buffer the magazine's fall. The disassembled gun removes the danger of handling a fireable gun in an unsecured area.

In the next chapter we'll discuss how to dryfire safely, but for now, let me stress that you must never practice reloads during the same session you are practicing draw and dryfire routines or any other dryfire trigger control skill. The body performs the skills you teach it and habituation can override conscious thought, making it all too possible to forget and carelessly load a gun during a dryfire practice session.

Live-fire practice routines

Just like your smooth trigger pull, clearing malfunctions is a habituated skill, and one more crucial to the semi-auto shooter. Revolver shooters simply give the trigger another pull and hope the fault was in the ammunition, not the gun. You can reinforce your speed and ability to clear semi-automatic malfunctions on the range using dummy cartridges. Produced by Precision Gun Specialties,[1] the bright orange Saf-T-Trainer dummy rounds can be interspersed with live rounds in a magazine, simulating a failure to fire. When a trigger pull produces a click instead of bang, the student performs a malfunction clearance drill.

Load several magazines at random, mixing in three or four dummy rounds with the live ammunition. Have a friend load the magazines, or mix several magazines until you cannot anticipate in what order the live and dummy rounds will come. The element of surprise makes the train-

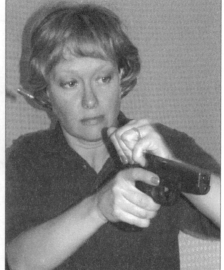

When a dummy round is hit, the first step is a crisp tap to the base of the magazine (left) to assure it is properly seated, followed by manually cycling the slide (right) to load the chamber or eject the faulty round. Next the shooter assesses the need to fire and responds.

ing realistic. In addition to rapidly performing the clearance drill, watch your front sight during the dummy round's trigger pull to observe any flinching if you've anticipated the shot. Making the conscious connection between your flinch and what happens to sight alignment when you flinch is a valuable training epiphany. Attaining this realization, the shooter is able to feel the flinch BEFORE it happens and focus their attention on making a smooth trigger pull and surprise hammer fall.

Malfunction drills are a valuable part of your practice training. Clearing malfunctions increases your understanding of how your gun works and increases your gun-handling capability. Repeating clearance drills imprints the correct motions on your mind, and should the weapon malfunction during a class or a match, you will be gratified by a skilled, smooth response that puts your hands in motion to get the gun back in the game. More important, if the gun fails on the street, your rapid, trained reaction may save your life.

It feels great to reach the skill level at which you can bring the gun up to the target and drill out an inch-or-two hole in the center. It is a great affirmation that your practice has paid off in an important survival skill. Now it is time for you to be sure you can perform that skill with adequate speed and under stress, on the move and on demand. Ask your instructors about intermediate and advanced training that teaches the tactics of armed

The author remembers with great fondness the Second Chance Combat Shoot bowling pin match, when it was hosted by soft body armor inventor Richard Davis.

defense. Instruction you now need includes use of protective cover, tactical movement, low-light marksmanship, one-handed shooting, weak hand shooting, and realistic scenarios and simulated defensive situations. Ask for training in quick or partial sight pictures for fast, close-quarters shots. These are some of the abilities you need to add to your survival skills.

When you go shooting with friends or practice alone, make the accuracy of each round fired of paramount importance. Take care to avoid habituating poor technique. Even when shooting just for fun, shoot with a strong grip, stance, and precise sight alignment. If shooting with others, set up a friendly competition with some kind of stakes. Every shot outside the X ring can "cost" a quarter's donation to a charity or an organization like your area's grass roots gun rights lobby. With shooters of varying skills, establish a handicap, like the more skilled shooter firing left handed to make it truly competitive.

Games to induce the "rush"

Joining a practical shooting league is a great way to stay in practice. The largest organization providing combat shooting competition is the International Practical Shooter's Confederation (IPSC) represented by the United States Practical Shooter's Association, in the States.[2] An IPSC match generally consists of five or six stages of fire with targets arranged to simulate assailants and innocent bystanders or other challenges. A good stage will include targets that move or drop when hit, sight line obstacles, use of cover or firing from a kneeling or prone position. It is excellent practice and always shows me areas where my skills need improvement.

When competing one must remain aware that the match is a game, not realistic training for an actual armed encounter. Game rules often require the shooter to engage targets under conditions that would produce disastrous result in real life. I like to remind myself "This is a game. I am here to practice drawing, reloading and shooting accurately and to have fun. This is not tactical training."

Newer to the competitive shooting world is the International Defensive Pistol Association,[3] formed in an effort to return combat shooting to more practical equipment and courses. Although the rules differ from IPSC, the new discipline is similar, with stages of fire shot on scored paper targets and reactive steel targets. Gear is strictly regulated to keep it compatible with realistic self-defense guns and holsters.

Other competitive shooting events include bowling pin matches. It sounds a little weird, but shooting the wily bowling pin has become very popular. It is surprisingly practical. The bowling pin, at about 15 inches tall and three to four inches wide, is similar in size to the vital area on a human assailant we call the "center of mass" argues Massad Ayoob. Bowling pins are reaction targets—when hit, they react. Well-aimed hits will push the pin off a special, two-tier steel table. Sloppy hits will merely knock them over. You can learn a lot about the balance between speed shooting and precision shot placement by shooting bowling pins. Tables of five to eleven pins comprise the shooting "stages" in a bowling pin match. If speed and accuracy are to co-exist, the shooter must follow the front sight from one pin to the next without looking up to see their hits.

Ask your local gun range about bowling pin matches as well as Police Pistol Competition (PPC) shooting. PPC uses unmoving paper targets, and requires precise shot placement and timing. All four sports are excellent places to test your skills against other shooters. Consider this: if in competition, you miss or are the slowest, could you survive against an armed assailant on the street?

Speed and smoothness

Most shooting competition uses the shooter's time as part of the scoring formula, recognizing that the first bullet that hits a vital spot may change the outcome of a street fight. You need to develop speed, yet not at the expense of accuracy.

Competition induced stress includes shooting for score against skilled shooters, shooting under time constraints and other elements specified by the match director.

Finally, speed is not a product of haste, it comes from eliminating all unnecessary motions in your shooting. It comes from smoothness. Never rush your movements to the point that they become jerky. The tension of hurrying will steal the smoothness that is the trademark of champion shooters.

1 Precision Gun Specialities, Inc., 154 E Condensery Rd., Sheridan, MI 48884 517-291-5170 or purchase from Brownell's, 200 S. Front St., Montezuma, IA 50171 515-623-4000.
2 The International Defensive Pistol Association, 2232 CR 719, Berryville, AR 72616 870-545-3886.
3 United States Practical Shooting Association, P.O. Box 811, Sedro Woolley, WA 98284 and the International Practical Shooting Confederation, P.O. Box 972, Oakville, Ontario, Canada L6J 9Z9 905-849-6960.

17

Eliminating Dryfire's Dangers

You don't need to go to the range to practice a smooth, controlled trigger pull, speed reloads, or draw and dry fire skills. Champion pistol shooters all practice dry fire, because despite one's level of skill, flinching is an unavoidable human physiological response to extensive live fire. Dryfire is the cure, and is inexpensive because it requires no ammunition. It is practical: with planning, you can safely do it almost anywhere. Best of all, it lets you ingrain a perfect trigger pull without the aversive stimuli of the gun firing, so the practice habituates the body to pull the trigger smoothly without flinching.

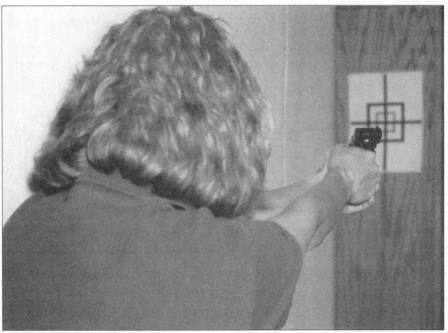

Step 1. A proper place to dryfire requires a safe backstop, like an old Kevlar® vest or a fully packed bookcase as shown here. If you cannot assure the safety of what is beyond the wall, do not dryfire.

Dryfire practice, however, is a two-edged sword. Valuable in that it is without question the best way to develop trigger control, dryfire is extremely dangerous unless performed under very stringent safety rules. This may be the reason nearly every gun owner's manual warns against the practice. With rimfire guns, like a .22 LR pistol or rifle, the warning stems from mechanical causes and should be heeded.

With shotguns and rifles, too, there is potential for accelerated wear to the firing pin. "Snap Caps" or other inert, dummy cartridges are recommended as a way to avert mechanical problems, yet these, too, are hazardous because live and dummy ammunition may be inadvertently mixed. With center fire handguns, like your self-defense pistol, the manufacturer's warning is rooted in safety and liability concerns.

Far, far too often, dryfire is practiced carelessly, with disregard for basic firearms safety. The danger of a negligent discharge and the subsequent liability is the reason behind manufacturer's warnings against dryfiring. Those dangers are very real and should not be ignored.

Dryfire entails all of the steps of discharging a gun with one crucial difference: the absence of ammunition. In one careless moment, live ammunition is all too often loaded in the gun during a dryfire practice session. People have been injured and killed, property damage incurred, and private gun ownership earned one more black mark, all because dryfire was not practiced safely.

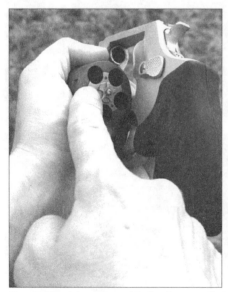 

Step 2. Check by sight and feel to be sure all ammunition is removed from the gun, magazine and shooter's person, then double check before beginning to dryfire.

Establish a safety net

If dryfire practice consists of going through all the steps of firing your gun away from a safe range, why is it condoned and even encouraged? Dryfire CAN be performed safely, if the practitioner complies with uncompromising rules of safe dryfire practice every time he or she dryfires.

The best compilation of safe dryfire rules I've ever seen was developed by Pierce County, WA Sheriff's chief firearms instructor Bill Burris. Well over a decade ago, this law enforcement professional recognized the benefits and dangers of dryfire. His recommendations were so successful that they are currently part of the Washington State Criminal Justice Training Commission's police firearms instructor curriculum and were published nationally beneath Burris' byline.

Burris developed a seven-step ritual for dryfire that protects against accidents because, as the term "ritual" implies, the same steps are executed each and every time dryfire is practiced. With Burris' permission, we share this practice method, with his ritual delineated by bold type and quotation marks.

Step 1. **"SELECT THE PROPER TIME AND PLACE."** There are appropriate circumstances under which dryfire may be practiced, and there are times and places where any dryfire is dangerous and negligent. Several years ago, a local motel posted a sign in the lobby "No Firearms Allowed." When I heard of it, I was annoyed, but that feeling changed to shame, when a match shooter later confessed that another shooter, in town for a championship match, had discharged a round in a room of that motel. Need I say more?

When I was a student at Gunsite in 1995, students were issued a square of bullet-resistant Kevlar® toward which they were to practice the dryfire exercises assigned at days' end. I suspect that famous, well-attended shooting school feared a similar reputation-spoiling problem.

Firearms expert Massad Ayoob lectures that a proper dryfire location must include a backstop that will stop a bullet from the most

Ammunition is removed from the practice room and placed in a secure spot.

powerful cartridge your practice firearm could discharge. In your home a
basement wall backed by earth is best, however a heavy, masonry wall or
fireplace will suffice. In the absence of impenetrable housing construction,
a fully-packed three or four foot bookcase can be carefully substituted,
establishing an aiming point on one end, where a shot would have to travel through all of the books.

Dryfire is best practiced alone. If another person is present, they
should hold an active role in the practice and must perform the dryfire ritual steps, too. If you live with family members or roommates, they should
not be present during dryfire. Television, radio or other distractions should
be turned off, and if interrupted by the telephone or doorbell, re-initiate
the ritual from the beginning to ensure the safety of the dryfire.

Finally, as with all shooting activities, complete sobriety is demanded.

Step 2. "REMOVE ALL LIVE AMMUNITION FROM THE TRAINING AREA."
Pointing the gun in a safe direction, empty the cylinder or remove the magazine and clear the chamber if it is a semi-automatic. Many of the injuries
inflicted during gun handling occur after a magazine has been removed,
but a cartridge is left in the chamber of a semi-auto. Make a visual and manual inspection of the gun,
both looking and feeling
inside the chamber(s) and up
the semi-auto's magazine well.
Repeat the inspection to be
doubly sure.

As Burris advises, move
the unloaded ammunition
plus any loose cartridges or
boxes of ammunition to a different room.

Step 3. "GO INTO PRAC-
TICE MODE." As we've dis-
cussed, in dryfire you do
things that would be extremely dangerous without the protections of the Dryfire Ritual.
As you prepare to dryfire, Burris recommends stating aloud
"This is practice. The gun is
not loaded."

*Step 4. "Perform practice." A coin balanced on the
front sight reveals any jerking when the trigger is
pulled in dryfire.*

The audible utterance grants permission to perform dryfire under the safe, ritualized circumstances, while emphasizing that these actions would ordinarily be unsafe. Make the statement aloud two or three times.

Step 4. "PERFORM PRACTICE." Dryfire practice can consist squeezing the trigger smoothly while maintaining a precise sight alignment, or it can include drawing, presenting the gun and dryfiring. More elaborate practice can integrate dryfiring from behind cover or other "tactics," but only if the gun remains pointed into a safe, bullet-absorbing backstop.

Have a practical goal. If you wish to develop a smooth trigger pull, building up hand and arm strength in the process, that simple goal is good enough. Pursue it with complete concentration and intense focus to avoid forming bad habits during the practice session.

The practice period should last no longer than you can concentrate completely on the training. Dryfire doesn't offer much feedback. If, after five or ten minutes, your mind wanders, it is time to stop! On the other hand, if you are working with a partner, concentration may last longer, because there is more feedback in the shared experience.

Step 5. "RETURN TO REALITY MODE WHEN PRACTICE IS OVER." Remember the audible, verbal statement that released us to safely engage in dryfire practice? When the practice time is over, you need to withdraw from the dryfire mind-set and acknowledge that pulling the trigger can cause death, injury or other damage.

Say aloud, so you can hear the statement: "Practice is over. If I pull the trigger, this gun will fire." Repeat the statement emphatically several times.

Step 6. Put the gun away or secure it in its usual condition.

Step 6. **"PUT THE GUN AWAY IMMEDIATELY."** The final step is of extreme importance, because after ritual dryfire you are accustomed or habituated to doing things with a firearm that are ordinarily very dangerous. It is all too easy to pick up a loaded gun for "one last dryfire," and find out tragically that the gun is loaded. Unless the practice gun is the home-defense weapon, lock it away and do not handle it for several hours. If you commonly keep a loaded gun in the home for defense, load it, put it in its holster or lock box and do not touch it for several hours. It is too easy to revert to practice mode.

On a related topic, I have no patience with those who leave guns laying around on tables, shelves, desks and in other easily accessible places. Even if you are the home's sole occupant, this kind of carelessness encourages reckless gun handling and is an invitation to theft or an accident involving a visiting child. The defensive handgun belongs in a holster, stored in a safe or locking box or secured in a carry device like a holster purse, fanny pack or holster brief case.

Basic safety rules not suspended

Without a full understanding of how the Dryfire Ritual functions, one might think that the Universal Rules of Firearms Safety are suspended during ritual dryfire. Absolutely untrue. During dryfire it is of even greater importance to refer back to Chapter 12 and apply each of the four Universal Rules of Gun Safety to the situation.

Dryfire, like any activity with a firearm, is not for the irresponsible. On the surface, recommending dryfire practice and adherence to gun safety rules appears in conflict. If after careful study you cannot integrate safety rules and ritual dryfire, please, for heaven's sake, do not dryfire. Better yet, adopt a non-firearms method of defense.

However, if you are willing to approach gun use with great care and caution, dryfire is the fastest, least expensive path to increased smoothness, speed and accuracy.

18

Carrying a Gun When You Need It

With so much violent crime occurring on the street, how can a gun kept in the home protect you when you are outside? Can you predict when you will become the target of a violent criminal? A chore as innocuous as a trip to the store can throw you into contact with an assailant. It is unwise to assume that a familiar shopping center, post office or other public facility is danger free. Can you guarantee beyond doubt that your car will reach your destination trouble free? Can you be certain of the character of every person in the parking lot or of the tow truck driver if your car breaks down?

Of course not. Mercifully, most of us go about our day-to-day duties without defending ourselves. Nonetheless, the one woman in three statistically predicted to become a victim of violence in her lifetime can't select the moment the attack will come. *We simply cannot predict when or where we may need to protect ourselves.* I won't play roulette with my daily well-being, so I carry a gun whenever it is legal.

The "art" of concealed carry is more complex than stuffing a revolver

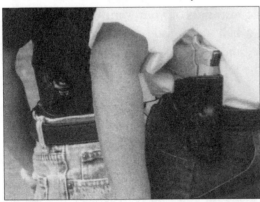

Individual build governs holster choice. Left, the author carries an HK P7M8 comfortably in a Rosen ARG, while firearms instructor Vicki Farnam was happier with the same manufacturer's women's holster, the "Nancy Special" for S&W 3913 LadySmith.

in your handbag or in the waistband of your jeans! Newcomers to the world of armed self-defense are dazzled by the array of holsters, gun bags, and other carry devices marketed. I could write another book on the topic alone, but Jerry Ahern has already done so in *CCW: Carrying Concealed Weapons*, 157 informative pages and over 125 photographs on this extensive subject.[1]

There exists no utterly comfortable way to wear a concealed handgun. The best we can hope for, first and foremost, is complete concealment of the gun. Comfort can be fine tuned with different holsters, maybe even using various models of one brand of handgun for various situations. Winter clothing will accommodate a larger, generally higher capacity handgun than the lighter garb of summer. Two guns, one large, the other small, with comparable locations for safety and magazine releases can make it easier to carry a gun all the time.

Unfortunately, it may take several purchases to find the right holster for you and your gun. Nearly every gun owner I know jokes about wanting to have a holster garage sale. Like me, they own several holsters per gun, some they know they will never use again. The following principles may keep new gun owners from spending money and accumulating way too many holsters, as you try to find one that works.

Start with the basics

Among experienced armed citizens, the primary holster choice for concealed handgun carry is generally some variety of high-quality belt holster. A lot of women have tried holsters made for men and given up prematurely on the idea of using a belt holster. Before you give up, try one of the belt holsters made specifically for women from makers like Kramer Handgun Leather,[2] Blade-Tech[3] or Mitch Rosen.[4] Other ladies have found the cross-draw holster is a good belt rig alternative. Like any other personal-safety issue, learning to wear a holstered gun and becoming accustomed to its presence, is not altogether easy. It takes effort, patience and ingenuity.

A belt and holster place some restraints on your wardrobe. Casual garb is more likely to accommodate a belt and holster with minimal fuss. I've been at this for nearly a decade, and to this day, I own several expensive pair of suit trousers on which the loops are too small for the belt that fits most of my holsters.

There are numerous belt holster variations, but you should insist on one with a rigid mouth that remains open after the gun is drawn. Sometimes, a spring steel band will be enclosed in leather to keep the holster open for safe, one-handed holstering. Other holsters rely on very stiff construction, like Greg Kramer's premium-quality horse-hide holsters.

This is an important feature should you find it necessary to hold an assailant at gun point. What will the police perceive when they come on the scene? How will they know you are the victim, not the assailant? Trust me, the gun in your hand marks you as an unidentified threat of some kind. You can avoid a mistaken-identity shooting by discretely holstering the gun the moment before the law officers arrive. The rigid, open top allows you to holster the gun without looking, so you can keep your eyes on the assailant. Rigid nylon holsters, like the Bianchi[5] Accu-mold line, and gear made from other synthetic materials like Kydex® approach the performance of leather, and are often less expensive. You should, whatever the material, insist that the holster remain open at the top when the gun is drawn.

A better fit

For the womanly figure, I like a concealment holster positioned in what is called the appendix carry, tucked in the concave curve between abdomen and strong-side hip. It was recommended to me when I was first carrying a five-shot revolver and when climate allowed an over shirt or vest to conceal the gun I continued to use it when I carried the larger Glock 23. Although the gun seems obvious to the wearer in this position, it is not a place where men stare.

For the same reason, cross draw holsters work well for women. A woman's figure is studied in the buttocks or bust line. The abdomen is not subject to that much scrutiny. Although care must be taken to do so safely, the appendix carry is very fast from which to draw and the only downside I discovered was that it required a closed vest or shirt to conceal it.

Women are substantially shorter through the torso than men. Recently, a 5' 8" tall friend described trying out her husband's paddle holster. We laughed as she indicated the spot in her armpit to which she reported the

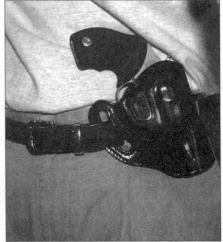

The cross draw holster (right), this one from Galco International, uses the bust line to lift garments over the gun for excellent concealment, as does the appendix carry, shown above left, with Wild Bill's[10] version of David Workman's under-the-shirt holster design.

grips of her Glock 23 extended, yet we *were* happy she hadn't paid $80 to buy the holster only to discover that men's high-rise holsters rarely are functional for women. In belt holster selection for women, one of my leading criteria is a holster that does not open any higher than the beltline. While many, many very nice holsters are eliminated from my shopping list by this rule, those that remain are easier to draw and carry.

Mitch Rosen's Ayoob Rear Guard holster is an excellent example of a very high quality holster that sits low inside the trouser waistband for the best-possible concealment. While many find an inside the waistband holster uncomfortable, Rosen and Ayoob's design eliminate a lot of the problems by angling the gun at an extreme cant. For several years, I carried a Heckler & Koch P7M8 in the Rear Guard, and at times, would check to see if I'd forgotten to put on the gun. It remains the only gun and holster I've ever worn that I could literally forget I had on.

Orca Custom International, a Washington State manufacturer, makes a very comfortable rigid nylon holster, the Bodyguard, that also sits low inside the waistband.[6] If I am carrying a small, flat semi-automatic like the Kahr K9 or Glock 26, I like an Orca holster tucked right behind my strong-side hip. This allows me to conceal the gun while wearing an open vest or big shirt over a tank top or t-shirt. In this mode of carry, one learns not to lean over in public, since the butt of even a small gun makes a recognizable outline even when covered by fabric. In the grocery store, for instance, I'll squat to pick up items on low shelves instead of just bending over to collect them. Choose a good quality holster from a reputable manufacturer. Readily available choices include Bianchi, Galco, Blade-Tech and DeSantis.[8] Spend a few more dollars and you can have the workmanship of a Milt Sparks, Greg Kramer, or Mitch Rosen rig.

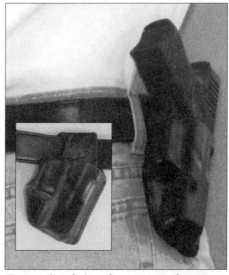

Some holsters come outfitted to accommodate several widths of belts. My Milt Sparks Executive Companion, for instance, has two screws that attach the belt loop to the holster.[7] A smaller loop is sold for 1-inch belts and costs $7.50, which I gladly spent, knowing some

Kramer drop holster fits woman's short torso.

trousers wouldn't accommodate my inch-and-a-half gun belt. And speaking of belts, your common dress belt isn't going to last long under the weight of your gun and holster. Budget $60 to $75 for a good gun belt produced by a reputable holster manufacturer. A sturdy belt, like Galco's Contour Concealable, is critical to successful belt holster carry, as it eliminates most of the holster's movement.[9] The contour cut lets the belt snug to your curves with surprising comfort and having worn contour-cut belts for years, I cannot see why a woman would try to carry a holstered gun on anything else.

The new concealed carry practitioner is uncomfortably aware of the gun and holster, especially during the break in period. It takes self control to avoid fiddling with the gun, holster and clothing. In public you may only give the concealing garment a pat or pull when alone, upon standing up or getting out of a car or at other times when adjusting one's clothing would be normal without a holstered pistol. Press through this disturbing period by practicing concealed carry at first in privacy.

Not everyone is willing to endure the initial discomfort of breaking in an inside the waistband holster. Female figures, especially ladies with a tiny waistline and curving hips, may find an IWB intolerable, although a radical angle (cant) provides some relief. If a belt scabbard is worn on the outside of the trousers, you will need to exaggerate concealment techniques: rely on bulkier clothing, heavier fabrics, and roomier fashions. With a belt scabbard, the trouser fabric won't cover the bottom of the holster, so the covering garment must be considerably longer, too.

Alternatives to the belt holster

It takes a few years to replace ordinary garments with those that will accommodate your belt, holster and gun, so it might be good to start with more than one carry method, including a sturdy "belly band" that holds the gun tight against the torso with wide, Velcro®-secured elastic. Sources include DeSantis, Gould & Goodrich, Bianchi and other well-known holster companies.

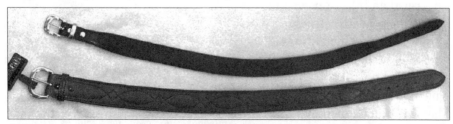

Galco's Concealable Contour belt (top) and Bianchi contour cut belt (bottom).

Gould & Goodrich also makes a wide elastic belt that works on the same principle, designed to be worn outside the clothing, with a false buckle on the front.[11] Tucked beneath a blazer or cardigan sweater, the Gould & Goodrich Lady Bodyguard looks like a wide fabric belt. The gun is carried at or behind the hip, in a sewn-in holster-shaped with a Velcro®-secured thumb strap to keep the gun in place. It works great with guns like a .38 Special air weight revolver or the thin .380 semi-automatic Colt Mustang, and with sufficiently concealing garments, will accommodate small semi-autos like the Kahr Mk9 or Smith & Wesson's 9mm Chief's Special. I use my Lady Bodyguard for all-day seminars or trade shows, where a blazer and skirt are de rigeur. I can virtually forget the super-light titanium revolver the belt holds securely at my hip. Another alternative to a belt-holstered gun is the shoulder holster.

The majority of shoulder holsters sold will not conceal a defensive handgun on a woman's body, because it is carried horizontally and the muzzle extends beyond the back. Trust me, the distinctive outline of the muzzle or the angle of the holster's leather sheath can be mistaken for nothing but a shoulder holster–something everyone has seen repeatedly on TV cop dramas.

Invest the time and make the effort to shop for a vertical shoulder holster if this is an on-body carry method you favor. Choices from well-known manufacturers include Uncle Mike's[12] and Bianchi International. The gun is carried beneath the non-dominant side arm with the muzzle pointing down and the pistol's grips forward. A good harness should distribute the weight of the pistol and spare ammunition. Concealment, of course, requires a jacket or loose over-garment, as well as some care that a collar covers the material of the harness.

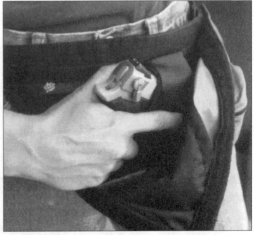

My friend Jane, who introduced me to the Milt Sparks Executive Companion inside-the-waistband holster carried her Glock in the traditional position, behind her strong side hip. She is taller and has a trimmer waistline than I, and her gun concealed comfortably in that position. Nonetheless, the last time I saw Jane, on a

DeSantis makes this fanny pack with its fast all-Velcro® enclosure in a variety of colors.

humid July day in western Washington, she was toting a .38 Special revolver in a belly bag holster. Hot weather will be a determining factor in how you carry your gun. I also sometimes concede to hot weather by tucking my semi-automatic into a specially designed belly bag. I prefer nylon to leather, since it has a more common appearance that does not shout "GUN!" Some holster fanny packs have wide Velcro® straps to secure the gun, an elastic band to hold an extra magazine in place, plus a cord for a downward rip to unzip the carry pouch and expose the gun for the draw. Others have a built-in holster attached to the back panel of the bag.

Choices include Bianchi's roomy nylon pouch with side pockets, an unusual detail I appreciated. I like a small pocket to serve exclusively as magazine pouch or place to tuck pistol permits and identification papers or other objects I don't want mixed with other things. DeSantis was the original designer to use Velcro® on fanny pack pockets, a design they've patented. For years, I've used their Gunnysack II, an extremely well-designed fanny pack with a full rip-away front panel that reliably exposes the holstered gun for a fast draw.

Men do have it easier in a few regards. Not only do men's rest room lines move faster, men don't have to give birth, and they can wear ankle holsters with nearly all of their trousers! An ankle holster is one of the hardest-to-detect modes of concealed carry. I'm always a little jealous as I watch my husband tuck his .38 Special air weight revolver into an ankle rig deeply concealed beneath his dark dress socks.

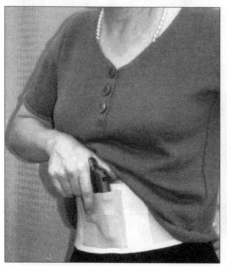

Vertical shoulder holster blends pistol's outline with torso of even a small woman. The draw from a belly band is greatly eased if the carry device is worn beneath a roomy open-bottomed sweater or blouse.

Women's fashions change every season. When slim-cut trousers are the rage, the ankle holster reverts to a gentleman's carry option. However, boot cut jeans, painter pants, straight-legged trousers and cuffed chinos will generally camouflage a Colt .380 ACP semi-auto carried in a trim elastic holster worn on the feminine ankle. While drawing from this method is a bit slow, it allows you to remain armed in an office where blouses and dress slacks are the daily uniform. Of course, you must sit carefully, avoiding crossed legs that expose the gun. An inch or two of extra length at the trouser hemline will assure that when you sit, the fabric will not ride up and reveal your handgun tucked on the inside of your calf right above the ankle bone. For really casual wear, a pair of jogging pants gathered with elastic at the ankles hides an ankle holster best of all.

Drawing your handgun from an ankle holster requires practice. The right-handed "defender" takes a big step, left-leg forward. The left hand lifts a handful of trouser leg on the thigh above the knee, where the hand can rest and support the weight as the right hand snakes down and snatches the gun from its holster on the inside the left ankle. The defender then simply straightens the torso enough to align the sights on target and is ready to shoot. The feet are already in an aggressive shooting stance. If the pants are too tight to grab and lift, drop to the non-gun knee, grab the pistol and shoot from a kneeling position.

Holster purses

I'm very uneasy with a gun carried off the body, but reality takes its toll on idealism, and I have to admit that there are times when a purse or holster bag is the only real option for keeping a gun in easy reach. At a dress-up affair, a woman carrying a pretty sequined or beaded purse is inconspicuous, however a woman who cannot take off her jacket can become pretty uncomfortable. I concede: a gun purse is a good solution under limited circumstances.

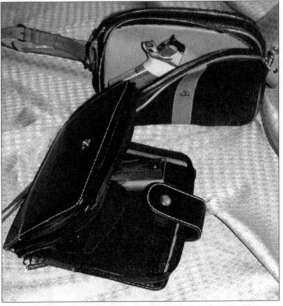

Galco's holster-bag (top) and Strictly Anything's Planner Plus[13] (bottom) are concealment devices that mimic everyday styles.

Some will ask why they can't put the gun in their normal handbag. There are several very good reasons to use a holster handbag. The first is the presence of other objects that become caught in and foul the gun's action, or worse yet, may disengage the gun's safety making it more at risk of negligent discharge. This is not just a problem for amateurs. I still remember my amazement when at an American Society of Law Enforcement Trainers conference, as I listened to a trainer describe the tribulations of an off-duty female law enforcement officer who drew a revolver from her purse to find an eyebrow pencil jammed down the barrel.

The second reason for using a purse specially designed to carry a gun is drawing speed. Pulling a handgun from a conventional purse is terribly slow, as the defender fumbles with the latch or zipper, then dredges through the other personal effects trying to reach the weapon. A gun purse has a separate pouch that is inaccessible from the rest of the bag, often with a sewn-in holster to hold the gun in the same position all the time. At a minimum, this separation protects your gun from open view when you reach in to get your wallet, lipstick or other common purse contents. To

Top-opening Coronado California Case allows a draw stroke that is much like that of the cross-draw method.

draw, insert your hand, grasp the butt and present the weapon in a cross-draw manner. If the gun purse does not have a dedicated pouch and a built-in holster, don't purchase it. There are plenty of very good gun purses that have built-in holsters and fast, positive closures that make getting to the gun in an emergency fumble-free.

The best fast-draw design I've seen is the two-compartment bag (shown to the left) from Coronado Leather,[14] which, in my wardrobe, has replaced a similar purse from DeSantis that is no longer manufactured. The Coronado purses look like a nice, casual handbag in colors and styles any woman would happily carry. The front section holds your personal goods; the back section is large enough to contain up to a medium-sized semi-automatic or K-frame revolver. The draw is very similar to the up-and-out draw of a conventional belt holster, and therefore is considerably faster than bags that tuck the gun horizontally in a center section between two pockets.

For business events, I've been very happy with the handsome portfolio marketed by Guardian Leather.[15] It has two large pockets for papers and books, and a hidden compartment in the middle for your gun. With this design, the woman reaches cross body, separates the Velcro® closure, grabs the gun butt and makes a cross-body draw. This takes some practice, and is a few seconds slower than the California Case's design. Velcro® tabs secure a holster sized to fit your gun, making it easy to change the holster if you decide to carry different guns in the bag.

When I bought my first holster briefcase, I ordered two holsters–one for my Glock and one for a .38 Special revolver, but in a bag this size, it seems ridiculous not to carry the higher capacity, bigger caliber Glock, since it fits in the bag just as easily as a five-shot revolver. Really, the only constraining factor is the weight you can carry on your shoulder. I found the fully loaded Glock 23 with spare magazine is just about the maximum for me, and my shoulder is sore after long business days.

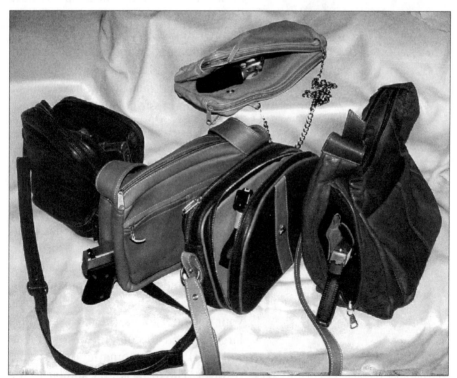

A variety of manufacturers make holster purses, with different drawing styles, some faster, some more secretive, but all with separate gun compartments and built in holsters.

The greatest difficulty I have in justifying gun purses is the question of proper response to a purse snatching. Experts agree that the best defense against muggers or purse snatchers is to give them the purse or wallet, so long as the woman is allowed to escape unharmed. A run-by purse snatching can turn into an ugly ground fight if the woman struggles to keep her bag. However, the good advice to give up a snatched bag is drastically altered by the presence of a deadly weapon in the purse. We know we must not use deadly force to stop property theft, yet we also endorse the need to keep guns out of criminal hands.

The best decision is to use the holster purse only in social or business circumstances where no other alternative exists. If unexpected circumstances put you at risk of a purse snatching, carry the holster bag crossbody, and tuck that bag in tight to the front of your body where the savvy criminal knows it is more difficult to grab. Try other holster methods, including belly bands, shoulder rigs and ankle holsters before falling back on holster bags for every day use. It is, in my opinion, a last resort.

If you decide to tuck a gun into a handbag–one specially designed for a gun–you must be committed to keeping that purse on your body , if seated, or between your ankles at all times. A purse hung off the back of a chair can be stolen or may attract the curiosity of a small child. Neither is

Boxy blazers and patterned vests all help break up outline of concealed handgun. Another great alternative is Coronado Leather's carry vest, (above, left) featuring built-in holsters.

acceptable when the purse contains a gun. A purse left on a host's coat tree or couch is also accessible to unauthorized hands. If you carry in a holster handbag, when you are in the car lodge that bag tightly between the seat and console or the seat and your locked door, where it won't shift as the car moves. The gun is a serious responsibility. If you aren't willing to keep it with you at all times, you must leave it safely locked away.

Clothing for concealed carry

A cute 25-year old student complained that she couldn't carry a concealed handgun. She didn't like the feel of a fanny pack, nor would an in-the-waistband concealment holster fit inside the tight blue jeans she favored, she had concluded. The question sounded like a challenge: "tell me how to carry my gun with no hassle, and then I'll take your advice to carry it all the time." Fortunately, there was an answer for this one: if you want to show off your rear, buy boys or men's jeans–they still fit tight in the seat, but they're cut roomier through the waist and will accommodate an inside-the-waistband holster and gun for most women.

A lot of armed people find themselves buying clothes to fit the gun. We select pants that have a little extra room in the waist. Our trousers have waistbands with belt loops for a sturdy belt and straight, loose legs to hide ankle holsters. We buy boxy blazers that are more loosely fitted to hide either a belt holster or shoulder holster. Others have adopted the casual photographer or hiker's vest to hide the gun, or wear oversized shirts over tank tops in the summertime. Any jacket with an elastic band at the bottom, bomber jackets and baseball jackets work well for belt holster concealment, too.

It's not really as much trouble as it seems in the beginning. After a while, fitting the gun into your clothing style becomes as natural as making sure you have white underwear to wear with white slacks.

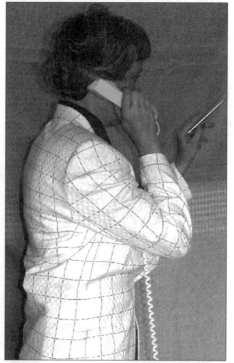

Practice with a new holster in private reveals problems like the gun and holster "printing" through the fabric of covering garments.

Break it in

I like to break in a holster by wearing it around the house so I can adjust the gear if it begins to rub or gouge. A new holster, worn immediately in public, can inflict considerable discomfort with no opportunity to make adjustments. I'd rather find out where it rubs and where it needs to be adjusted in privacy before taking it public. I also recommend several hundred "dry" repetitions of drawing the unloaded gun from the holster, assuming a shooting stance and dry firing, when breaking in a new holster.

The body, according to physiologists, needs 2,000 to 5,000 repetitions of any movement before it becomes habituated. Remember when driving a manual transmission car was nearly impossible? Now, if you drive that kind of car regularly, shifting is as automatic as tying your shoes. After around 5,000 repetitions, drawing and firing your handgun becomes just as smooth, too. You can get a good start on those repetitive movements by practicing with an unloaded gun. Skills to develop include a fumble-free draw, being sure none of your motions allows the gun muzzle to cross any part of your body during the draw. Be sure you are learning to draw while keeping the trigger finger outside the trigger guard until the sights are on target and you've decided to shoot.

Practice with any holster or gun must be accomplished with the weapon unloaded. Put all the ammu-

A light-weight bicycler's vest (left) uses a gathered waistline that camouflages the gun well. In a suit-and-skirt environment, a textured sweater covers a Glock in a shoulder holster.

nition in a box or drawer in a different room. Double check to see that the chamber or cylinder is empty and apply all the other principles of the dry-fire ritual detailed in Chapter 17. Learning your safe way around your new holster will take some time and practice. Practice in complete privacy, without distractions or the danger of inadvertently pointing your gun at a family member.

First holster choices

Holster selection can be a confusing job for the new gun owner. At the very beginning, the individual might be best served by obtaining an inexpensive belt holster molded from Kydex® for training, a belly bag for summer, or gun purse if your life includes a lot of dress-up events. As your advancing classes and training prepare you for armed self-defense situations, go shopping for a good leather holster with a rigid, open top. You'll need to budget between $60 and $100 for this chore, yet with your advancing skill you will recognize the tactical advantage a good holster offers for both concealment and for drawing the gun quickly.

If practicing concealed carry, I believe you need to invest in one very high quality holster, a belt and magazine pouch or speedloader holder, all from the same manufacturer, so they fit together perfectly. Beyond this basic rig, optional products like a holster handbag, a safe pocket holster like that made by Ahern Enterprises, an elasticized belly band, or a shoulder holster represent the variety that make it possible to be armed and protected whenever and wherever legal.

Society's expectations about a woman's appearance increases the challenge of concealed handgun carry, yet with several serviceable carry rigs, lots of patience and your own feminine ingenuity, going armed on a daily basis is surprisingly manageable.

Sources for products shown in this chapter:
1 Ahern Enterprises P O Box 186, Commerce, GA 30529, 706-335-5715.
2 Kramer Handgun Leather, P O Box 112154, Tacoma, WA 98411, 253-564-6652.
3 Blade-Tech, 3060 S 96th, Tacoma, WA 98499, 253-581-4347.
4 Mitch Rosen's Extraordinary Gunleather, 300 Bedford St., Manchester, NH 03101, 603-647-2971.
5 Bianchi International, 100 Calle Cortez, Temecula, CA 92590 800-477-8545.
6 Orca Custom International, Inc., P O Box 1065, Centralia, WA 98532, 360-748-4557.
7 Milt Sparks Holsters Inc., 605 E. 44th, #2, Boise, ID 82714 208-377-5577.
8 DeSantis, P O Box 2039, Hillside Manor Branch, New Hyde Park, NY 11040 516-354-8000.
9 Galco International, 2019 W. Quail Ave., Phoenix, AZ 85027 602-258-8295.
10 Wild Bill's, P O Box 1941, Garner, NC 27529, 919-779-9456.
11 Gould & Goodrich, P O Box 1479, Lillington, NC 27546 919-893-2071.
12 Uncle Mike's, P O Box 1690, Oregon City, OR 97045, 503-557-0536.
13 Strictly Anything, 6751 N Blackstone Ave., #220, Fresno, CA 93710, 800-209-7904.
14 Coronado Leather, 120 "C" Ave., Coronado, CA 92118 800-283-9509.
15 Guardian Leather, P O Box 277, Newton Centre, MA 02159.

19

The Home-Defense Shotgun

While the handgun is an easy firearm with which to learn shooting skills, it is not the most powerful in the selection of defensive weapons from which the home occupant or business owner may choose. It comes first to mind in discussion of defensive firearms, because the pistol's small dimensions provide the portability and concealability valued by the individual legally entitled to carry a concealed firearm for personal defense. Other defensive functions, including home-defense or protection of a place of business, may be served as well or better by a light rifle or a shotgun.

Rifles and shotguns have many good characteristics for the ensconced defender–that is one who by circumstances needs to remain in position and fight instead of fleeing. Because the operating systems of rifles and shotguns differ significantly, let's start with the shotgun, a common home-defense long arm. The shotgun comes in many configurations, some specifically appropriate for shooting sports, others designed for law enforcement duty. We will concentrate on adaptations of the latter for home-defense.

The shotgun is a formidable defense tool in trained hands.

Looking back at our discussion of handgun ammunition in Chapter 14, you will remember that there are no absolute guarantees with the self-defense firearm. With the shotgun, variables affecting the end result are numerous, influenced by accuracy, gauge of the shotgun ammunition, distance to the assailant, not to mention the combatants' size, weight, disposition clothing, and more. There is much to understand with the defensive shotgun.

The shotgun is unique in its ability to fire shells containing varying numbers of pellets, different sized shot, slugs, and in some guns even shells of several lengths for a magnum or standard charge. It is really quite a versatile defense tool that can be a lot of fun with which to train.

The great advantage of the home-defense shotgun is its simultaneous delivery of multiple projectiles at reasonably high velocities. The effect of twenty .25 caliber pellets of #3 buckshot moving at around 1200 fps from a 20 gauge shotgun is completely different from firing nine single shots of .25 caliber handgun ammunition into an assailant; likewise, nine .33 caliber pellets of 00 buckshot from a 12 gauge is NOT the same as nine hits with a .32 caliber pistol. The physical trauma of multiple projectiles penetrating simultaneously causes neural shock, and, some hypothesize, this stops assailants who have not yet lost sufficient blood to be incapacitated by the more conventional means of blood loss or neurological injury.

When innocent life is threatened, the overwhelming concern must be to stop the attack quickly. We are not worried about the eventual survival or demise of the assailant; seeking only an immediate cessation of the attack. Used to stop violent attack, the shotgun is effective indeed when used with accuracy and skill.

Pros and cons

I believe the shotgun, loaded with proper ammunition and employed correctly, is great for home-defense. However, before depending on any equipment, you need a clear understanding of its advantages and pitfalls: when it will work best and when other tools would serve better.

The home-defense shotgun is best employed when the home's occupants can take refuge in a pre-arranged, protected area, and defend themselves from a single point. The multiple projectiles that make the shot shell so effective are equally dangerous to innocents if they miss the intruder and penetrate walls of occupied rooms. Handgun ammunition poses the same danger, of course, however the hazard is compounded by the multiple pellets each shot shell contains. Later, we'll discuss shot patterns, how they spread over varying distances, and the penetration potential of various shotgun loads.

As a defensive weapon, the shotgun seems best suited to childless couples or single occupants, or in home layouts where those to be protected are sure to be clustered behind the defender. The shotgun works well if those responsible for home-defense are located at the head of a hall that precedes all other bedrooms, or can defend the family from the top of a staircase, if all the residents are on the upper floor.

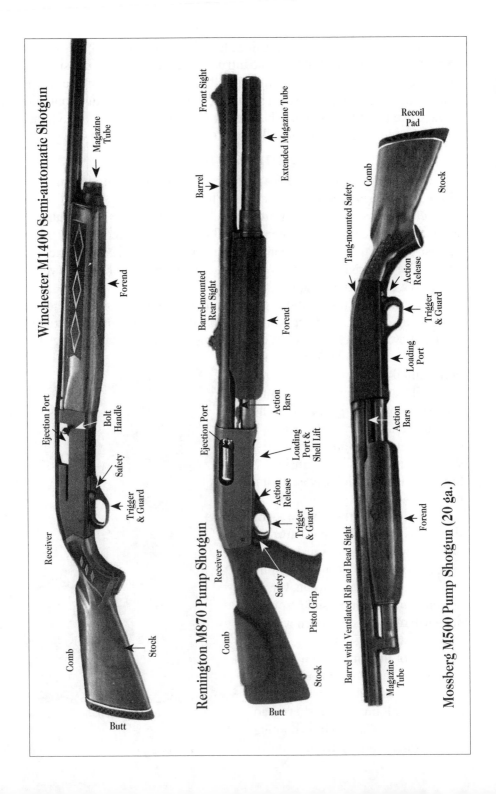

Winchester M1400 Semi-automatic Shotgun

Magazine Tube

Forend

Ejection Port

Bolt Handle

Safety

Trigger & Guard

Receiver

Comb

Stock

Butt

Remington M870 Pump Shotgun

Front Sight

Barrel

Extended Magazine Tube

Barrel-mounted Rear Sight

Forend

Action Bars

Ejection Port

Loading Port & Shell Lift

Action Release

Trigger & Guard

Receiver

Comb

Safety

Pistol Grip

Stock

Butt

Mossberg M500 Pump Shotgun (20 ga.)

Recoil Pad

Comb

Stock

Tang-mounted Safety

Action Release

Trigger & Guard

Loading Port

Action Bars

Forend

Barrel with Ventilated Rib and Bead Sight

Magazine Tube

In any home-defense plan, the downfall of the shotgun will be its weight and length. If you must hold a home intruder at gun point with the shotgun for more than ten or fifteen minutes, its weight will become onerous indeed. 12 gauge shotguns weigh around seven pounds; 20 gauge shotguns average five pounds. Compare that weight to your one to two pound handgun when deciding which home-defense tool will work best for you.

Debunking myths

You may have read elsewhere that the shotgun can be fired accurately without taking time to align the sights. This is not true. At home-defense distances like five yards, it is entirely possible to completely miss a human-sized target if the sights are not used! Skill with the shotgun, like any other defensive firearm, requires competent instruction, dedicated practice, sighted fire and trigger control. When these skills are mastered, however, it becomes a devastating weapon.

Like any of the myths about shooting, any degree of unsighted accuracy depends on achieving the same body position in relation to the target each and every time. This is not likely during self-defense, where the shot may have to be made from a position behind low cover or down a stairwell and almost certainly against a moving target or while the shooter herself moves. In personal experimentation, taping over the shotgun sights to force unsighted fire, I can usually hit fairly accurately from four to five yards so long as no movement by either the target or shooter is involved. I have further experimented firing upward from a prone or kneeling position, as one might if using protective cover, it becomes nearly impossible to estimate where the shot pattern will hit without using the sights.

What of the times when it is not so easy to hit without using the sights? What liability exists if those experimental unsighted shots had been fired anywhere but a shooting range where an earthen berm

Contrary to popular myth, a manually operated shotgun CAN be cycled with only one hand, should injury steal the use of a hand or arm in an emergency.

absorbed the pellets not caught by the target? And what could a living, moving target have done between a second shot and the first miss or blast in which only one or two pellets nicked the edge of the target? These are serious questions. The logical answer is simply learning proper shotgun technique, which includes using the shotgun's sights.

Others have written that one big disadvantage of the shotgun is that it requires two hands to operate. This is not entirely true, either. Certainly, with only one hand, it is faster and easier to fire a pistol than a shotgun, still, with advanced training, one can operate the shotgun with just one hand, including cycling a pump shotgun.

Does the home-defense shotgun still interest you? There is much to be said in its favor. No small argument is its benign image. Gun control activists have overlooked the shotgun, equating it with genteel sports like bird hunting or the refined shooting sports of trap and skeet. Possession of a shotgun remains legal in some areas where handgun possession is a serious criminal infraction.

There's a lot more to learn about shotguns before buying your own for home-defense. Considerations include shotgun selection, appropriate gauge (caliber equivalent), ammunition and shot patterning, and shooting techniques for this effective defensive firearm.

Shotgun selection

Just as handgun fit is crucial to accuracy, the shotgun must also fit the

shooter. Women face a challenge in finding shotgun stocks that are sufficiently short. One great advantage to the 20 gauge shotgun is the ready availability of "youth models," short-stocked shotguns that operate just like the full-sized models. Most full-sized shotguns have a 14-inch or longer length of pull (the measurement from end of stock to trigger), while youth models are usually 13 inches.

While it is more difficult, shotguns and rifles can be fired one handed, and training should address how to fire and operate the gun one-handed in case either the right or left hand or arm is injured in a defense emergency.

If the shotgun's stock is too long, the support arm is nearly hyper extended, instead of bent at the elbow for strength needed to hold up the shotgun and pull it in tightly into the shoulder. Without strong support from the non-shooting hand, the shooter leans back at the waist, attempting to balance the weight of the shotgun over her hips. If merely holding the gun was required, this would succeed, however when firing the shotgun, a shoulders-back stance is disastrous. When strong stance is compromised, the recoil's effects are intensified. If the over-large shotgun is a pump action, working the slide can pull the shotgun out onto the shoulder joint, where it must either be re-positioned before the next shot, or it will recoil painfully into the joint.

By now, you can see the necessity of proper stock fit. As a general rule, when the butt of the shotgun is held in the elbow crook of your bent arm, the first joint crease on your index finger should fully contact the trigger. The 20 gauge youth shotguns fit this dimension perfectly for a lot of women, and should be seriously considered when buying a home-defense shotgun. If a youth model is too short, you can add a recoil pad like the Pachmayr Decelerator, which not only dampens the felt recoil enormously, but adds length to the stock.[1]

Alternatively, the entire stock can be replaced with one with a 13-inch length of pull, like those sold by SPEEDFEED®.[2] Requiring no gunsmithing to install, this replacement stock screws onto the Remington pump or semi-auto shotguns with relative ease, and is available with or without a pistol grip for 12- or 20-gauge guns. A more expensive alternative is to buy a full-sized shotgun with a wood stock, then pay a gunsmith to cut the stock to size.

Pump or autoloader?

There is another variable in shotgun selection: type of action. For defensive use, we choose between semi-automatic and pump-operated shotguns, although the sporting world also includes side-by-sides and over and unders. The choice between a pump or semi-automatic shotgun is similar to choosing between a semi-automatic pistol and a revolver. The semi-auto shotgun employs some of the gas created by firing the shell to automatically eject the empty case and chamber fresh ammunition after each shot; the pump requires the shooter to pull the forend back to eject the empty shell, then pump it forward to recharge the chamber.

Racking the pump gun's action to eject the empty shell and chamber another round, the shooter manually controls the supply of ammunition. On a smoothly finished pump shotgun this operation can become as automatic as shifting an automobile's manual transmission: you learn to do it almost without thinking.

The great advantage of manual operation is the gun's ability to cycle the variety of powder charges as found in different brands and kinds of ammunition. A number of semi-automatic shotguns will not cycle low-powered bird shot, an inexpensive choice students favor for training. The pump shotguns just don't care, since they need not harness the gases or the recoil-impulse generated when the shell is fired to operate the gun. A pump-action shotgun can be forced to cycle when dirty or unlubricated, since it is the shooter that does the work.

On the down side, the pump action shotgun may produce more felt recoil than a semi-automatic shotgun of the same gauge. Most semi-automatic shotguns use these gases in the operating cycle, channeling gas through small holes in the barrel to cycle the action. As a generalization, an autoloader recoils slightly less than a pump shotgun.

There are, however, two types of semi-auto shotguns, and one does not bleed off any of these gases. Typified by the Benelli and Beretta, some semi-auto shotguns cycle the action using the recoil impulse or the energy from the rearward thrust of the burning gases. A recoil- or impulse-operated shotgun will hit just as hard as a pump-shotgun.

Spending more money

There are several modifications, accomplished by custom gunsmiths, that can tame the recoil. A common modification to the shotgun is a mercury recoil reducer installed in the stock. This is a popular customization to auto-loading shotguns, especially the competition 12 gauge. Gripmaker Hogue[3] markets the recoil-reducing CompStock, an assembly of springs, chains and levers that buffers recoil, especially with 12 gauge slugs. Unlike mercury recoil reducers, the Hogue stock can be installed at home. The only downside, is the length of pull, which is around 14 inches at time of this writing, too long for many women.

A barrel modification called back boring causes a similar effect by redistributing the gases created by the burning powder, and as a side benefit, re-arranges the pellets into a tighter shot group that does not spread as quickly in flight to the target. Best in the business for this after-market modification is Hans Vang, inventor of the Vang Comp System.[4]

Major modifications aside, a competent gunsmith can do much to simply "slick up" the operation of your shotgun. On the pump gun, this means smoothing away any rough places on the action bars and related working parts. Some of the same effect can be accomplished by pumping the action thousands of times, which could be accomplished practicing dry fire.

Extensive dry fire isn't recommended for shotguns, however, as it is feared that the long firing pin may crack from vibrations that run through the metal during dry fire. If your manual shotgun cycles roughly, however, you can do everything but pull the trigger, racking the action repeatedly until the parts wear themselves into a smoother fit. The action release lever will have to be used if the trigger is not pulled, otherwise the action will remain locked closed.

Another common after-market modification is shotgun sights. Many shotguns come from the factory with no rear sight whatsoever: just one or two beads on a ventilated rib running along the top of many sporting shotguns. Slug guns, set up for deer hunting, are the common exception, wearing better buckhorn or pistol style sights.

I believe a self-defense shotgun absolutely requires a good set of sights. Variations include a rear notch and front blade that are very like pistol sights; or a ghost ring rear sight that is much like an aperture sight, commonly used with a blade front sight. In my opinion, the Express Sight designed by Ashley Emerson and marketed by Ashley Outdoors[5] can't be beat on the shotgun. The latter three are excellent choices for the combat shotgun, although the beads will suffice for those who will simply pursue basic competence with their home-defense shotgun at relatively short dis-

Bead sight

tances.

Your skill with your defensive shotgun will be only as good as the practice and training time you put in with your equipment. Good technique is the first step in finding that the shotgun is enjoyable for training and informal practice. The second step is setting up the shotgun so it is comfortable. We've already discussed the mechanics, so let's outline some of the accessories that make a difference.

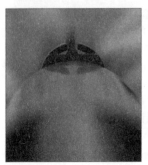

Rifle sights

Ghost-ring sights

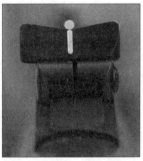

Express sights

Before you set out to replace the recoil pad on your shotgun, look at your undies. Metal parts on brassiere straps are downright dangerous beneath the butt of a recoiling shotgun! My favorite cure is the PAST Heraean Shield[6] recoil pad for women, which is secured beneath the bra strap with several Velcro® strips. Another cure is to wear a sports bra without any metal, but that won't offer any recoil protection.

If the recoil really bothers you, consider having a gunsmith fit a Pachmayr Decelerator butt pad on the end of your shotgun. This incredible accessory absorbs and distributes the recoil like nobody's business—it is well worth the price!

Technique eases the pain

An unfortunate number of men and women get the enthusiasm knocked out of them when they are given a shotgun, without instruction in proper technique before they discharge this powerful firearm. Perhaps this is why the 12 gauge shotgun is no longer in favor with many law enforcement officers. Has the weapon changed? Of course not. Most cops are simply not adequately trained with the shotgun, a weapon system that requires skill and knowledge.

If introduced to the shotgun by an unskilled "coach" the beginning shooter may relate the above sentiments. Listen up, this is important: firing the shotgun doesn't have to hurt! Let's look at why people get bruised shooting the shotgun and see if we can prevent bad first experiences, as well as offer techniques that will make shooting more pleasant.

Just like the pistol, there is a proper grip for the shotgun. Because of the shotgun's weight, there is a tendency to encircle the stock with the shooting hand thumb, a habit I fight to this day. That would work, if just holding up the gun was required. Unfortunately, when the shotgun moves back under recoil, a "wrapped" thumb can strike the nose with considerable force.

Although counter-intuitive, the straight thumb of the shooting hand is the key to avoiding socking your own nose during recoil.

Rule #1: To avoid nosebleeds on the shotgun range, point the shooting-hand thumb toward the muzzle.

Other dangers to avoid are too-long fingernails. I have seen the nails of the shooting-hand gouge the cheek when the shooting hand and face come too close during recoil. Nose-bleeds and cheek gouges don't happen to everyone: variables include the length of the stock and where the shooter cheeks the comb.

Find the shoulder pocket

Improper placement of the shotgun on the shoulder joint is the leading cause of shooting discomfort with the self-defense shotgun. A lot of folks learned to shoot a rifle as the first gun they ever fired, and attempt to apply the traditional rifle marksman's stance to the shotgun. Unlike a rifle, the defensive shotgun will be fired with heavily recoiling buckshot and perhaps even slugs. If fired with the butt against the shoulder joint, the collar bone or lower, on breast tissue, it will hurt!

To locate the proper spot for the shotgun butt, try the following exercise which I learned at Clint Smith's Thunder Ranch:[7] Put your middle finger in your shooting-side armpit; flatten your hand, and let the thumb point up. The area the thumb touches (midpoint between the armpit and center of your chest) is called the shoulder pocket. Raise and lower the shooting-side elbow, and feel the musculature move up and down the chest. If the butt of the shotgun is placed where your thumb touches, those muscles help protect against bruising.

It is my experience that squaring your shoulders to face the target is the best protection against the shotgun slipping out

X marks the spot! The shoulder pocket is magic for avoiding bruising and pain from the shotgun's recoil.

onto the shoulder joint during multiple shots. A bladed stance invites the shotgun to slip out of the shoulder pocket.

Rule #2: Find the shoulder pocket, and pull the butt of the shotgun against it firmly. This rearward pull is exerted with the strong hand, which also operates the safety and the trigger. Do not discharge the shotgun unless it is pressed tightly into the shoulder pocket, with the torso squared to the target!

Many shotgun trainers teach that raising the shooting-side elbow enhances the protection of the shoulder pocket. At Thunder Ranch, I was told the raised elbow keeps the shotgun in the pocket, so it cannot move onto the shoulder joint. Some circumstances do not permit the raised elbow, however, including extending the elbow beyond cover or conceal-ment. Personally, as a weakling, I favor a lower elbow position, for more strength with which to pull the stock into my shoulder. You can choose what works best for you.

Why is it so important to press the butt of the shotgun tightly in the shoulder pocket? The shotgun's recoil is considerable. When the shotgun is pressed tightly against the shooter's chest, the jolt of the recoil is like receiving a hard shove. It rolls you back, but does not injure. If the recoil-ing shotgun is held loosely or is actually slightly away from the shoulder, it comes back with brutal impact, and is like taking a full power, fisted punch. Which would you prefer?

Body position

There is little we can do to eliminate recoil in the defensive shotgun, yet the power of the weapon is both its strength and disadvantage. Proper grip and shoulder position mitigate most of the discomfort, yet the shoot-er must still contend with the rearward thrust, which can throw a slightly-built person off balance unless body dynamics and strength are harnessed to tip the equation in our favor.

If the shotgun shooter's legs are locked and rigid, the recoil punches the shooter back, pressed rearward all the way from the feet up. On the other hand, if the knees are bent, the legs act as shock absorbers, allowing the shooter to flex with the recoil, then spring immediately forward to regain the shooting stance.

I prefer a deep bend in the forward, non-shooting side knee, with less in the rear, shooting-side leg. The deep flex of the forward knee brings the shoulders well forward of the hips, and puts the hips forward of the rear knee and foot. The aggressive, forward-leaning posture puts all the weight of the body behind the recoiling shotgun, and uses that weight to bring the muzzle down and re-assume a shooting position for follow-up shots.

Which brings us to **Rule #3:** Lean aggressively into the shotgun to enjoy recoil control and maintain balance.

The final element of body positioning for successful, pain-free shotgun shooting is the placement of the cheek on the comb of the stock. Firm pressure between cheek and stock is essential. If the cheek is slightly off the stock, the blow can be debilitating when the shotgun recoils and strikes its operator in the jaw. Just as the stock is pulled tightly into the shoulder pocket, a firm cheek "weld" is an important way to avoid shooting pain.

An excellent after-market product for both carbines and shotguns encourages a consistent cheek weld, while reducing the amount of recoil felt on the cheek and jaw. An adhesive-backed pad, made of rubbery Sorbothane® is marketed as the Cheek-eez pad through the Brownells catalog.[8]

Rule #4: Press your cheek firmly to the stock, contacting the comb in the same place every time. There is a secondary advantage to developing a cheek weld that is a repeatable every time the shotgun comes to your shoulder. If you cheek the comb the same place every time, your use of the shotgun sights will be consistent and once the proper position is memorized, the cheek weld is the key to quick sight acquisition.

As we discussed earlier, the most common shotgun sights are a single bead, double beads, ghost-ring sights or rifle-style sights. When you cheek the stock, the sight alignment should be similar to the earlier illustrations. If the sights are out of alignment when you bring the shot-

Strong shotgunning stance counteracts the recoil's rearward thrust seen here and allows small shooter to maintain balance and control for multiple shots, even with the 12-gauge.

gun up on target, experiment with cheeking the stock on a different part of your face. Where the cheek contacts the comb will vary from individual to individual, depending on face shape, length of neck, and how well the shotgun fits the individual. I press the comb of the stock right below my upper mandible, while others contact the stock at the jawline.

Unlike classic riflery, the shotgunning stance positions hips and shoulders square to the target.

Keeping it loaded

Non-emergency loading of the shotgun consists of filling only the magazine tube. Most shotguns in common use do not have internal firing pin blocks, so are at risk of accidentally discharging if they fall or are dropped with a shell in the chamber. Indeed, this feature which is standard on later model Mossbergs, is the exception, not the rule.

This is why we do not leave the home-defense shotgun sitting in a corner or on a shelf with a loaded chamber. If the danger of home invasion is so great that there is no time to chamber a round, the problem will not be solved by a firearm. That danger should be addressed by good locks, solid doors and windows, and other precautions.

Unlike the procedure for handguns, loading the shotgun is a relatively slow and dexterity-intensive job. The shotgun's magazine is a tube beneath the barrel, nearly always accessed through the bottom of the receiver. On most shotguns, the action must be closed before the magazine can be loaded. Unmodified shotguns usually accept four rounds, although an extension to the tube may accommodate seven or eight shells. If the tube only accepts one or two shells, take it off and check for a block, commonly installed to make the gun legal for bird hunting.

Louis Awerbuck teaches his students to "trace" the final half inch of the trigger guard with the tip of the shell, guiding it into the magazine tube. On shotguns like the common Remington 1100/11-87s this brings the front of the cartridge in contact with the carrier release, which must be depressed to open the loading port. On other shotguns, his method gives an index to guide the shell into the loading port, even in the dark. Awer-

buck gained recognition teaching at Gunsite in its heyday, then began his own instructional firm, Yavapai Firearms Academy. He travels to locations all throughout the U.S. and his training is well worth the expense. He is also author of the useful book *The Defensive Shotgun: Techniques & Tactics* published by Desert Publications.[9]

Once the shell is inside the loading port, use your thumb to push on its base until it is in the magazine tube completely. Pushing against the pressure of the magazine spring, you'll feel the cartridge catch when it goes past the shell stops. Con-figured slightly dif-

Louis Awerbuck (left) teaches a dynamic shotgun class dealing with realistic targets, movement and other shooting problems.

ferently on various shotguns, the shell stops are small metal claws on either side of the mouth of the tube that keep the shells inside the tube despite the pressure of the magazine spring. Take a look now at your unloaded shotgun and find the shell stops; we'll revisit them later.

If the shotgun is brought into action, you will need to chamber a shell. Cycle the shotgun's action to move a shot shell from the magazine tube, onto the shell carrier and up into the chamber. With the pump gun, that will mean depressing the action release and pulling the forend all the way back to put a shell on the carrier, then pushing it forward so the shell is lifted into the chamber and the action locked closed.

On most semi-automatics, pull back the operating handle until the action locks open. This brings a shell out of the tube, and if you look in, you can see it sitting on the carrier. Depress the carrier release, and the action will slam closed, chambering the shot shell. Benellis and Berettas use a different sequence, due to their tactical advantage of being able to leave a shell on the carrier with the action closed. Hitting a small button mounted on the side of the receiver puts a shell on the shell lift where it can sit indefinitely until the shooter racks the action to load the chamber.

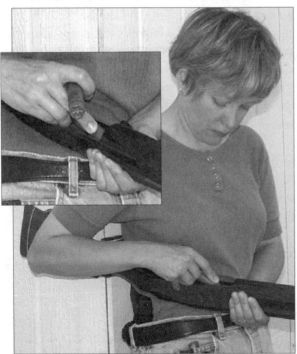

Topping off

The newly chambered shell came from the magazine tube, reducing that reserve by one. Unless the need to shoot is immediate, load another shell in the tube. Any time there is a lull in the shooting, top off that magazine tube. According to Clint Smith at Thunder Ranch, the shotgun's greatest downfall is its relatively small ammunition capacity. Keep the magazine tube full, reloading at every opportunity, he urges.

Ayoob's off-shoulder loading method is very, very sure and could be performed in darkness with good success, even with two shells in the hand, illustrated in the inset.

Smith and others teach students to reload while keeping the gun on the shoulder, pointing at the target. The shooting hand remains in position, ready to fire, while the shells are inserted with the non-dominant hand. I know women of considerable shotgunning skill and experience who report they lack the physical strength required to reload a shotgun in this manner. I felt less "disadvantaged" after reading Massad Ayoob's comments in his excellent book, *StressFire II–Advanced Combat Shotgun*,[8] where he calls this reloading method "difficult and awkward."

While I acknowledge the tactical value of loading with the muzzle on the target, I suggest the shotgunner, who after adequate practice, concludes she has insufficient strength to perform the technique quickly and smoothly, should move on to a method which serves her better. One choice is the off-shoulder loading Ken Hackathorn offers as an alternative (shown below). Keeping the muzzle pointed toward the threat, Hackathorn uses his support hand to hold the shotgun just slightly away from his torso. The dextrous dominant hand grasps the shotshells, from a strong side pocket or belt holder, and deftly feeds them into the magazine tube. Loading with the dextrous dominant hand is one of the advantages of this method, because it is faster and less prone to fumbles like dropping the shells.

Ayoob teaches grasping the *receiver* (the barrel will be hot after fir-

ing), and turning the gun over, loading port up, and stuff it full (see page 195). Alternately, you may lodge the stock's comb beneath your armpit, continue holding it on target with your shooting hand (finger outside trigger guard!) and load with your non-dominant hand.

Because the shotgun is slow to load by any method it may not be practical to reload an empty shotgun during a fight. If you have a handgun available, dump the empty shotgun and grab the smaller weapon.

Hackathorn's version of off-shoulder loading is less strength intensive than reloading with the shotgun mounted on the shoulder and uses the more dextrous dominant hand to accomplish loading the shells.

Unloading professionally

Now its time to discuss proper unloading. "Can't I just pump the shells out of my shotgun to unload?" a student always asks during our defensive shotgun classes. You could, but there is a better way that first empties the chamber, then keeps it empty for maximum safety.

First, remove the round from the chamber. Engage the safety and open the action, being careful to maintain safe muzzle direction. The chamber round should eject; you can catch it if you open the action slowly. With most shotguns, this step will have positioned a shell on the carrier. Roll the shotgun over, so the ejection port faces down. The shell on the carrier should fall into your hand. Carefully check by sight and feel to ascertain that the chamber is indeed empty.

Watching carefully to assure the chamber remains empty, close the action. The chamber should remain empty as you close the action, because you have removed the shell from the carrier. On most shotguns, new shell shouldn't feed from the magazine tube without fully cycling the action. Turn the gun over, so you look down into the loading port. With the tip of your finger, depress the shell stop. The shell may remain in place, constrained by the shell stop on the opposite side. Use your thumb to wiggle the shell free. When it pops past the shell stops, slip it out of the loading port and repeat the process until all the shot shells are out of the magazine tube.

Before declaring the shotgun unloaded, open the action again and double check both the chamber and magazine tube visually. Insert your finger into the empty chamber for a manual inspection. Reach lower and feel for the magazine follower to be sure a shell is not present. A brightly colored follower, like those manufactured by Hans Vang and others, give a more certain visual inspection.

If the gun is simply being stored, the magazine tube should be empty so the compressed metal spring does not take a "set."

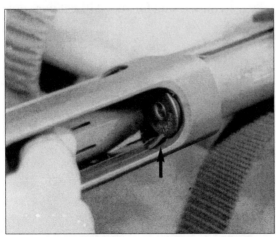

The shotgun's shell stops (indicated by arrow) hold the shells in the magazine tube. To unload, they must be overcome manually.

Don't be discouraged if this unloading process is difficult at first. The thumb and fingers seem too big for the limited space inside the loading port, yet it feels like you need three hands to get the job done! Persevere, and you will learn how to jimmy the shell stops, carrier and shell into position where the shell pops out easily.

Learning how to properly unload your shotgun is important. It keeps you from having to chamber and manually eject each round when you need to unload the shotgun, reducing wear and damage to the shells. Safety must come first, over any perceived inconvenience! PUMPING THE SHELLS OUT OF THE MAGAZINE TUBE IS THE MARK OF AN AMATEUR.

Shotgun ammunition

Like the handgun, the shotgun is just a launching platform for the working part of the home-defense equation, the ammunition. All you really need is a reliable firearm that has sufficient power to do the job for which it is purchased. If that job is home-defense, stay with 12 or 20 gauge shotguns. Defensive shotgun ammunition needs adequate penetration to provide "stopping power." And while a primary concern is stopping an assailant, with the home-defense shotgun, we also must guarantee that all the projectiles strike the target.

Shotgun ammunition choices range from slugs to buckshot to small game loads and bird shot. To give you an idea of the differences within just one category, Federal Cartridge Company sells a half dozen different slugs in weights ranging from the $1\,^3/_4$ ounce 10 gauge slug, $1\,^1/_4$ or 1 ounce slugs for the 12 gauge; a $^4/_5$ ounce slug for the 16 gauge; the common $^3/_4$ ounce slug for the 20 gauge; and finally a $^1/_4$ ounce slug for the .410 caliber shotgun.

The list is several times longer for buckshot, since it comes in seven different sizes of shot, and may be loaded in either 3-inch "Magnum" shells or 2 $^3/_4$ inch "Maximum" shells for 12 gauge, 16 gauge or 20 gauge shotguns. On the topic of birdshot and field loads, the choices are as numerous as the different gauges multiplied by ten or

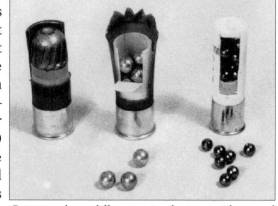

Cut-away shows different projectile sizes inside several different shells. (L-R) 12 gauge 1 oz. slug, 12 gauge 00 buckshot, and 20 gauge #3 buckshot.

more sizes of shot and BBs used to hunt everything from tiny doves to large geese.

Of all the choices in shotgun ammunition, we need to study two categories for home-defense: buckshot and slugs. Some will advise you to load your home-defense shotgun with bird shot "because it won't go through the walls." That statement is incorrect, false and dead wrong! We have fired birdshot through three layers of half-inch sheet rock. Whether it would penetrate the body cavity is questionable, yet there remains potential for harm to delicate tissue like eyes.

However, that is not my argument against such advice. Even without intervening obstacles like walls, penetration by field, game, or bird shot is too shallow to reach vital organs on an adult-sized assailant, a problem compounded by thick clothing, obesity or heavy musculature. In bare ballistic gelatin, birdshot will penetrate just six to eight inches, but performance is seriously impaired by placing multiple layers of fabric on the face of the gelatin block. By comparison, 00 buckshot can penetrate up to 16 inches on bare gelatin, and manages to penetrate 10-12 inches beyond fabric layers.

The larger the projectile, the deeper the penetration. This is certainly the case with the next kind of shotgun ammunition we'll discuss—slugs. The one ounce, 12 gauge shotgun slug is capable of devastating stopping power. Some folks, including Marty Hayes, director of The Firearms Academy of Seattle, have gone so far as to recommend loading only slugs in the 20 gauge shotgun—bypassing buckshot altogether. Personally, I would temper that advice, commenting that the slug is simply designed to do a different job than buckshot.

Slugs best serve the shotgunner's long distance and extreme accuracy shooting needs. With decent sights, a skilled operator can hit accurately with a slug out to 100 meters, farther than we might anticipate using the gun in home-defense, yet a very real necessity for law enforcement officers or for hunters. Slugs can also penetrate glass, wood, automobile panels, needs more common to law enforcement duties.

Buckshot choices

With buckshot, penetration is influenced by size and velocity of the projectiles, more than the gauge of shotgun from which it is fired. Larger buckshot is recommended where heavy clothing or intervening obstacles may interfere with penetration. It would be difficult to anticipate an obese or leather-clad assailant, however the differences between summer and winter weather in many areas can indicate heavy clothing.

Because body mass is also impossible to predict, it might be more sensible to load the home-defense shotgun with a medium-sized buckshot like the common 20 gauge #3 buckshot, or #1 buckshot in the 12 gauge. While penetration is not likely to be as deep as with the more common 00 buckshot, the smaller shot simultaneously introduces a lot of projectiles creating a devastating wound channel.

The following chart lists common buck shot sizes, with the largest shot shown first. To help you compare, the size of the shot is described here in caliber, which you will remember from handgunning is the measurement of the projectile at its greatest diameter.

Shot Size	Shot Shell Description	Caliber of Pellets	Qty in Shell
000 buckshot	3-inch Magnum 12 gauge	.36 caliber	10
00 buckshot*	2 $^3/_4$-inch Maximum 12 ga.	.33 caliber	9
0 buckshot	2 $^3/_4$-inch Maximum 12 ga.	.32 caliber	12
#1 buckshot	2 $^3/_4$-inch Maximum 12 ga.	.30 caliber	16
#2 buckshot	3-inch Magnum 20 gauge	.27 caliber	18
#3 buckshot	2 $^3/_4$-inch Maximum 20 ga.	.25 caliber	20
#4 buckshot **	2 $^3/_4$-inch Maximum 12 ga.	.24 caliber	27

* With 00 buckshot, 3-inch Magnum shells contain 15 pellets; 2 $^3/_4$-inch Magnum shells contain 12 pellets.
** With #4 buckshot, 3-inch Magnum shells contain 41 pellets; 2 $^3/_4$-inch Magnum shells contain 34 pellets. The magnum shells recoil viciously, in my opinion, and are to be avoided.

Buckshot choices range from (L to R) a 12 gauge shell containing #4 buckshot, the 20 gauge's #3 buckshot, 12 gauge #1 buckshot, 0 buckshot, 00 buckshot and 000 buckshot (all 12 gauge) in different caliber pellets and with varying quantities per shell. Shot spread will vary with the different sizes, pellet quantity and gauge, as well as the shotgun itself.

In choosing buckshot, you will sometimes face additional choices. For example, #4 buckshot is sold in Magnum 3-inch cartridges containing 41 pellets, $2^3/_4$-inch Magnum shells with 34 pellets, and $2^3/_4$-inch Maximum shot shells with just 27 pellets. The last, 27-pellet shell will recoil less than the Magnum cartridges, which must push the heavier payload of more pellets. And, if you've chosen the 20 gauge, the #3 buckshot recoils considerably less than 00 buckshot from a 12 gauge.

Shot spread

Until we understand how buck shot behaves after it exits the shotgun's barrel, the idea of simultaneously unleashing from nine to 27 pellets seems pretty risky. Testing your own shotgun is the key to knowing where and how it will hit with different brands and sizes of buckshot. The distribution of the shot pellets striking the target is called "patterning." Every shotgun will pattern differently, and the same shotgun will pattern differently with different ammunition. Only hands-on experience at the range will show you what to expect from your own shotgun and the ammunition you have chosen.

Expect the buckshot pattern to expand at approximately one inch per yard between the muzzle and the target. That means that shot fired across a seven yard bedroom should cluster in a six to eight inch circle, depending on ammunition and the shotgun. Two additional factors affect how tightly the shot patterns. The first is the shot pellets, the second is the addition of a choke tube, which can be used to constrict that column of shot as it leaves the shotgun barrel. Another method to tighten shot groups is backboring, which lengthens the forcing cone and changes how the shot travels down the barrel. Hans Vang of Vang Comp Systems is the leading source of this defensive shotgun modification.

Since we're addressing ammunition, let's discuss how the shot itself affects the size of the pattern. Shot can be either copper-plated or bare lead. (Steel shot is also sold, but as it is used in game loads, not buckshot, it is not applicable for self-defense purposes.) The harder copper-plated shot reduces denting that can occur while the shot is being propelled down the barrel. A dented pellet that is no longer spherical will "fly" erratically, expanding an otherwise good shot pattern.

One example of copper plated shot is Federal's low-recoil Tactical Buckshot or their standard-recoil Premium Buckshot. At a product introduction, I was able to see for myself the good condition of the Federal copper-plated buckshot after it had traveled down the barrel of a Benelli Super 90 shotgun, penetrated several layers of fabric, and stopped about a foot into a block of 10% ballistic gelatin.

Is it confusing?

While much of the foregoing is intended to broaden your understanding, I've included it to give you an overview of shotgun ammunition. At the risk of oversimplification, I believe it boils down to home-defense choices of a 20 gauge or 12 gauge shotgun, determined by your strength, stature and how much recoil you can control. For home-defense, I would load the shotgun's magazine tube with buckshot, and keep some slugs available for unexpected circumstances.

The 16 gauge shotgun would also make a fine home-defense weapon, but the owner may have trouble finding a readily available variety of ammunition, especially at budget prices like those that come along at large chain stores and gun shows. And, like any other defense weapon, the shotgun is only as effective as the shooter's training, practice and confidence which comes only from training and regular practice.

Tactics for the home-defense shotgun

As discussed at this chapter's beginning, the shotgun is an excellent survival tool for the defender ensconced in a safe room, prepared to defend self and family if the intruder ignores warnings and breaks through the door. This scenario presumes that the defender knows the direction in

#4 Buckshot fired 10 yards from the target using 12 gauge shotgun.

#1 Buckshot fired 10 yards from the target using 16 gauge shotgun.

which the shotgun pellets will travel and is certain no innocents are in the path of the shot. The shotgun is best applied to home layouts where children's rooms lie behind the defender. In home layouts where rooms are scattered throughout the home, young children will need to be quietly evacuated to the safe area before firing begins. If, within the constraints of your circumstances, this does not seem possible, the shotgun may not be your best choice.

In apartments, safe rooms must be arranged so the area into which the pellets will fly is backed by bullet stopping material, something in short supply in urban housing. While nothing short of heavy concrete or masonry construction gives full bullet stopping ability, careful shot placement into known uninhabited directions is necessary for those who plan to use the shotgun's multiple pellets in home-defense.

The shotgun is not the best weapon to take prowling through your house to check out a noise in the night. Not only are house searches dangerous, the long muzzle of the shotgun may alert a waiting intruder to your approach, so he may grab and lever from your hands. The shotgun's size makes it more difficult to move quietly, avoiding furniture, lamps and other household objects. Return to lesson one: don't search your house if you believe you have an intruder in the home!

00 Buckshot fired 10 yards from target using 12 gauge shotgun; 2 slugs in the head.

#3 Buckshot fired from 10 yards with 20 gauge shotgun; two 20-ga. slugs in head.

Weapon retention techniques have been developed for the shotgun; if you adopt this weapon you owe it to yourself and your loved ones to get the proper training in its use and retention. Know how to accurately shoot your shotgun, and know how to keep it in your hands if the assailant tries to take it from you. One advantage of the "Arm Tuck" shooting stance (shown below) taught by Massad Ayoob (who credits its development to Bill Groce) is the ability to withdraw the muzzle somewhat while remaining in a firing stance.

The shotgun, handgun or rifle each has defensive advantages and tactical disadvantages. Serious self- and home-defense practitioners often pursue proficiency with more than one defensive weapon system available, to increase the chances that they and their family can survive criminal attack.

1   Pachmayr, 1875 S. Mountain Ave., Monrovia, CA 91016 818-357-7771.

2   SPEEDFEED®, P O Box 1146, Rocklin, CA 95677. 916-630-7720.

3   Hogue Inc., P O Box 1138, Paso Robles, CA 93447 805-239-1440.

4   Vang Comp Systems, 234 Orange Ave., Goleta, CA 93117. 805-964-7956.

5   Ashley Outdoors, 2401 Ludelle St., Ft. Worth, TX 76105 817-536-3517. www.ashleyoutdoors.com.

6   PAST Corp., 210 Park Ave., Columbia, MO 65203. 314-449-7278.

7   Training resources quoted: Thunder Ranch, HCR 1, Box 53, Mountain Home, TX 78058. 830-640-3138; Lethal Force Institute, PO Box 122, Concord, NH 0330, 603-224-6814; Yavapai Firearms Academy, P O Box 27290, Prescott Valley, AZ 86312 520-772-8262.

8   Brownells, 200 S Front St., Montezuma, IA 50171 641-623-4000 www.brownells.com.

9   Desert Publications, P O Box 1751, El Dorado, AR 71731.

10 Police Bookshelf, PO Box 122, Concord, NH 03301. 603-224-6814.

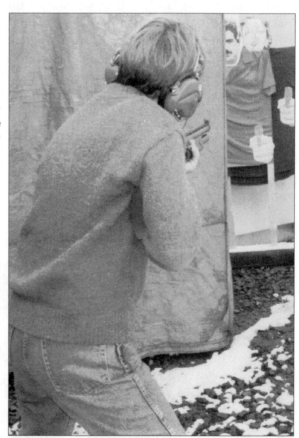

In Ayoob's "Arm Tuck" shotgunning stance, the comb of the shotgun is pressed firmly into both the front and rear tendons of the armpit. The barrel is seen in the lower peripheral vision and can thus be roughly aimed.

20

Rifles & Carbines

While the handgun is versatile and portable, the home defender can put the bulkier rifle or shotgun to very effective use defending herself and her family. In some emergencies, a rifle fills a role in the self-defense armory that can be filled by no other firearm. This truth is reflected by municipal and rural police agencies' addition of a light rifle to the patrol officer's weaponry. Although I am a vocal proponent of the shotgun's capabilities, I cannot ignore the value of the rifle in circumstances like the Los Angeles Bank of America robbery February 28, 1997 in which police engaged two well-armored criminals in a high-round count gun fight. This is only one of a number of notable examples of criminals using body armor that is likely to stop handgun bullets.

Is there any place for the light rifle in the private citizen's self-defense arsenal, or is it best carried by cops, sheriffs and soldiers? I asked John and Vicki Farnam, who responded with a story.

A woman and her children were in their remote Montana home when a warning came over the radio that authorities believed an escaped, dangerous prisoner was in their

The Ruger Ranch Rifle (Mini-14) is a .223 caliber rifle that has none of the militaristic appearance that seems to so alarm legislators and anti-gun activists.

area. The announcement put the woman in a heightened state of awareness, so she was prepared when some while later she spotted a lone figure walking up her mile-and-a-half driveway.

Standing on her porch, rifle in hand, she ordered the man to come no closer. The stranger ignored repeated verbal warnings, and when he kept coming, the woman shot him in one knee. With determined aggression, the man continued to approach the home. Her second shot took out his other knee. The woman held him at gunpoint for law enforcement officers, who confirmed her fear that she had indeed encountered the escapee.

The rifle extended this woman's perimeter of safety dramatically. The escapee would have been too close for the safety of the family if he had approached to within the distances most handgunners would confidently make a shot into a moving aggressor. The tactics of this situation underscore the very real danger of being overrun by the aggressor and sometimes their accomplices, as well. People who are shot with a handgun can remain aggressive and assaultive for some time before the wound incapacitates them. In this dangerous time gap, the home defender can be killed or seriously injured if the invader is too close. The rifle extends the effective marksmanship range to prevent this danger.

Federal legislation restricting features available on the AR-15 style rifle has run the cost up in recent years, until what was once an affordable home-defense carbine, has become a major equipment investment.

At the same time, we can legally and ethically shoot only a person we have clearly identified as a deadly danger to ourselves or other innocents. The rifle's ability to control distance must be balanced by the home owner's clear-headed analysis of the situation.

"We're hearing the term 'urban rifle' to describe a rifle used for defense between 30 and 150 meters," Farnam elaborated. These distances allow target identification and verbal warnings, both vital elements of legally justifiable self-defense. At even closer distances, if circumstances allow all-out escape, it is heartily recommended.

As you know, I am a enthusiastic advocate of the personal defense shotgun. Having admitted that, even I will point out that most shotguns are effective only out to 12 to 14 yards with buckshot, unless the shooter has a safe backstop behind the assailant which she knows will absorb a buckshot pattern that has spread beyond the size of the assailant's body. A slug can certainly be substituted in such circumstances, but unless they have shot the weapon extensively with slugs the shotgun-armed home defender may lack confidence in their marksmanship, especially at longer distances. Because they are discomfited by the recoil, few shooters practice enough to realize the long-range capacity of their shotgun loaded with slugs.

A rudimentary rifle or carbine is unhampered by the problem of shot spread, and smaller calibers are almost free of recoil. Over and over, we see beginners' faces light up after firing their first shot through a .223 carbine. The comparatively light recoil of the rifle or carbine has another advantage, that of nearly instant recoil recovery and the ability to accurately deliver rapid, multiple shots. For this task, it will be hard to surpass the .223 Rem. caliber (5.56x45 metric). This medium sized caliber will generally show muzzle velocities of 3,000 feet per second for the common 55 grain bullet.

Rifle ammunition balances the momentum equation on the velocity side, not the mass element. Even so, an assailant may be hit with a .223 bullet without immediate incapacitation. The harder-recoiling .308 Win. (or metric 7.62x51) is capable of a more decisive result, but its compromises eliminate some of the advantages of a defensive carbine.

Overpenetration of larger caliber rifle bullets must be considered, too. Most hunting rounds are capable of penetrating wall after wall of modern housing construction. This very real hazard makes selection of ammunition that will not over penetrate exceedingly crucial with any rifle, even a .223. In *Ultimate Sniper*,[1] author John Plaster reports that a .308 bullet that has gone through a body maintains the power of a .357 Magnum handgun bullet, although it has lost half of its velocity. These concerns should serve as very serious warning to those considering a rifle for home-defense in a multi-person household, apartment building or densely populated area. Remember, even if your reason for discharging a firearm is completely justified you remain responsible for harm inflicted beyond your immediate threat.

Further, few semi-automatic rifles are chambered for the larger caliber, and tend to be considerably more expensive than the .223 carbine. The .308 rifle will be heavier than most .223s. Finally, the concussion of firing a .308 inside a confined space is exponentially more disorienting and deafening than doing so with a .223, which is certainly bad enough. For the same reasons, other hunting rifle calibers like the 30-30, .30-06 or 7mm Magnum should not be considered suitable for home-defense.

So many rifles

Semi-automatic rifles that work well for ensconced defense scenarios include the ubiquitous "black rifles," derived from Eugene Stoner's original AR-15 design. Although Colt's Manufacturing was long the primary source of AR-15s, Olympic Arms, Bushmaster, DPMS, Armalite and others have all but eclipsed the financially-troubled Colts at the time of this writing.

The prevalence of state and federal gun restriction laws has put the price and availability of the AR-15 and its clones out of reach for some shooters. A very serviceable alternative is the semi-automatic Ruger Mini-14 or Ruger Ranch Rifle chambered in .223 Rem. It is not too heavy and is short stocked for a good fit for small-statured shooters right out of the box.

The Ruger Ranch Rifle, the civilian version of the Mini-14, is drilled and tapped for scope rings, so installing optical sights is easily accomplished, depending on the use envisioned. For home-defense distances, the rifle's rudimentary peep sight should serve just fine, however if you begin to enjoy practice and casual competition with your Ruger, I expect the sights will be the first thing you wish to upgrade.

Both the Ranch Rifle and AR-15s are box magazine fed, with general availability and affordability of 20 and 30 round magazines still good as this is being written. The 10 round magazines currently legally manufactured will serve just fine for the home-defense purpose, with the larger capacity magazines valued for competitive and sport shooting. This feed system makes reloading or switching to specialty ammunition a quick, relatively simple task, which is not true of other rifle operating systems.

Radical caliber change

An alternative "urban" rifle is a carbine chambered for a pistol cartridge. "Some people argue that a carbine is just a big, clumsy handgun," John Farnam contends "but that's not true." He noted that this kind of carbine has a considerably longer sight radius than a pistol, that most handgun bullets develop much higher velocities in the long barrel and these guns generally have sights far superior to the handgun.

The pistol-caliber carbine recoils considerably less than a handgun firing the same cartridge and is relatively quiet when discharged. These features make them very pleasant firearms with which to practice and simply enjoy recreational marksmanship. Farnam reported that he has seen women shoot hundreds of rounds comfortably with such carbines, becoming deadly accurate in the process. Excellent "companion" guns to the handgun, they allow the owner to keep one caliber of ammunition on hand for use in both weapons.

The carbine offers good accuracy to 100 meters, for threat management where an assailant has been clearly identified and has disobeyed warnings to leave. One of the older choices for this kind of firearm is the Marlin Camp Carbine, chambered for 9mm or .45 ACP pistol cartridges. Most civilians won't shoot enough rounds to wear the Marlin out, although Evan Marshall reported that some Michigan police departments had attempted to put the Marlin Camp Carbine into service and found it would not stand up to the rigors of law enforcement training and day-to-day use. Farnam recommended the HK 94 as

The Marlin Camp Carbine in .45 ACP packs a punch, yet is fun and easy to shoot, guaranteeing more enthusiastic training and practice.

an alternate, although you will pay much, much more for this weapon than the popular little Marlin.

Likely a better alternative comes from Sturm, Ruger & Co., which in 1996 released a 9mm carbine in a sleek synthetic stock that was quickly followed by a .40 S&W version. Resembling the .22 LR 10/22, greatly beloved of competitive shooters, the Ruger Carbine uses the same box magazine as do Ruger pistols, and is available with a ghost ring rear sight or can be fitted with telescopic sights. The entire outfit is light weight, durably-made, and very, very pleasant to shoot.

Another pistol caliber carbine that deserves thoughtful consideration for home-defense is the manually operated lever action. While we think of this firearm as the province of those fun-loving cowboy action shooters, it has the potential to serve the serious duty of defense, too.

Common calibers include .38 Special, .357 Magnum, .44 Special and .44 Magnum, with cartridges generally loaded in a magazine tube banded beneath the barrel. A round is chambered by working the lever, although due to the nature of the gun's safety mechanism (it has only a cross bolt

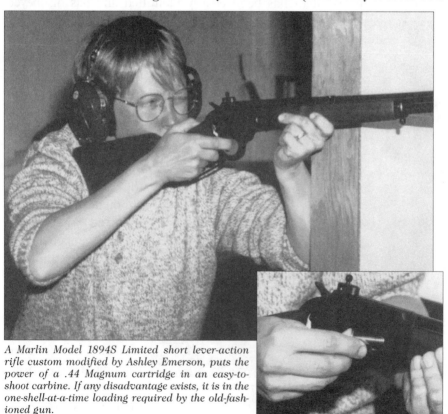

A Marlin Model 1894S Limited short lever-action rifle custom modified by Ashley Emerson, puts the power of a .44 Magnum cartridge in an easy-to-shoot carbine. If any disadvantage exists, it is in the one-shell-at-a-time loading required by the old-fashioned gun.

safety) I would do with the lever-action carbine as I do with a shotgun: store it chamber-empty until ready to use.

On initial consideration, it might seem that a manually operated gun like a lever-action carbine or a pump shotgun may be too slow for self-defense, although that cycle differs little from the pump shotgun. With practice and habituation, the manual cycle to remove the empty shell and replace it with fresh ammunition can become smooth, natural and quick. The reload *will* be slower, because only one cartridge at a time can be loaded into the magazine tube, introduced through a tiny loading port.

Pistol caliber carbines are not universally loved and accepted, because despite their rifle-like size, the ballistic performance of these guns will never approach that of a .223 or .308. However, I believe they deserve serious consideration for home-defense for their user-friendly operating systems, handgun ammunition compatibility, easy aiming qualities, milder noise and recoil when discharged, and the tendency for hollowpoint pistol ammunition's to stop inside the assailant's body. Without doubt, the pistol caliber carbine is less powerful, yet that very factor is attractive to people who will not or cannot engage in live fire practice more than four or five times a year.

Sighting issues

Probably the most common rifle accessory is optical or telescopic sights. Because rifles have seen more traditional service in hunting and competitive sports, a telescopic sight or "scope" has been the common response to increasing the ability to see and aim at distances of 100, 300, 500 yards or more. With defensive rifle uses occurring within the 10 to 50 yard range, and 100 yards an extreme distance for justifiable defense by a private citizen, in this venue most scopes can represent more liability than advantage.

Not only does the addition of a scope, scope rings and bases add to the weight and bulkiness of the rifle, it introduces a fragility to the sighting system that is not present with fixed, iron sights. In addition, the field of view through a telescopic sight is much narrower than our 360° world, making it possible to *Modern optical sights like the Trijicon ACOG* completely overlook a second *have limited magnification and a lighted dot* assailant. Finally, on the popular *with which one aims, instead of cross-hairs.*

and common AR 15 style rifle, scopes are commonly mounted on the carrying handle, placing them very, very high, especially difficult for use with the smaller female facial structure.

Fixed iron sights, while preferred for home-defense, also have their own challenge. The greatest one is learning and remembering that the rifle, designed for more distant targets may not hit the exact spot covered by the iron sights at closer distances. Primarily a concern for the AR 15 rifle system, on which the rear sight is mounted atop the carrying handle several inches above the barrel. Called "mechanical offset" and perhaps comparable to parallax between the viewfinder and lens of a camera, an across-the-bedroom shot with an AR-15 will strike several inches below the point covered by the front sight.

Competent training and serious practice lets the rifle owner commit these disparities to memory, and if a precise shot is required at close distances the shooter will compensate for the mechanical offset by holding the sights an inch or two higher than the spot they wish to strike. If these possibilities seem obscure, let me admit that more than one police officer

Mechanical offset occurs at the close distances likely in home-defense, because the sights are located several inches above the barrel, "offsetting" the close range impact. In this illustration, the line drawn from eyes, through the aperture rear sight and across the top of the front sight shows the shooter's aim point, while the actual impact would occur at the point at which the muzzle contacts the target.

has put a crease across the hood of a patrol car behind which they took cover before shooting. The mechanical offset of their AR-15's sights gave a clear sight picture, but the barrel itself was obstructed by the car body, a difference forgotten in the heat of an emergency. Consider also the need for an ocular-cranial shot to a hostage-taker or the very real possibility of an armed assailant partially protected by a brick wall or other obstacle before dismissing the challenges that mechanical offset can cause in real-life self-defense. Practice on both near and far targets ingrains the modifications to sight picture that must be made to compensate for mechanical offset.

If discussing home-defense, it is difficult to imagine any viable threat beyond 50 yards, unless the carbine's role includes "protecting" a garden, livestock and pets. While it is common to sight in, or"zero," a rifle or carbine to hit precisely at a 100 or even 200 yard distance, it may be more reasonable for the home-defense rifle owner to sight their gun in for 50 yard targets. Even then, a rudimentary understanding of bullet trajectory, mechanical offset and such factors is necessary.

Upon leaving the rifle's barrel, the bullet begins a slightly upward path of travel, called its trajectory. After the bullet reaches the apex of a gentle arc, it will begin to drop. Naturally, different bullet weights and calibers have flatter or sharper trajectories and begin their descent at different distances.

Thus, the rifle and carbine shooter's task is to zero their gun and defense cartridge at a reasonable distance. From muzzle contact distance to the 50 yard zero suggested above, the bullet will *rise* to intersect with line of sight (the point on the target on which the sights are precisely aligned). Most .223 ammunition will strike only an inch or two higher at the 100 yard line, and begin to drop at that point.

Training issues

In addition to the pure marksmanship issues associated with the light rifle, there are additional lessons to be learned if this is the tool with which you intend to defend self and family. One of the biggest impediments to women enjoying rifle shooting is the weight of the gun compared to their

-- Line of Sight
— Bullet Trajectory
100 yards
Sighted in for 50 yards

A depiction of bullet trajectory shows the difference between line of sight and actual bullet impact before and beyond the distance at which the rifle is "zeroed." In the drawing, bullet drop is somewhat exaggerated for illustrative purposes.

upper body strength, not so great an issue for the male shooter. Adaptive techniques that run counter to classic competitive rifle methods can help the female shooter overcome the problem of all that outboard weight.

Perhaps the most simple cure is taking a braced or a kneeling position whenever possible. In addition to stabilizing the gun, it reduces your own target size and should be considered if circumstances allow you to ensconce and fight from a protected position from which you need not move. In addition to taking a lower position, be sure the support arm is directly beneath the stock, maximizing skeletal support, as well as exploiting the natural strength of the bicep.

Traditional marksmanship coaches have taught rifle shooters to stand upright, with the rifle centered over legs and feet, shoulders angled back behind hips and the spine in something of an S-curve. This position is very relaxed and perfect for the slow pace of classic competitive courses of fire. Introduce the stress and rapid-fire requirements of a home-defense emergency, however, and the marksman's position deteriorates.

Two decades ago Massad Ayoob developed his combat handgun system, dubbing it StressFire, to indicate techniques that succeed when stress and adrenaline affect the body. He applies many of his basic StressFire concepts to the rifle, including taking a tight grip on the rifle and leaning the upper body dramatically forward. A deep, wide stance provides excellent balance and makes the weight of the rifle seem less onerous. Deeply flex the forward, support-side leg for further stability.

A wide stance goes a long ways to eliminate the troublesome wobble of the rifle sights across and on and off the target. If sight wobble is unchecked, the shooter usually tries to snatch the trigger when the sights cross the target, a reaction that results in trigger jerk and abysmal accuracy. Instead, Ayoob has developed several radical techniques that further steady the rifle long enough to make an accurate shot.

The most unusual of the two he has dubbed the "Rifle Isosceles," and although it looks and feels odd, it is extremely effective. Traditionally the rifle shooter is quite bladed to the target. In Rifle Isosceles we square the hips and shoulders to the target. Instead of tucking the support arm beneath the rifle, it locks straight out. Instead of bending the legs for balance, the knees are locked. Functional for only short periods of time, this unique stance will stabilize the rifle against the tremble of adrenaline and to a good degree, the ragged breathing of physical exertion.

Coupled with the StressFire rifle stance, Ayoob teaches a grip modification of which I have made extensive personal use. The non-dominant hand usually supports the forend, with the elbow as completely beneath the rifle as possible. This is an excellent, traditional shooting technique

that will work for all rifles. Shooting an AR-15, I use Ayoob's "Death Grip" method extensively, but it is not recommended for other rifle types on which it will disrupt feeding reliability

The shooting hand clutches the pistol grip firmly, while the support hand takes a hard grip on the magazine well and pulls too, firmly. The effect is something like the isometric tension of the Weaver handgun shooting stance, and compensates nicely for limited upper body strength.

An entire book could be written on additional riflery techniques, and indeed many qualified authors have written works worth the reader's time.[1] I present these vignettes in this context to underscore that rifle shooting techniques for most women, whether with a rifle or handgun, must address the particular issues of upper body strength, overall body size and physique to enhance the female shooter's control on the gun.

The rifle's appeal

Evan Marshall believes the rifle fills several roles in civilian self-defense. Many people simply find the "long gun" easier to accept. They've been socialized to perceive rifles and shotguns as legitimate, having seen their

Ayoob teaches ambidextrous use of the rifle to maximize protective cover when it exists on the non-dominant side. Sighting with the non-dominant eye is taught when the shooter is able to do so.

fathers and grandfathers hunt, he points out. Yet, some are simply unwilling to learn to shoot the shotgun. They've been told the recoil will be painful, and they may be unable to find suitable training. The smaller caliber rifle appeal to this person.

Some jurisdictions deny citizens the right to own a handgun. Because of the social acceptance of hunting sports, owning a rifle or pistol-caliber carbine may remain permissible. In the wake of strict laws on firearms possession in Canada, we've seen an increase in home invasions and burglaries. As government and society attacks American gun owners' rights, the skills and ability to defend home and family with a less impugned firearm

than the hand-gun may well become vital. Either the shot-gun or the rifle, in the hands of a determined, trained individual can do much to assure the safety of innocent citizens and those in their care.

1 Suggested reading: *The Fighting Rifle,* Chuck Taylor, 1984, and *The Ultimate Sniper, An Advanced Training Manual for Military and Police,* Maj. John L. Plaster, USAR, Ret.1993. both published by Paladin Press, Gunbarrel Tech Center, 7077 Winchester Circle, Colorado 80301. 800-466-6868, 800-392-2400. *The Farnam Method of Defensive Shotgun and Rifle Shooting,* John S Farnam DTI Publications, Inc. P O Box 18746, Boulder, CO 80308 970-482-2520.

Modifications to classic riflery methods, including what Ayoob teaches as the "Death Grip," eases handling the weight of the carbine.

21
Tactics to Survive
What You Can't Avoid

We've discussed the importance of avoiding trouble, however women must still be prepared for dangers that we can't avoid. Having a handgun doesn't make the danger go away–it only provides a tool that helps you control it, much as a fire extinguisher gives you the chance to stop a fire before your house burns. Further, possession of a self-defense gun is not enough, you must know you can fire it accurately, keep it loaded and operating, and that the tactical choices you make are the safest available to you under the circumstances.

Because entertainment is obsessed with violence, we see thousands of portrayals of victimization: assaults on attractive, helpless women who are raped or murdered because they had no defensive plan, skill or weapon. I believe women are being trained by television to be victims. As you watch the repeated television scenes of men assaulting woman, mentally envision an appropriate response from the victim: imagine how you would respond. Affirm now that you will fight back viciously to avoid being hurt. Prepare your mind to survive, to direct your body to fight off the assailant.

Mental preparation comes from making *The Decision* to survive as detailed in Chapter 2. Training with your defensive firearm and planning what you would do if faced with a violent assailant prepares your body to respond quickly when your mind recognizes danger. Those who have not trained and planned out ways to fight off a lethal assault freeze in terror or react hysterically, unable to mount a counter-attack. Defense training ingrains defensive skills with or without firearms. Practice and repetition record them in the muscle memory so the body can respond to attack without step-by-step direction from the mind.

In the discussion of rape, I am personally disturbed when victims and those who counsel women talk about the kinds of injury women are willing to endure *before* fighting back. A report coming from the southern states tells of a woman who, when abducted, elected not to use a revolver she carried in her purse. She felt she could accept sexual assault, and it was not until the rapist escalated the violence that, deciding she could not accept death, she drew her gun and killed the man. She endured extreme emotional repercussions, including months of immobilizing fear in which she was unable to leave her bedroom. She bore the condemnation of a small town that sympathized with a dead assailant and believed lies spread by the rapist's family. She survived a legal nightmare, forced to argue and prove her right to shoot a man who was trying to take her life.

And yet, I do believe she was fortunate to be alive. Many who do not fight off an assailant from the first indication of lethal assault lose the narrow advantage that tactical control of the situation might have given them. They are killed, too often after hours of anguish and torture.

The first step of tactical readiness is your determination not to be a victim. Decide that from the first indication of danger you will fight. Decide that your life is worth defending. Making that determination should lead to a decision to get good training, not just in how to shoot, but in threat management and fighting skills, too.

Survival tactics

Did some of the physical self-defense information in Chapter 9 give you a fresh respect for edged weapons? The first rule of survival is controlling the distance between you and the assailant. Against contact weapons like bludgeons and knives, the distance you can create to escape or draw your gun may well determine your survival. Remember, protective cover against contact weapons consists of obstacles that impede your attacker. If the threat is made with a firearm, however, good tactics suggest you protect yourself behind bullet-stopping cover. Protective cover is often confused with concealment. Anything from draperies to a sheet rock wall provides concealment, but will not stop a bullet. In taking cover, we seek objects sufficiently dense to impede a bullet–a heavy gauge dumpster, a retaining wall, a large tree or automobile engine block.

Develop a cover-conscious mindset. Look around in restaurants, walking down sidewalks, in department stores and banks. Try to recognize objects that would stop bullets. Envision crouching behind the cover. Could you return fire without endangering other innocents? In your home, practice shielding yourself behind heavy furniture like a solidly filled bookcase, then expose only the arms and only as much of the head as necessary to aim your gun at an assailant. If nothing else is available, even the lumber in a door frame is preferable to full body exposure, however the home-defense conscious individual will arrange furnishings to provide good cover in hallways, at stair heads and in bedrooms.

If attacked on the street, cars, large trees, buildings and other environmental objects provide some safety in which to hunker down and return fire. If you use a car, crouch behind the engine block for best bullet-stopping protection. You may read that few handgun bullets penetrate a car door, and films of the FBI shooting up old 1960s vintage cars, show few bullets penetrating to strike a paper target in the driver's seat. However, a number of years ago, I watched John Farnam fire several .45 caliber bullets in one door and out the opposite side of a Volkswagen Rabbit, and although this excellent instructor emphasizes the limited power of handgun ammunition, we learned that the light construction of modern automobiles can't be trusted to stop a bullet.

The trouble with crouching behind the bulk of the engine block is that the only way to return fire is to rise and expose your head and shoulders as you take aim and shoot or expose legs and feet around the bumper. When possible, get behind a heavy wall or something larger than a car. In extremely exposed conditions, employ utility poles, large trees, concrete construction and other heavy fixtures to protect your body's central mass and if absolutely nothing is available, use movement or a low crouch to make yourself a harder target to hit.

A crouch behind a car takes advantage of its immediate, if limited, protection. The crouch keeps the shooter mobile and able to run to better cover if a second assailant flanks her.

If you shoot from behind cover at an assailant, avoid predictable actions that the assailant can second-guess. If you repeatedly peek out in a full standing position, he can simply approximate the position at which you last appeared, line up his gun sights on that spot and shoot when you next peek out. Instead, if the cover is vertical, take a shot from full standing, drop to a crouch for a follow-up shot, and so forth. Behind horizontal cover, scuttle from side to side keeping your assailant off guard and confused.

A common use-of-cover error is peeking out and ducking back behind cover repeatedly, instead of carefully exposing only as much of the eye as necessary to view a limited area, carefully clearing the next small portion and so on. Once you are sure the danger is NOT in the area you have viewed, look beyond that space, and do not yield back the area you have just cleared by letting it out of your view.

Using cover, even in a limited area search, is best done slowly and methodically and with extreme caution. Bobbing and ducking in and out of cover accomplishes little. In real life–compared to training scenarios–a live intruder is likely to fire through walls if he has seen you. If you perceive a threat, engage it appropriately with verbal commands and with gun fire if necessary. Ducking back behind cover telegraphs a lack of decisive control and may cost you dearly.

When using cover, especially outdoors, remember the vulnerable area behind you. Don't be so focused on the assailant in front of your gun that you forget he may have a companion approaching from behind. During lulls in the action, reload and take a 360° danger scan to be sure no one else is approaching from other directions. Consciously fight the natural compulsion to tunnel in on the perceived source of danger. This

Effective use of cover means keeping everything but gun and eye protected as much as possible.

is one of the tachy psyche effects addressed in the third chapter. Like many training facilities, we teach students to physically turn their heads, looking left, right and behind after a stress shooting drill. While it is important to search for additional dangers, the physical activity also helps dispel the tunnel vision that accompanies a lethal assault.

On the move

If your assailant moves or an accomplice approaches, you may have to leave the relative safety of your bookcase, brick wall, or engine block, and move to a different place of cover. This is no time to imitate the movies,

where a gunman makes his way stealthily down a hall, gun muzzle pointing upwards. This is a good time to mimic a jack rabbit dashing across a busy highway. At this moment, your future is as questionable as the bunny's.

If overrun, locate a different source of cover, then sprint to it. During movement, decock the gun or engage its manual safety and take your finger all the way out of the trigger guard. It doesn't belong on the trigger unless you have your gun raised and aimed at a target you have decided to shoot. The stress and activity of your dash could cause a negligent discharge. Don't point the gun skyward, as also "taught" in the movies. Particularly, in urban situations, the responsibility for all your bullets equals the safety of innocent people who live nearby. Be assured that a bullet discharged at an upward angle can return with sufficient energy to do harm, as has been the case in cities like Portland, OR, where a gang-related shooting resulted in an unlikely death quite some distance from the altercation. Keep both hands on the grip, and pull the gun in tight against your mid-section. This "civilian" ready position

Maintaining a steady shooting stance while using cover requires training and practice. denies the gun to an assailant who may grab it, yet keeps it instantly ready. In this position, a close range shot is as fast as thrusting the gun into your line of vision, seeing it silhouetted against your target and pulling the trigger.

The same technique is advisable if, ignoring all advice, you have decided to go through the house searching for the source of a disturbing noise. Find a safe place where you can't be flanked to survey the area for danger. Instead of standing in a doorway, staring at the entire room, use the door frame and adjacent wall to shield you from view of a possible intruder. Remaining behind this concealment as much as possible, look out into a limited area and be sure it is empty, before moving further away from your concealment to look deeper into the room. Called "slicing the pie," this method is illustrated below.

When satisfied that the area is clear, move rapidly to the next cover, gun tucked in close to your body. When approaching doors, if you believe

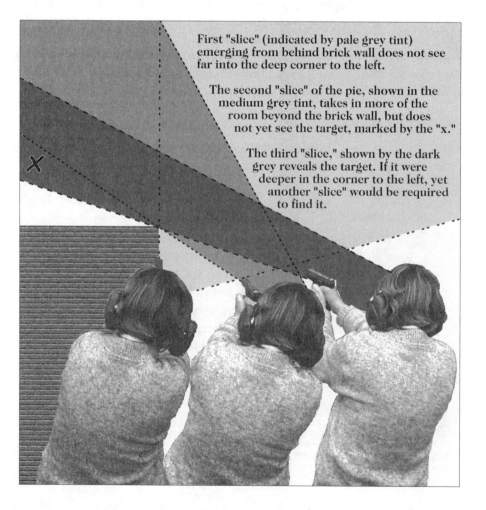

First "slice" (indicated by pale grey tint) emerging from behind brick wall does not see far into the deep corner to the left.

The second "slice" of the pie, shown in the medium grey tint, takes in more of the room beyond the brick wall, but does not yet see the target, marked by the "x."

The third "slice," shown by the dark grey reveals the target. If it were deeper in the corner to the left, yet another "slice" would be required to find it.

the area behind you is free of threat, remain on the outside, and roll out the eyeball nearest the cover and peek quickly into the next room.

Jim Cirillo, survivor of multiple armed confrontation during his service with the New York Police Department, calls using just one eye to search beyond cover the "Hammerhead Shark method." Like the shark, expose only as much of your head as necessary to align one eye with the gun sights. Tilting the forehead back and looking across the bridge of the nose exposes even less of the cranium, as taught by Massad Ayoob. Using cover effectively is rarely comfortable, and often somewhat contorted, however it is worth the effort to learn use of cover methods and learn them well.

Do these search techniques sound terrifying? Clearing a house of dangerous intruders is better left to a trained police team and their canine assistants.

Shoot and move

If there is one noteworthy change defensive shooting instructors have instituted in the past decade, it is teaching self-defense practitioners to move away dynamically, should a self-defense emergency require an armed response. Learning from tragedies detailed in both police and private citizens' after-action reports, I am firmly convinced that failing to move, whether away from the threat or toward cover, is very dangerous indeed.

If you've experimented with moving and shooting, you've probably concluded that you can shoot accurately or move quickly, but not simultaneously. One of several things may happen: you are compelled to pause as you aimed and fired the gun, or the impulse to make the gun fire when the sights cross the target spoiled a smooth, surprise trigger break. Based on such experiences, many have concluded that moving and shooting are mutually exclusive. Effective movement technique, however, overcomes these impediments. The key is changing HOW you move.

Let's start with the feet and legs that provide our mobility. When human beings walk, the upper body bobs up and down as each foot hits the ground and lifts off again. The bouncing motion is accentuated at greater speed. The pistol, extended at the end of the arms, also moves with the jolt of each foot fall, enough to jerk its small sights completely off the target. Our first concern, then, is curtailing upper body movement while the legs remain in motion.

The upper body is not responsible for the undesirable motion. To blame are the feet and legs as they step and strike the ground. Striding on rigid legs is no solution, because locked knees will only intensify the up and down jog of even a quick stride. Instead, a deep and sustained knee bend is the key to reducing the up and down motion of any biped's gait.

Taught for years as the "Groucho Marx" walk, the deeply bent knees that mimic the comedic gait of this famous entertainer serve as shock absorbers to cushion the bounce. The more deeply flexed the knees, the smoother is the glide of the upper body. When teaching this skill, I tell students "if it doesn't feel extreme, you're not doing it right!"

This gliding gait is an elemental skill taught by Ken Hackathorn, who is famous for classes emphasizing moving and shooting. Students are shown to contact the ground with the heel, then roll weight to the toe when moving forward. This natural sequence is consistent with the way we walk, and serves best when advancing. When retreating, however, the hazards of unseen ground require touching toe first, then rolling the weight back to the heel. In any case, when walking backward, toe to heel reduces bounce, again a necessary goal of the moving shooter.

The Groucho Marx walk goes a long way toward smoothing the shooter's gait, still, the sights can be steadied even more if the shooter's arms

Moving quickly backward or laterally away from the target may regain the initiative when the assailant is dangerously close or cover too far for immediate protection.

are bent, as well. Speed shooters often fire from a locked-elbow Isosceles stance, using the rigid limbs to overcome recoil. However, when movement is added, locked arms accentuate the natural up and down bob. The best shooters know and use a variety of stances, and can change from an Isosceles to the Weaver position when movement disrupts the sight picture.

At close ranges, explosive retreat to the rear or to either side is about the only way to regain the initiative against an already drawn gun or other weapon. Because running backwards is slower, retreat may be best accomplished by moving in the step and drag technique. Long taught to law enforcement officers for a variety of defensive tactics applications, step and drag movement allows the skilled practitioner to cover ground very rapidly without simply turning and fleeing. Like the Groucho Marx walk, the knees remain bent, so the shooting platform of torso and arms remain sufficiently steady to produce effective hits.

In step and drag movement, the leading foot takes a big step in the direction of travel. As soon as it is planted, the other is brought quickly to the first. As soon as that foot is on the ground, the lead leg takes the next lunge. Practice is needed to produce smooth, steady motion, with beginners prone to dip with the lead leg's first stride and rise as the other foot moves. Smooth it out by bending the knee of the weight-bearing leg more deeply throughout the stride. This valuable movement pattern gives the shooter the ability to cover rough terrain quickly and surely, even in poorly lit conditions.

The step and drag method of movement is highly recommended at The Firearms Academy of Seattle for police applications because the torso remains frontal to the target, maximizing body armor. Further, it keeps the shooter in position to deliver accurate shots. Finally, unless cover is directly behind, the line of attack is better disrupted by moving away at an angle.

Trainers disagree on the question of how to move while shooting. Some favor the protections of a well-practiced step-and-drag pattern, while others believe in the natural toe-forward step buffered by the deeply bent knees of the Groucho Marx walk. In reality, mastering both methods is good insurance.

We live in a 360° world. Movement can be toward any of the points on the compass and infinite degrees in between. On a shooting range, safe muzzle direction generally restricts the realistic practice of moving to cover, all out retreat, and shooting during this kind of movement. An innovative match director, instructor or practitioner can find ways to mimic real life and challenge marksmanship skills, however.

Regardless how the lower half is moving, the upper body–your torso, arms, and head–becomes the "gun turret" of the "tank," an analogy used by Massad Ayoob. The "turret" moves laterally to keep the gun sights on the target as the angle between the moving shooter and target becomes increasingly oblique. The arms holding the gun in a two-handed grip will need to bend more deeply to keep the gun aimed at the target, and the two-handed grasp may need to be sacrificed when moving to the non-dominant side.

In altering how we use feet, legs, and arms, we've been working with gross motor skills. In addition, the moving shooter must perform the small motor skill of working the pistol's trigger smoothly. If the gross motor movement skills were learned well, the sights should float steadily on the target during rearward, angled or lateral movement.

If the shooter has not eliminated the bounce or jog in their gait, they will fail miserably when trying to fire at the fleeting moment the sights cross the center of the target. In their haste and excitement to catch the shot while the sights are on target, trigger control is lost. If the sights wander on and off the target, return to practice smooth, proper foot movement, bent knees, turreting torso and bent arms. Perfect the carriage and there will be sufficient time for a partial sight picture and smooth trigger squeeze.

When the movement has been refined to a glide, learning to squeeze off the required number of shots while moving in any

Real-life confrontations have taught us that not all defensive shooting will be done from a perfect shooting stance.

direction is surprisingly easy. You may have received the old advice of triggering the shot at the exact moment the foot touches the ground. The choreography required to accomplish this feat is far too intricate to accomplish during a competitive stage of fire or a defensive emergency. Besides, attempting to work the trigger as your foot touches down has the same effect as trying to fire the instant the sight picture is on target.

Fight the impulse to take a step, pause and fire, then take the next step. Speed, whether in pursuit of better match score or in running for safety, does not allow this luxury. If you wish to stand and shoot, dash to your shooting position, then stand and deliver. Moving and shooting means just that: firing the gun while you are in motion. With practice and proper movement technique, what once seemed impossible is quite manageable.

Moving marksmanship is not a skill learned at full speed. It takes deliberate practice, started at a slow pace with care taken to fire while in motion. After breaking through the mental barrier to firing with feet in motion, add a little speed and then a little more speed. Only with time and safe practice does this become a natural response.

Close encounters

If face-to-face with an assailant who has a drawn gun, don't try to draw your own in response unless you are in rapid motion or behind cover. Without cover or retreat, the assailant's advantage is too great. He can shoot you before your gun ever leaves the holster. Even a respectable 1.5 second draw can't beat a gun already in the hands of an "amped-up" assailant.

At face-to-face distances, you're basically staring death in the eyes unless you have learned disarming techniques. At a minimum, take immediate action to get off the line of force—in this case, out of the bullet's path. The addition of a "parry" to keep the gun's muzzle off you is the next step in handgun disarming. Even the first two steps, applied aggressively, can open a window of opportunity to fight off an armed assailant. Another element in disarming techniques engages the assailant verbally, distracting him from your intent to take away his weapon. John Farnam writes that speaking creates an impression of self-assurance, granting a bit of a psychological edge, letting the assailant know that although you face his handgun, you are not frightened into immobility.

Faced with multiple assailants, control the most immediate threat first—focus on the most dangerous weapon, or if the assailants are not armed, the nearest or one acting most aggressively. A study of body language and pre-assaultive cues is invaluable, whether faced with a single threat or a small group of people who have not yet revealed their intentions.

If the danger is so serious that you must use your gun, you may need to shoot the most dangerous assailant first, then take aim on other members of the gang while determining if they are continuing to attack. With practice, the shooter can move from one target to another with smoothness and control. Learned and practiced on three or four targets in a row, the shooter fires the first shot, and instead of regaining the sight picture on the same target, lets the recoil move the sights onto the next target, fires the next shot, and lets the recoil carry the front sight to the next target.

If the last assailants disengage and flee, you must let them go. To shoot a retreating criminal is not necessary, nor is it moral, or legal. As a fight is broken off, be it against one or several assailants, scan the nearby area to be sure there are no others closing in and to ascertain the compliance of any wounded or remaining attackers.

A gunfight may require more than one magazine or revolver cylinder of ammunition. Jim Cirillo relates one case in which a patrolman was a mere fourteen or fifteen feet from a felon. Both men emptied their revolvers at each other without hitting. "The guns were just going click, click, click," Cirillo relates. The officer began to search in his pocket for ammunition and came up with car keys, a nickel and a dime, which he attempted to load, duplicating the police range procedure of stowing extra qualification ammunition in the pocket. The officer became flustered, and when he remembered that his ammunition was in a pouch on the belt, fumbled and spilled the rounds on the ground. When the officer knelt to retrieve the ammunition, the felon rushed him. Having put several rounds in the revolver's chambers, the officer closed the cylinder and began pulling the trigger. After several pulls, the loaded chambers lined up and the officer was able to strike the attacker in the chest at close range.

Inexperienced shooters claim they would count their shots in a gunfight, so they'll know when to reload. Under the stress of a lethal encounter, no one, no matter how experienced or hardened, can afford the distraction of counting the shots they've fired, even if it were possible to have the presence of mind to do so. Much of the time, the indication that the gun is empty comes when pulling the trigger has no effect. Cover would be a nice thing to have when it's time to take that two to ten seconds out of the fight to reload your gun. If none is available, angled or lateral movement while reloading increases your chances of survival. Prior practice reloading could make the difference between survival and dying at the hands of a freely advancing assailant.

The foremost rule of gun defense is to shoot no faster than you can hit the target. In view of the physical fight-or-flight adrenaline rush that takes place in an emergency, it's not surprising that in encounters involving police officers and criminals, only a fraction of the bullets fired hit. Unfortunately, only accurate shots can stop the danger. Your sights must be lined up on the assailant and remain undisturbed during the trigger pull. In most cases, several, perhaps many, shots will be required to stop the assailant.

Television misinforms and misleads us to expect one handgun bullet to spin an assailant off his feet and halfway across the room. In the informative book, *Handgun Stopping Power* co-author Evan Marshall relates an

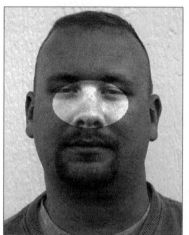

incident where a fighter took seven or eight rounds of .45 ball ammunition in the torso, then caught a city bus to the nearest hospital. Could this person have continued a killing assault if he had wished? Absolutely. Beyond the anachronism of non-hollow-point ammunition, Evan cites case after case of assailants continuing to fight after multiple hits from 9mm, .45 ACP, or .357 Magnum caliber hollowpoint ammunition. You must condition yourself to continue to fire your defense handgun until the threat ceases.

If several center-of-mass shots have failed to deter an advancing assailant, consider aiming the next shot at the head, or at the pelvis as recommended by Massad Ayoob. This large bone is integral to body support, and breaking it will drop him to the ground. If the assailant is armed, however, you cannot consider him no longer dangerous. You have only taken his mobility, not his ability to shoot.

Top: To be effective head shots need to aim at areas unprotected by the "helmet" of the skull. Bottom: From the back, the medulla oblongata is a tiny target in the brain stem that can produce an instant shut down if it can be hit. All else is admirably armored by thick, curved bone.

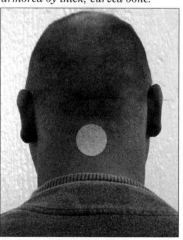

Instant stops are difficult to achieve, requiring exactly placed shots to the brain's medulla oblongata at the base of the skull. The brain can also be accessed by exact shots through the eye sockets, or with less probability, through the mouth. At any tactically-safe distance, achieving this level of marksmanship under high-stress conditions is very difficult.

Shoot to stop

Advice to shoot merely to frighten or wound an assailant is dangerously wrong. Amateurs giving that advice recommend "just injure the criminal," implying that shooting his legs is more justifiable than employing deadly force. Merely pointing a gun at a human being is employing lethal force, regardless of your aim point or intent. By producing a firearm, you have escalated an argument, robbery, or other lesser crime into a deadly force incident. Don't misunderstand: you need not and should not wait for an assailant to fire the first shot if innocent life is endangered. However, if you decide to shoot, you must be convinced that you are in immediate and unavoidable danger of death or crippling injury. If that is your conviction, aim at vital areas with intent to stop the threat that initially caused you to draw the weapon. Never fire unless you believe your life or the life of another is at risk.

Additional hazards lurk in the warning shot. You have told your assailant that he is facing a gun without a determined human behind it. Sensing your lack of resolve, he may advance and take your gun, or draw his own and shoot you, recognizing that you cannot bring yourself to harm him. Finally, you are responsible for injury your warning shot may cause another person. Remember, handgun bullets can pass through wood, windows, and other barriers quite easily.

A street assailant obeys no rules of engagement and subscribes to no code of fairness! Your confirmation of danger may be a punch that knocks you flat on your back. This scenario is an excellent argument against small-of-the-back holsters and a warning to learn physical skills to recover from

Survivor of multiple line-of-duty gunfights, Jim Cirillo teaches his students to fire with great accuracy from several "fallen" positions, as he demonstrates above.

being knocked down, as well as learning to shoot from a variety of positions.

Firing from a fallen position may be necessary if you have been injured in the fight. Jim Cirillo teaches prone shooting methods as part of his Downed Officer Survival Course. In extreme, close-in assaults, one would simply line up the sights on the assailant and pull the trigger. At greater distances the gun can be braced atop or between the drawn-up knees as the body contracts into a fetal position. I have found Cirillo's braced-gun positions extremely accurate.

In addition, learn to fall and roll out of your assailant's reach. Martial arts, as an adjunct to handguns, again proves valuable. Training halls have mats to break the fall, and any good school can teach students how to fall without injury, and how to roll up and regain their balance, as well as teaching good kicks and traps to execute from the ground with feet and legs.

If you are hit with a bullet, continue to fight for your life. Remember that very few handgun wounds are immediately lethal. What will prove lethal is if you stop fighting and let your attacker walk up and kill you. Ignore the fear, ignore the blood or pain, and center your front sight on the assailant's chest and keep pressing the trigger in controlled, rapid fire. When the assault stops, check your wounds, apply pressure where needed and get medical attention. People who have been hit by handgun bullets report the initial sensation was like taking a hard punch. Under the fight-or-flight adrenaline rush, they often do not realize they've been shot until later, when the blood draws their attention to the gunshot wound.

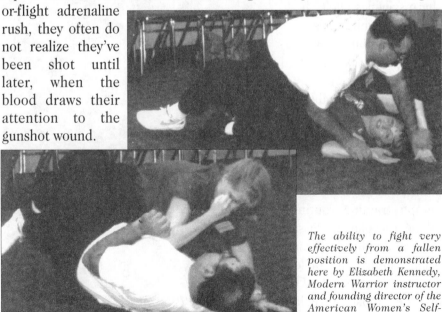

The ability to fight very effectively from a fallen position is demonstrated here by Elizabeth Kennedy, Modern Warrior instructor and founding director of the American Women's Self-Defense Association.

Controlling an assailant

If your shots put an assailant on the ground, don't assume that he is incapacitated. You must maintain your distance, and preferably stay behind cover, while taking control of the situation. Check the assailant's hands for weapons that he could use to renew the assault. Do not approach a fallen assailant or attempt to tie him or restrain him. This is still a dangerous human who wishes you harm. This is a time for control; you don't want a negligent discharge of the gun to allow his heirs to allege that you vengefully "finished him off" after he no longer posed a threat. Have your double action gun's safety off with the weapon ready to fire in double action mode. Single action handguns should be on-safe, with the thumb riding atop the safety for a quick flick into "fire" mode. Keep your gun fixed on the assailant, and keep your finger outside the trigger guard to avoid a startle response that might make you unintentionally fire the gun.

Don't let the assailant engage you in conversation; limit your communication with him to brief, forceful commands. Short, sharp syllables elicit obedience while minimizing the amount of time your nervous system is occupied with the speech act. Humans are capable of only limited simultaneous activity. It is nearly impossible to continue coherent speech and fire a handgun at the same time. We choreograph training routines, taking role-playing "assailants" at dummy-gun points using dummy guns or low-velocity paint pellets. One of the most revealing lessons comes when order-

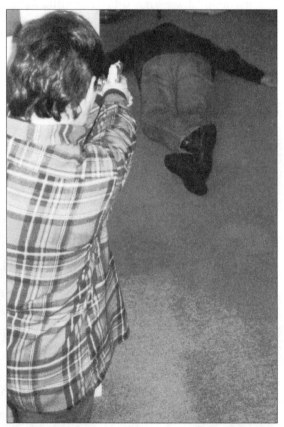

Placing a subdued assailant in a controlled posture from which he cannot see you helps interrupt attempts on his part to distract you.

ing the assailant to assume a hands-above-head position. While the command is being voiced, role-playing "assailants" can usually draw their dummy gun and "shoot." The other student is often incapable of returning fire while speaking their commands. In practice, students are often far more compliant than a real life burglar or intruder.

Stress causes "motor mouth," making advance memorization of a very brief set of commands preferable. Practice and emphasize the necessity of delivering the commands slowly, distinctly and clearly. Yelled at the warp-speed symptomatic of adrenaline and fear, many verbal the commands are unintelligible. Neither the perpetrator nor the witnesses will be able to report what actions were ordered, when law enforcement investigates the situation in the aftermath. "A crazy woman ran in and started screaming gibberish," they will recount.

Delivered in command voice, expelled forcefully from the diaphragm, the commands are brief and explosive. The first:

"DON'T MOVE!"

when forcefully delivered has a nearly physical force that can bring action to a temporary standstill. Then:

"DROP THAT WEAPON!"

is the next command if you see a gun, knife or bludgeon in his hands. If not, it may be appropriate to command,

"DON'T TOUCH THAT WEAPON!"

Assuming he intends to draw a weapon he carries, improvise a bludgeon from any object he can reach, or grab for your drawn handgun you would now command:

"SLOWLY, RAISE YOUR HANDS."

If you find you must hold an assailant at gunpoint until help arrives, order him to take slow, controlled movements that you can monitor. Keep any movements you order slow and controlled. Deny any opportunity for the assailant to rapidly turn and renew his assault on you. With his hands at waist level, an assailant can pull a gun from his belt and fire before you have time to react.

What then follows, as taught at Lethal Force Institute, are orders to slowly turn and face away from you, kneel, cross ankles and slowly drop to the floor, lying face down with hands and arms fully extended. Know where his hands are at all times. Keep distance and objects between you to increase your zone of safety against a surprise attack. When he is prone and facing away from you, you can scan the area for accomplices, reach for a nearby telephone, and dial 911. At the last moment, you can safely holster your own weapon before the police come through the door.

If surprised by the police and ordered to drop your gun, you must comply immediately. The first officers on the scene have no way to determine if you are the home owner or the intruder. By working your way into a safer area, some distance away from the assailant, you will have less worry about dropping your gun where the intruder can grab and use it.

Further discussion of holding an assailant at gun point appears in *In The Gravest Extreme*,[1] by Massad Ayoob, an excellent primer for tactical information. Formal training in handgun tactics is essential for the person who carries a gun for self-defense. Lethal Force Institute or instructors trained by Ayoob, and John and Vicki Farnam are all excellent sources of training. These and other tactical skills are taught in classes by our own Firearms Academy of Seattle, as well. Additional written material recommended is Farnam's *The Street Smart Gun Book*,[1] along with Gabe Suarez's book *Tactical Advantage*,[2] published by Paladin Press.

Having practiced and thought out what you would do if assailed under varying circumstances is important. As John and Vicki Farnam are fond of saying during their training courses: **"Have a plan."** Predetermine how you would respond if a knife wielder rushed at you on a crowded street. Think about how you would react in a deserted street at midnight if approached by a threatening person. See the images in your mind. Feel your body ready to make the appropriate response.

Some might say this constitutes pre-meditation. An attorney with whom I am friends counsels his clients to establish a safety-conscious lifestyle. Instead of arming only for criminal assault, he teaches us to carry fire extinguishers and emergency flares in our cars, install back up fire detectors and fire extinguishers in our homes, and make overall safety a way of life. Careful, responsible people, he stresses, are far easier to defend, when he can demonstrate that it was their life-long practice to prepare for all kinds of dangers, not just criminal attack.

---

1 Ayoob's *In the Gravest Extreme* and Farnam's *The Street Smart Gun Book* are published by Police Book shelf, P O Box 122, Concord, NH 03301.

2 *Tactical Advantage*, by Gabriel Suarez, published by Paladin Press, Gunbarrel Tech Center, 7077 Winchester Circle, Colorado 80301. 800-466-6868, 800-392-2400.

22

Kids & Guns

Possession of firearms carries considerable responsibility. While learning to avoid becoming the target of criminal assault, we would be greatly at fault if we fail to take safety precautions to balance the gun's dangers against its great power to save threatened human life.

When faced with the hot topic of children and guns, the element of gun owner responsibility has never been more crucial. Exploiting a society that puts children's needs near the top of our legislative agendas, those who would take guns from the hands of private citizens have used child safety to fortify their gun banning agenda. Even so, the notorious lies told in this effort do not absolve each gun owner from the responsibility to keep their guns out of children's hands, as well as help their own children grasp the precepts of firearms responsibility at an early age.

Numerous women have concluded that the danger possessing firearms poses to their children exceeds their danger from criminal predators. These families have fallen victim already, victim to the lies propagated by gun ban advocates. I believe it is entirely possible to possess defensive and sporting firearms while raising a well-adjusted family that will share your values of personal responsibility.

Are the statistics right?

We are told repeatedly that guns are responsible for the deaths of up to 17 children per day, an alarming "sound bite" for any parent. Fatality figures for young people are not sorted to eliminate youths shot while committing a crime, or even 19 and 20 year olds killed during gang and drug activities, according to researcher Dave Kopel. Writing in *National Review*, he points out that the daily death rate for children 14 years and younger is 2.6 per day, and for children under ten, 0.4 per day.[1] Even with the incidents of fatal gun accidents at its lowest level since 1903, anyone responsible for a child's well-being must surely ask "what steps can I take to assure my child won't be injured with my firearms, or by guns owned by other families?"

For every parent who has decided keeping their children strictly away from guns there is a child who is curious, perhaps even fascinated, by firearms, a widely propagated symbol of adulthood and power. We have television to thank for this misapprehension, and we have ourselves to blame for the great influence television has on most children. The American Association of Pediatrics estimates that American children and teens view from 22-28 hours of television per week, viewing enactments of 10,000 rapes, murders and assaults per year. Media reform activists point out that in nearly three-quarters of the dramas, aggressors went unpunished; in well over half of the scenes, the victim was not portrayed as feeling pain; and in over a third of the scenes, violence was portrayed as humorous.

In families accustomed to heavy television use, parents sometimes argue "I tell my kids TVs not real. We know the difference." Yet psychologist and researcher Lt. Col. David Grossman suggests just the opposite. Having spent part of his service career analyzing how the military taught recruits to overcome their natural resistance to killing the enemy, he now is a leading voice arguing that violent television and video-games have overwritten the natural resistance to killing in American youth. Grossman proposes that children as young as 18 months undergo desensitization to killing while watching television. These little minds are unable to distinguish between reality and the images on TV, he explains. The adult emphasizes that "It's only TV," yet the little child absolutely cannot tell the difference, even if they tell their parents they understand the difference. "A three year old child('s) ... brain is not cognitively developed enough to distinguish fantasy from reality," he writes.[2]

The only gun handling most children witness is to draw, point, and shoot, as learned from cartoons and by actors portraying criminals and police officers alike. Put a gun in the hand of a young viewer and the TV-trained response is to point the gun at a person and pull the trigger. Kids have been taught this deadly response in their own living room, sometimes in the presence of their parents.

TV drama gives guns an attractive mystique. Shown in the hands of the popular actors, they represent power, command respect, and are integral to the climax of the show. Is it any wonder that children want toy guns to play with? Is it any wonder that children sneak out their parents' guns when the parents are away, and experiment with holding and aiming (and sometimes tragically firing) these deadly weapons?

Prevention's the best cure

The Center for Disease Control reported that handgun and long gun accidents killed 20 children ages 1-4 in 1997, compared to 34 children under age of 5 killed in gun mishaps in 1984. The National Safety Council states that handgun accident fatalities took the lives of between 50 and 55 kids under the age of 15 in 1980.[3] *Gun accidents are preventable.* You can keep your children out of these statistics.

What a tragedy it is when a child is killed or injured with a firearm obtained by a parent for the defense of that very child! Terrible misunderstanding couples with uneducated carelessness to allow these horrors. One common gun myth suggests that children can't pull a heavy double action revolver trigger or rack the slide of a semi-auto to get a cartridge into the chamber. That may be true under "test" circumstances, but children are cunning and will figure out how to use leverage, pushing the slide against another object, pulling that heavy trigger with both fingers, and applying other yet-unthought-of ways to load and fire the weapon. The same principle can apply to some safe boxes that use gimmicks to secure the gun.

These parents have exposed young McKenzie to guns from babyhood, and to this five-year-old, they have little mystery or attraction. Although she enjoys the one-on-one attention of shooting with her mom and dad, she prefers to color pictures after 10-15 minutes.

Hiding the gun is absolutely ineffective. As a child, didn't you find where your parents hid your birthday or Christmas present at least once, probably repeatedly? A locking safe or safe box with key is about the only effective "hiding" place. Keys must stay on the parent's person, however, not be left where the child can pick up and use them.

An acquaintance of mine, relating how she taught her son about gun safety, emphasized "demystifying guns is the best way to be certain a child's curiosity is handled in a safe way." Commenting that she was a "good kid," this same woman confessed that she got into her father's locked gun cabinet on a regular basis as a child, for she knew the location of the key!

Dispel the myth

In addition to keeping children safe with the family's guns, parents must prepare their children for the day they find an unsupervised gun in someone else's home. The best way is to remove the firearm's attraction. Tell your children a gun is an emergency rescue tool, much like the fire extinguisher or rope and ladder used to save lives during a house fire.

When TV or a film shows gun use, discuss it with your children. If the portrayal was inaccurate, for example, if a gun-wounded hero appears the same evening with just a bandage over a shoulder wound, explain to your children that in real life that person would be (a) dead (b) unable to use the arm (c) hospitalized for a lengthy period, but definitely not back on patrol! Explain that death is a very real possibility when a firearm is used. A gun's impact can be demonstrated in safe live fire at an outdoor shooting range. Fire into melons or water jugs to illustrate a bullet's destructive power. While actual ballistics are different, this is an impressive way to introduce young children to the handgun's purpose: destruction.

Repression has never decreased attraction. Your child's fascination with guns will only increase when you tell him or her that guns are "just for adults" and that they must never, never touch one. Children crave adult experiences. Find safe, appropriate ways to give your kids responsible involvement with your firearms. Your child's first hands-on experience with your guns can be during cleaning. Make the weapon safe: put all ammunition in a separate room, then invite the child to help you clean the gun.

Show the child how the gun works, and how to check that the gun is empty, emphasizing the first two rules of safe gun handling:

TREAT EVERY GUN AS IF IT IS LOADED.

NEVER POINT A GUN AT ANYTHING YOU ARE NOT WILLING TO SHOOT.

Your example is the most effective teacher. Enforce safe muzzle direction, do not allow the gun to "sweep" family members while you prepare to clean it. Decide what "help" the child can offer: perhaps by cleaning semi-auto's feed ramp or scrubbing the front of the revolver's cylinder with a nylon toothbrush. Older kids can "detail" the crevices and small recesses with cotton swabs.

Having taught the children to treat every firearm as if it is loaded, instruct them to leave any gun where they find it and get an adult to secure it. It may be appropriate to let your children know you will reward their safe behavior if they leave any place a gun is brought out without your express approval. Do not try to teach them to unload guns. The potential for disaster is too great.

Should children shoot?

Children of shooters will probably want to go to the range with their parents and will soon ask to fire the guns. Under direct parental supervision, the child may be allowed to first watch and hear the guns being fired.

Selected gun cleaning tasks bring parent and the young child together in safe, supervised experiences with firearms, dispelling some of the attraction of the gun for the little one.

Be sure to put hearing protection muffs and safety glasses on the little ones, even if they are only at the range to observe and enjoy time with mom.

On the range, begin drilling the other rules of safe gun handling. Explain the reasons for these rules and be sure you demonstrate them perfectly all the time.

KEEP YOUR FINGER OFF THE TRIGGER (AND OUTSIDE THE TRIGGER GUARD) UNTIL THE GUN SIGHTS ARE ON TARGET.

BE SURE OF YOUR TARGET AND WHAT IS BEHIND IT.

Hands-on participation at the shooting range can be something of a rite of passage, or in other families is undertaken as early as the child is cognitively able to understand sight alignment. I know several families that introduced their four and five year olds to shooting, at ages so young one parent had to help the little guy or gal hold up the firearm. When children of any age are introduced to shooting, start with dryfire as a way to communicate basic skills. At this stage, you must be in physical contact with the child to help them learn muzzle control skills. For children, I strongly prefer the rifle to small caliber handguns because the long barrel makes it

Taking a child shooting was once a rite of passage, the departure from which we are now paying the price of youthful irresponsibility with firearms and other deadly weapons.

so much easier to enforce safe muzzle direction. The rifle is easier to aim and shoot accurately, so the child's experience is positive.

Plenty of parents have done a fine job, however using a .22 LR pistol already owned by the family. Very young children will get the most out of small caliber firearms like the .22, especially if the parent's goal is to pass along enjoyment for the shooting sports.

While an adult's idea of fun at the range may last for three or four hours, as little as fifteen or twenty minutes may be enough time, especially for small children. When their attention wanders, it's time to stop. Parents have told me that their children become easily bored with traditional paper targets. Spinning or dropping steel plates and Pepper poppers are more fun, if available at your range. Less formal targets, like clay birds, aluminum cans, balloons and other objects make shooting more interesting; however, be sure to clean up afterwards!

Not until the child has attained the maturity to assume personal responsibility and to understand what death means should they be allowed to handle firearms without the parent in direct contact. The age will vary from child to child. A gauge of a child's understanding can be something as simple as their safe behavior as pedestrians or with bicycles on the street in front of your home. A careless or risk-taking youngster has no place on a firing range–wait a year or so until they have matured a little. If, however, your child demonstrates an understanding of life and death on the street, you can use that metaphor to be sure they understand the lethality of careless gun handling.

The NRA's Eddie Eagle program for young children teaches gun safety. and is highly recommended.[4] If your children are extremely interested in your guns, offer to enroll them in an organized youth shooting program. Attend or volunteer to help with the classes to be sure the gun-handling is safe. Some NRA gun clubs have junior leagues that let the children learn and compete in a well-supervised atmosphere. State fish and game departments usually sponsor hunter education classes that are good resources for gun safety instruction, too.

As your children demonstrate that they understand life and death, and the firearms' potential for tragedy, let them know that you will happily take them shooting when they ask and as soon as it is practical. Their half of the agreement is a solemn pledge never to touch a gun outside of your presence or without your your permission. The offer can extend to friends with parental permission, giving your child the ability to walk away from an unsupervised gun saying, "That's no big deal. My mom and dad take me shooting when I ask. If you put that gun down, I'll ask them if you can come along next weekend." If the offer fails, your child must walk away, and can do so with the prestige that they are allowed to use guns responsibly.

Younger children can begin their safe-gun attitudes with their toy guns. Use these toys as training devices to teach the four prime gun handling rules. Never allow your kids to point gun replicas at family members. A lot of us have grave reservations about even allowing toy guns in the home, however gun use is so integral to American culture that children denied toy guns will adopt other objects to substitute as guns in their play. I think it is more realistic to use toys to teach responsible gun handling. A leading female outdoors writer equipped her small son with a toy rifle to teach the habits necessary for a safe hunt. He would enjoy hunting with real firearms when he was able to demonstrate unfailing safe muzzle direction with the toy gun.

Living with guns and children

If you bought your gun for personal and home-defense, you need ways to keep that gun accessible for emergency use while keeping it out of reach of the children. One solution is to keep the gun holstered on the parent's body at all times, then locked in a bed-side drawer at night. Realistically, wearing a gun is rarely comfortable enough to continue inside the safe confines of your home. If the parent takes the gun off before bedtime, it must be secured in a locked box or gun safe immediately, not put atop the refrigerator or in an un-locked dresser drawer.

One of the fastest lock boxes I ever saw was the SafeGard™ Gun Vault recommended in the first edition of this book. The latches are concealed in two of four buttons that look like "feet" on the bottom of the box. To unlock the box, the adult pressed the appropriate "feet" and the lid popped open. It

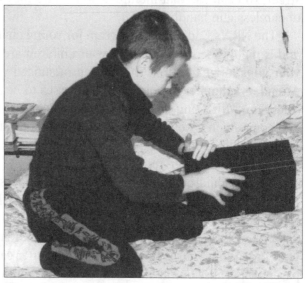

The author's nephew attempts to open the SafeGard™ gun lock box.

required quite a bit of coordination and strength to push the feet in the right directions, so young children were unable to access the gun.

Unfortunately, the manufacturer has disappeared from the firearms trade scene. Today, I would give serious consideration to the built-like-a-tank lock boxes made by R&D Enterprises.[5] The Simplex™ lock securing the lock box is simple only in name and appearance. Ron Venase, a parent and developer of these lock boxes, reports that the ability to program certain key combinations adds a great deal of child- and thief-proofing to the box.

Many of the more gimmicky gun storage devices marketed are simply too elementary. Tests with real children have shown most gun storage devices are all too easily defeated. A genuine safe, whether big or small, remains the best place to secure your guns when you're out of the house. The best safes have dials and keys, doubly protecting the contents. If a parent is concerned that an unruly adolescent might have figured out the safe combination, the key lock adds an extra ring of safety.

Your kids reflect your attitudes

Attitudes pass from one generation to the next. A surprising number of shooters want someone else to teach their children about guns. "He's started showing an interest in guns, but he won't listen to anything we say. Can you give him a class some afternoon after school?" is an appeal I've heard too often. Too little, too late, I think silently, and refer the caller to the National Rifle Association Education and Training Division, where an experienced youth coach can supply guidance.

How much better to dispel the attraction of guns when the children are young and will still listen raptly to their parent's teaching! If gun safety is a way of life for you, your children, too, will respect the power of the firearm.

The best argument made for disarming the American public is a tragic shooting by

The recessed door of the R&D lock box is further security against a prying attempt by a thief.

a child misusing the parent's gun. If you bring a gun into your home, please have the responsibility and maturity to keep it in your hands only. If you do not think you can keep your gun out of your children's hands, consider less deadly means of protection: oleoresin capsicum spray or large, mean dogs that love only your family. You must not endanger your children, yourself, and others by owning a gun without respecting its power.

1 Data edited by Don B. Kates, *Guns, Murder and the Constitution*, 1991.

2 Lt. Col. Dave Grossman, writing for Killology Research Group, www.killology.com/TwoLessons.htm, and for *Christianity Today* at www.christianityonline.com.

3 Center for Disease Control, *National Vital Statistics Reports*, Vol. 47, No. 19, June 4, 1999.

4 National Rifle Association, 11250 Waples Mill Rd., Fairfax, VA 22030, 703-267-1000.

5 R&D Enterprises, P O Box 293988, Phelan, CA 92329-3988, 800-467-4000.

23

Etiquette for Armed Citizens

Gang activity prevalent today has falsified the saying "an armed society is a polite society." Among legitimate gun owners, however, the statement must remain true. As you adopt the self-reliant life style of one who is truly able to care for herself, you'll realize the responsibility that your self-reliance carries.

Preparation and foresight are elements of the self-defense gun owner's life. Foresight means that we live our lives in such a way that our actions and activities don't demonstrate careless disregard for human life: our own or the lives of others. Simple things like the jokes we tell or the t-shirt slogans on our backs reveal attitudes that can come back to haunt us in a courtroom.

Jokes and slogans that indicate disregard for life or the lawful use of guns communicate that you don't intend to use your firearm in a judicious manner, whether or not that is your true attitude. Not only can this message be used by prosecutors following a self-defense shooting, it also fuels the anti-gun forces that threaten our right to possess guns for self-defense. Avoid intemperate remarks about use of guns and deadly force. Jokes and comments like "I would have killed that bastard myself," can surface in court as evidence that you wanted to kill someone, and hurt the reputation of all serious, careful self-defense practitioners.

A joke about telling someone to "make my day" may pop up if you ever have to face a violent assailant. Not only can such comments fuel your assailant's rage, they can come back to harm your legal defense if overheard by witnesses. "If you're judicious in your day-to-day comments, hard-to-defend phrases probably won't pop up under stress," advises Evan Marshall.

We talked earlier about keeping the gun out of sight, not showing it off to visitors in your home. When carrying a gun in public for self-defense you must be even more discrete. It is foolish to allow the gun or its outline to show outside of private areas in which you enjoy acceptance of your right to carry a gun. Moreover, in most jurisdictions, it is illegal to reveal the presence of your gun when carried in a public place. Allowing the gun to show is perceived as threatening, and often violates laws that give others the right not to feel endangered by the presence of armed people.

Beyond the law, it is unwise and risky to reveal that you are armed. In some folks, you may arouse harsh anti-gun sentiments, while others may see it as an opportunity to try to disarm you.

The gun must not be drawn and pointed at another human unless you believe you are in immediate and unavoidable danger of death or grave bodily harm. If you cannot justify your actions by these criteria, leave the gun in its holster and get away from the perceived threat.

Have a plan

Preparation means knowing what to do if assaulted. Decide how you will respond to a variety of circumstances: a break-in to your home, an assault against you in your home, an assault against another family member, an assault at work, in your car or on the street. Keep the plan private, except to work out details with roommates or family members who need to participate in the overall safety, evacuation and other survival plans. Think through your responses to various scenarios. If you realize you don't know what to do in response to different dangers, seek out further training.

Merely owning a gun for self-defense is not enough. The owner must become and remain skilled in its proper use and knowledgeable about when it may be used. The government and news media campaign against sensible people who own guns for self-defense makes it crucial that our use of the gun occurs only when no other avenue of escape or deflection exists.

When an innocent person uses a gun in self-defense, the news media gives scant mention or ignores the value the gun held for the survivor in their moment of danger. We live in a society that does not understand the awful, yet sometimes necessary, act of using a gun in self-defense. Every use of the gun is portrayed as criminal, bloodthirsty and unconscionable. The rights of criminals sometimes receive more attention than the rights of victims and the future victims the offender will assault.

Clearly the agony of the victims is not of sufficient importance to convince our leaders that violent offenders must be imprisoned permanently. So long as these abusers are set free to prey on the helpless, the numbers of atrocious attacks will increase. So long as television instructs the impressionable in rape, murder and violence, women will be targeted as victims of men without consciences. Until a majority of women say "Enough!" and assume the responsibility of using deadly force in self-defense, we will continue to be targeted.

For some, the gun will never be acceptable. These women must exercise a much higher level of prudence about their surroundings. Intermediate weapons like pepper sprays, the Persuader, and empty hand defenses are useful, and a high level of training and proficiency will be crucial.

Each woman needs to decide how she will protect herself and her family. Our right, and the right of our children, to survive unmolested, is worth protecting passionately. It is worth the time and expense of training and the cost of the tools–whether that be a gun or another weapon. It is worth the time needed to wrestle with the question "could I kill in self-defense?" And it is worth the effort to develop realistic self-defense plans we are capable of executing.

Victims and survivors

Two words have received extensive use throughout the foregoing pages. They are "victim" and "survivor." As this book comes to an end, take a minute to think about these terms and about yourself. The word "victim" indicates one to whom something is done. The term does not suggest any effective pre-emptive or defensive action, instead conveying that the person to whom the term is applied is the victim of actions against which they were powerless to defend.

When "survivor" is used in a sentence, the implication is less black and white. A survivor may have suffered injuries, yet somehow overcame the forces arrayed against her. Survival occurs on many levels: physical, emotional, spiritual and mental, and the latter two are often overlooked in our Western society's preoccupation with tangible, physical matters.

Leaders in the field of armed self-defense hesitate to use the term "victor" in describing those who face deadly danger and prevail. It has been suggested that no one "wins" when the worst happens and good people are forced to use lethal force. This view, however, overlooks the triumphs of pre-emptive action, of alert avoidance, of verbal intervention and all the other force options we've discussed as ways to avoid criminal attack.

I don't think I could overstate the value of a feminine attitude that, while not seeking out dangers, personifies a woman who is ready, able and willing to use defensive force to prevent injury and abuse to herself and her family. Beyond attitude and belief, this mindset takes form in physical activities like training, personal safety and crime prevention measures, and always remaining alert to unpredictable risks. This kind of woman is a survivor.

Keep your head up, keep your spirits up. Stay alert and aware; stay safe.